EXPLORATIONS IN SOCIOLOGY

British Sociological Association conference volur

Sami Zubaida (*editor*)	1	*Race and Racism*
Richard Brown (*editor*)	2	*Knowledge, Education and Cultural Exchange*
Paul Rock and Mary McIntosh (*editors*)	3	*Deviance and Social Control*
Emmanuel de Kadt and Gavin Williams (*editors*)	4	*Sociology and Development*
Frank Parkin (*editor*)	5	*The Social Analysis of Class Structure*
Diana Leonard Barker and Sheila Allen (*editors*)	6	*Sexual Divisions and Society*
Diana Leonard Barker and Sheila Allen (*editors*)	7	*Dependence and Exploitation in Work and Marriage*
Richard Scase (*editor*)	8	*Industrial Society*
Robert Dingwall, Christian Heath, Margaret Reid and Margaret Stacey (*editors*)	9	*Health Care and Health Knowledge*
Robert Dingwall, Christian Heath, Margaret Reid and Margaret Stacey (*editor*)	10	*Health and the Division of Labour*
Gary Littlejohn, Barry Smart, John Wakeford and Nira Yuval-Davis (*editors*)	11	*Power and the State*
Michèle Barrett, Philip Corrigan, Annette Kuhn and Janet Wolff (*editors*)	12	*Ideology and Cultural Production*
Bob Fryer, Allan Hunt, Doreen MacBarnet and Bert Moorhouse (*editors*)	13	*Law, State and Society*
Philip Abrams, Rosemary Deem, Janet Finch and Paul Rock (*editors*)	14	*Practice and Progress*
Graham Day, Lesley Caldwell, Karen Jones, David Robbins and Hilary Rose (*editors*)	15	*Diversity and Decomposition in the Labour Market*
David Robbins, Lesley Caldwell, Graham Day, Karen Jones and Hilary Rose (*editors*)	16	*Rethinking Social Inequality*
Eva Gamarnikow, David Morgan, June Purvis and Daphne Taylorson (*editors*)	17	*The Public and the Private*
Eva Gamarnikow, David Morgan, June Purvis and Daphne Taylorson (*editors*)	18	*Gender, Class and Work*
* Gareth Rees, Janet Bujra, Paul Littlewood, Howard Newby and Teresa L. Rees (*editors*)	19	*Political Action and Social Identity*
Howard Newby, Janet Bujra, Paul Littlewood, Gareth Rees and Teresa L. Rees (*editors*)	20	*Restructuring Capital*
* Sheila Allen, Kate Purcell, Alan Waton and Stephen Wood (*editors*)	21	*The Experience of Unemployment*
* Kate Purcell, Stephen Wood, Alan Waton and Sheila Allen (*editors*)	22	*The Changing Experience of Employment*
* Jalna Hanmer and Mary Maynard (*editors*)	23	*Women, Violence and Social Control*
* Colin Creighton and Martin Shaw (*editors*)	24	*Sociology of War and Peace*

* Alan Bryman, Bill Bytheway, Patricia Allatt and Teresa Keil (*editors*)	25	*Rethinking the Life Cycle*
* Patricia Allatt, Teresa Keil, Alan Bryman and Bill Bytheway (*editors*)	26	*Women and the Life Cycle*
* Ian Varcoe, Maureen McNeil and Steven Yearley (*editors*)	27	*Deciphering Science and Technology*
* Maureen McNeil, Ian Varcoe and Steven Yearley (*editors*)	28	*The New Reproductive Technologies*
David McCrone, Stephen Kendrick and Pat Straw (*editors*)	29	*The Making of Scotland*
* Stephen Kendrick, Pat Straw and David McCrone (*editors*)	30	*Interpreting the Past, Understanding the Present*
* Lynn Jamieson and Helen Corr (*editors*)	31	*State, Private Life and Political Change*
* Helen Corr and Lynn Jamieson (*editors*)	32	*Politics of Everyday Life*
Geoff Payne and Malcolm Cross (*editors*)	33	*Sociology in Action*
Pamela Abbott and Claire Wallace (*editors*)	34	*Gender, Power and Sexuality*
Robert Reiner and Malcolm Cross (*editors*)	35	*Beyond Law and Order*
Pamela Abbott and Geoff Payne (*editors*)	36	*New Directions in the Sociology of Health and Illness*
Claire Wallace and Malcolm Cross (*editors*)	37	*Youth in Transition*
Malcolm Cross and Geoff Payne (*editors*)	38	*Work and the Enterprise Culture*
* Sara Arber and Nigel Gilbert (*editors*)	39	*Women and Working Lives*
* Roger Burrows and Catherine Marsh (*editors*)	40	*Consumption and Class*
* Nigel Gilbert, Roger Burrows and Anna Pollert (*editors*)	41	*Fordism and Flexibility*
* Catherine Marsh and Sara Arber (*editors*)	42	*Families and Households*
* Lydia Morris and E. Stina Lyon (*editors*)	43	*Gender Relations in Public and Private*
* Colin Samson and Nigel South (*editors*)	44	*The Social Construction of Social Policy*
Joan Busfield and E. Stina Lyon (*editors*)	45	*Methodological Imaginations*
* Janet Holland and Lisa Adkins (*editors*)	46	*Sex, Sensibility and the Gendered Body*
* Lisa Adkins and Vicki Merchant (*editors*)	47	*Sexualizing the Social*
* Jeffrey Weeks and Janet Holland (*editors*)	48	*Sexual Cultures*
Sallie Westwood and John Williams (*editors*)	49	*Imagining Cities*
Nick Jewson and Suzanne MacGregor (*editors*)	50	*Transforming Cities*
* Kevin Brehony and Nazima Rassool (*editors*)	51	*Nationalisms Old and New*
* Avtar Brah, Mary J. Hickman and Máirtín Mac an Ghaill (*editors*)	52	*Thinking Identities*
* Avtar Brah, Mary J. Hickman and Máirtín Mac an Ghaill (*editors*)	53	*Global Futures*
* Paul Bagguley and Jeff Hearn (*editors*)	54	*Transforming Politics*
* Jeff Hearn and Sasha Roseneil (*editors*)	55	*Consuming Cultures*
* Sasha Roseneil and Julie Seymour (*editors*)	56	*Practising Identities*
* Julie Seymour and Paul Bagguley (*editors*)	57	*Relating Intimacies*

* *from the same publishers*

Consuming Cultures

Power and Resistance

Edited by

Jeff Hearn
Professorial Research Fellow
Faculty of Economic and Social Studies
University of Manchester

and

Sasha Roseneil
University Research Fellow
University of Leeds

First published in Great Britain 1999 by
MACMILLAN PRESS LTD
Houndmills, Basingstoke, Hampshire RG21 6XS and London
Companies and representatives throughout the world

A catalogue record for this book is available from the British Library.

ISBN 0–333–74716–X hardcover
ISBN 0–333–74717–8 paperback

First published in the United States of America 1999 by
ST. MARTIN'S PRESS, INC.,
Scholarly and Reference Division,
175 Fifth Avenue, New York, N.Y. 10010

ISBN 0–312–21882–6

Library of Congress Cataloging-in-Publication Data
Consuming cultures : power and resistance / edited by Jeff Hearn and Sasha Roseneil.
p. cm. — (Explorations in sociology ; 55)
Papers originally presented at the British Sociological Association Annual Conference, University of York, 1997.
Includes bibliographical references and index.
ISBN 0–312–21882–6 (cloth)
1. Consumption (Economics)—Congresses. 2. Consumers—Congresses. 3. Consumer behavior—Congresses. I. Hearn, Jeff, 1947– . II. Roseneil, Sasha, 1966– . III. British Sociological Association. Conference (1997 : University of York) IV. Series: Explorations in sociology ; v. 55.
HB801.C62825 1999
339.4'7—dc21 98–32039
CIP

---

10 9 8 7 6 5 4 3 2 1
08 07 06 05 04 03 02 01 00 99

Printed and bound in Great Britain by
Antony Rowe Ltd, Chippenham, Wiltshire

Contents

List of Figures

List of Tables

List of Plates

Acknowledgements

Consuming Cultures comprises revised versions of papers originally presented at the British Sociological Association (BSA) Annual Conference, held on the theme of 'Power/Resistance' at the University of York, 7–10 April 1997. It is one of four volumes, all published by Macmillan Press in 1999, produced from the papers given at the conference. The companion volumes are: *Practising Identities: Power and Resistance*, edited by Sasha Roseneil and Julie Seymour; *Relating Intimacies: Power and Resistance*, edited by Julie Seymour and Paul Bagguley; and *Transforming Politics: Power and Resistance*, edited by Paul Bagguley and Jeff Hearn.

The conference was one of the largest ever held by the BSA. Approximately 333 papers were presented, thus making the task of selecting papers for publication particularly difficult. We thank all conference participants for their patience whilst we read the papers; inevitably there were many papers that we would like to have included but were unable to in trying to make this and the other volumes into coherent collections. The contributors to this volume are particularly thanked for revising their papers so swiftly and efficiently in response to editorial comments and suggestions.

The conference theme of 'Power/Resistance' is both a long-established one throughout the history of sociology and one that has seen increased interest and re-evaluation in recent years. This sense of continuity and change was present throughout the conference. The four volumes bring together papers on major sub-themes that *emerged* from the conference. However, in addition there were many other concerns and issues that were debated at the conference, such as the growing amount of work on transnational, international and global issues. Even so it is probably fair to say that, with such a wide-ranging overall theme of power and resistance, these volumes give an indication of some of the preoccupations of sociology, particularly British sociology, in the late 1990s.

We are extremely grateful for all the work of the staff at the BSA office both in Durham and at the conference itself – Nicky Gibson, Judith Mudd, Jean Punton (until November 1996), and especially Nicola Boyne, who assisted the Organising Committee throughout in solving and resolving all sorts of interesting problems. We also thank the Conference Office and the Department of Sociology at York University for their advice and hospitality, and the student helpers at the conference for their invaluable assistance. Special thanks are due to Sarah Irwin, who was a member of the conference organising committee in its early stages, prior to the demands of motherhood. Our thanks are also offered to our colleagues at Leeds University, Manchester University and Åbo Akademi University for their support and encouragement, and to Valery Rose for her expert copy-editing. Our conference co-organisers, Paul Bagguley and Julie Seymour, were a joy to work with, and the overall shape of the four volumes and selection of the papers was decided collectively by all four of us.

Notes on the Contributors

Catrina Alferoff lectures for the School of Humanities and Social Sciences at Staffordshire University. She is currently undertaking cross-national research into the situations for older people in the labour market, based at Keele University in Staffordshire. Her principal areas of interest lie in new technologies, organisations, power and social change.

Kay Aranda is a Lecturer in Sociology and Social Policy in the School of Health Studies at Croydon College. As a nurse she has worked in the NHS and the voluntary sector, and her main interests are women's health, medicine and nursing. She is currently registered as a part-time postgraduate student at Southampton University researching community nursing discourses of equality and discrimination.

Michael Bull is a Lecturer in the Department of Communications at Anglia Polytechnic University. His main research interests are in the field of technology, experience and urban culture. His research into technology and Walkman use was completed in the Sociology Department, Goldsmiths College, where he worked up until 1996. He also specialises in the work of the Frankfurt School and has contributed to *The Routledge Encyclopaedia of Philosophy* (1998) in this area.

Tony Chapman is Head of Sociology at the University of Teesside. He teaches courses on the sociology of domestic architecture and urban life. His current research interests include the role of men in the domestic sphere; show homes; and energy conservation in domestic architecture. He is co-editor with Jenny Hockey of *Ideal Homes?* (Routledge, 1998).

Jörg Dürrschmidt is a Lecturer in Sociology at the University of the West of England, Bristol. He has completed a PhD on 'extended milieux' in a global city – a case study of London. His general research interest lies within the phenomenology of everyday life. His current research interests are focused on grassroots networks in the south west of England, and processes of microglobalisation within world cities.

Craig M. Gurney is a Lecturer in Housing at the Department of City and Regional Planning, Cardiff University. Previously he was a Lecturer in Urban Sociology at Sheffield Hallam University. His current research interests include a study of metaphor in discourses of urban and housing change; gender, sexuality and housing consumption; the social construction of home and home ownership; homeworking; and the housing careers of professional sportspeople. He has also published on home ownership and the meaning of home.

Barbara Harrison is Professor of Sociology and Head of Department at the University of East London. She is the author of *Not Only the 'Dangerous Trades': Women's Work and Health in Britain, 1880–1914* (Taylor and Francis, 1996). In addition to a continuing interest in the history of women's health, she has been working on various aspects of visual sociology and methodology over the past two years. She also teaches qualitative research methods.

Jeff Hearn is Professorial Research Fellow in the Faculty of Economic and Social Studies, University of Manchester, UK, and Visiting Professor in Sociology at Åbo Akademi University, Finland, and University of Oslo, Norway. He has published extensively on social and cultural issues, including film, popular culture, and media images of men. His most recent books are *Men in the Public Eye* (Routledge, 1992); *Violence and Gender Relations* (co-editor, Sage, 1996); *Men as Managers, Managers as Men* (co-editor, Sage, 1996); *Men, Gender Divisions and Welfare* (co-editor, Routledge, 1998); and *The Violences of Men* (Sage, 1998). He was a member of the Organising Committee of the 1997 British Sociological Association Annual Conference.

Gill Jones is Deputy Director of the Centre for Family Research, Faculty of Social and Political Sciences, at Cambridge University. She has an interest in all aspects of transitions to adulthood and inequalities in youth, and has published widely, including *Leaving Home* (1995) and, with Claire Wallace, *Youth, Family and Citizenship* (1992), both published by the Open University Press.

Lydia Martens is Lecturer in Sociology in the Department of Applied Social Science at the University of Stirling, and has research interests spanning the areas of gender, work and consumption. She is author of *Exclusion and Inclusion: The Gender Composition of British and Dutch Work Forces* (Ashgate: Avebury, 1997), and is currently involved in writing a book, with Alan Warde, *Eating Out: A Sociological Analysis*, to be published by Cambridge University Press in 1999.

Chris D. Martin is a Research Fellow at the Centre for Educational Sociology, University of Edinburgh. He is currently involved in comparative studies of education and training systems in the UK and Europe, and has research interests in youth and educational inequalities, and a particular interest in the secondary analysis of large data sets.

Shaun Moores is Reader in Media and Cultural Studies at the University of Sunderland. His previous publications include *Interpreting Audiences* (Sage, 1993), *The Politics of Domestic Consumption* (co-edited with Stevi Jackson, Prentice-Hall/Harvester Wheatsheaf, 1995) and *Satellite Television and Everyday Life* (John Libbey Media, 1996). He has also worked as a consultant author for the Faculty of Social Sciences at the Open University.

Martin O'Brien is Senior Research Fellow in the School of Education and Social Science at the University of Derby, UK. He works in the areas of social theory, social policy, social change and the environment. He is co-author, with Sue Penna, of *Theorizing Welfare: Enlightenment and Modern Society* (Sage, 1998) and co-editor, with Sue Penna and Colin Hay, of *Theorising Modernity: Reflexivity, Environment and Identity in Giddens' Social Theory* (Addison Wesley, Longman, 1998). Amongst other things, he is currently developing a project on the sociology of rubbish.

Gillian Reynolds lectures and researches for the School of Humanities and Social Sciences at Staffordshire University. Her research interests and publications include issues concerning identity, disability, work and charity; care in the community; technology, power and control; and research methodology.

Sasha Roseneil is University Research Fellow at the University of Leeds. Prior to this she was Lecturer in Sociology at Leeds, and Co-ordinator of Women's Studies, and in 1998 she was Visiting Fellow at the Australian National University. She is the author of *Disarming Patriarchy: Feminism and Political Action at Greenham* (Open University Press, 1995) and *Common Women, Uncommon Practices: The Queer Feminism of Greenham* (Cassell, 1998). She is co-editor of

Stirring It: Challenges for Feminism (Taylor and Francis, 1994). She has also written about media and political representations of lone mothers, about feminist cultural politics, and about the 'turn to culture' within feminist sociology. Much of her current work seeks to analyse the significance of the cultural transformations of post-modernity. She was a member of the Organising Committee of the 1997 British Sociological Association Annual Conference.

Rachel Thomson has worked in the voluntary sector and within academia. She is currently a Senior Research Fellow in the School of Education, Politics and Social Science at South Bank University, London. Her research interests include young people and sexuality, and sexuality in social policy, and she is currently involved in the ESRC-funded study *Youth Values: Identity, Diversity and Social Change*. She is a co-author of *The Male in the Head: Young People, Heterosexuality and Power* (Tufnell Press, 1998).

Mark Thorpe has for the last two years been Research Fellow in the Department of Geography at University College London. He has also worked for four years as an Associate of the Centre for Environmental and Social Studies in Ageing (CESSA), based at the University of North London. Following the completion of his doctorate on the construction and living of social relations in residential and non-residential institutions for older people, his current interests now include the growing significance of the 'Grey Market', and the material cultures of later life.

Alan Warde is Professor of Sociology at Lancaster University. His research interests include urban, economic and political sociology, but he has recently been working mostly on the sociology of consumption with particular reference to food. Recent books include *Consumption, Food and Taste: Culinary Antinomies and Commodity Culture* (Sage, 1997) and *Consumption Matters*, jointly edited with Stephen Edgell and Kevin Hetherington (Sociological Review Monograph, 1996). *Eating Out: A Sociological Analysis*, written with Lydia Martens, is nearing completion and will be published by Cambridge University Press.

1 Consuming Cultures: Power and Resistance

JEFF HEARN and SASHA ROSENEIL

Dream, desire, buy, consume, throw away! We consume to live; yet we also consume to do much more than just live. Almost anything can now be consumed: birth, 'growing up', holidays and of course marriage ceremonies can now be, not just photographed, but videoed for subsequent consumption; houses, décor, food and drink, sport, music, sex, bodies, clothes, pets, cars, care and people as well may all become objects of consumption; and even death is no escape, with consumer packages, with or without all mod cons, for the dying, the dead and the bereaved, and even now the possibility of visiting virtual graveyards on the Internet. We may wonder if we are in a world where consumption never ceases, even at the same moment as bare survival and starvation continue.

Consumption is one of the basic ways in which society is structured and organised, usually unequally, sometimes incredibly so. Differential powers, resources and life chances are routinely produced and reproduced by and through consumption patterns. Consumption not only takes place within culture and thus within specific cultures; it also produces culture and cultures. This is so in the general sense that consumption is part of and contributes to the wider culture of a given society or social group; it is also so in the more particular sense that it produces cultures and local sub-cultures centred around consumption and acts of consuming. Thus consumption is in culture but equally culture derives at least in part from consumption and consuming. Furthermore, consumption also constructs, even consumes, the consumer. Just as production produces both products and the producer, the worker, so too consumption has a dialectical form. People do consumption, and are 'done to', constructed, consumed by that consumption. Consumption is structure, process and agency.

This is especially clear when we think of the different and changing technologies that have become available for consumption: bartering, merchanting, the shop, shopping arcades, the department store, hypermarkets, malls, mail order, business services, brothels, cooperatives, credit unions, franchising, network selling, teleshopping, computer banking, Internet commerce, personal customising, eating in, eating out, drive-ins, fast food outlets, and much more. These and many technologies and modes of organising consumption do not just affect how consumption is done; they also affect and construct the person doing the consuming. They constrain the time and place of consumption, as well as constructing the senses of the consumer through their mediation of what they see, hear, smell and touch. This is perhaps clearest when one considers the transformation of visual cultures and consumption that has taken place since the end of the last century – in photography, advertising, film, computers, and so on. But it also applies much more generally in the construction of all the senses, for example, in the movements from music to musak, from easy listening to techno, from 'folk music' to 'world music', from Gregorian chant to trance.

Increasingly, the technology also exists and is exploited to monitor, aggregate, plot and profile consumers' actions, both individual and collective. The individual act of consumption is no longer just about the buying of that particular product at that particular time; rather it has also come to be understood as an item in the production of the overall consumption pattern of particular individuals and types of individuals. This is particularly clear in credit card transactions and the electronic surveillance that can accompany them. For those organisations that analyse, influence and construct markets in this way, consumers and consumer actions are necessary for their own production process. There is accordingly an increasingly complex interaction between consumption, culture, technology and the construction of the person and the person's senses.

Our dual concern with culture and consumption is also interesting conceptually. Culture and consumption are both well-established concepts in the sociological canon, and concepts that have enjoyed special recent favour. The idea of culture has long been one of the central concepts of sociology; it is also one of the most complex and contested in the social sciences more generally: 'it is … not neutral, it is historical, specific and ideological' (Swingewood, 1977: 26). According to Raymond Williams (1976: 76), it 'is one of the two or three most complicated words in the English language'.

Though this is not the place to chart the definitions and meanings of culture, it is useful to say something of the legacy of social anthropology in the construction of the concept of culture for the social sciences. The idea of culture developed in social anthropology and culturalist (as opposed to structuralist) sociology, to refer to the traditions, norms, values and everyday practices of particular societies and social groups. One of the most famous definitions of culture is that by Tylor (1871) in the book *Primitive Culture*: 'That complex whole which includes knowledge, belief, art, morals, law, custom, and any other capabilities and habits acquired by man (*sic.*) as a member of society.' Culture is here contrasted with nature. Linton (1940) also sought to address 'the whole': 'The sum total of the knowledge, attitudes and habitual behaviour patterns shared and transmitted by the members of a particular society.' This adds notions of 'habit', 'sharing' and 'transmission'. Kroeber (1948) expands on this as follows: 'The mass of learned and transmitted motor reactions, habits, techniques, ideas, and values – and the behavior they induce.' In some usages the concept has carried additional political connotations, often though not always of a conservative kind. Culture has also been presented as those elements of society that are in danger of being lost – to threatening material advances or some other change. Though these earlier uses have received critique from structuralist sociology, they remain with us, even if strongly contested.

In contrast, the idea of consumption is part of the conceptual apparatus of political economy and economic sociology more generally. However, while consumption or collective consumption has often figured as a category in macro-sociological analysis, as the reciprocal of production, it was not until relatively recently a popular subject for detailed, qualitative or ethnographic study. The reasons for these are complex but include, until the impact of feminist theory and practice, a relative neglect of those arenas of social life associated with women. Thus until at least the 1970s there was far more concern in the sociology of modern Western societies with the primacy of the 'public' world of 'production' than the 'private' world of consumption, with the clear genderings thereby implied. This has now been challenged, as have simple dichotomies between the public and the private themselves.

More recently still, both culture and consumption have become much more favoured terms within sociology. In the case of culture, and following the social anthropological tradition, it has been used as a way of talking about forms of social solidarity, collective class experience, the movement from tradition to modernity, and so on. From the 1960s British social anthropology itself was transformed through the work of the Manchester School in critically applying the insights of the discipline from the 'non-Western' world to British cultural milieux. For British sociology, the key shift in use of the concept of culture can be traced at least to the work of the Centre for Contemporary Cultural Studies at the University of Birmingham from the 1970s. It is interesting in both cases that the direction of these academic initiatives was with scholars born outside the UK – Max Gluckman in the former, Stuart Hall in the latter. The CCCS's and other critical analyses of the interrelations of culture with experiences and inequalities of class, gender, race and sexuality have been immensely influential well beyond British sociology. These important revisitings of culture through the lenses of Marxism, feminism, and critical studies of race and racism have in turn reformulated the whole discipline of cultural studies internationally.

Special mention should also be made of feminist critiques of culture and cultural studies (for example, Mulvey, 1975; Morris, 1988; Penley, 1988; Game, 1991; Franklin *et al.*, 1991). These have highlighted the implicit and explicit constructions of women through culture and cultural artefacts. They have also produced a critique of 'culture', at least as any kind of unified, agendered social or societal phenomenon. They have critiqued the idea of unified, shared totality or configuration; they have gendered culture; and uncovered the way a concept of culture can obscure men's domination and construction of women (Moore, 1987), not least through the association of women with nature, and men with culture (Ortner, 1974). Feminist and profeminist cultural studies have also attended to the implicit and explicit construction of men and masculinities in culture.

The notion of culture has also been reinvigorated from other debates and directions, notably in the turns to discourse, difference and deconstruction promoted in the various forms of poststructuralism and postmodernism. Culture has come to be seen as a central feature of late modern or postmodern society with its own realms of signification, symbolic production, consumer culture and semi-autonomous, multiple cultures (Foster, 1985; Lash, 1988; Jameson, 1991; Lash and Urry, 1994). In a related way the increasing attention to globalisation has meant a reconsideration of culture, but now with the clear understanding that local cultures are themselves set within complex global relations, and new cultures are developing within the contradictions of the local and the global (Scott, 1997). Increasing numbers of people now live between cultures and across cultures. Methodological and epistemological debates have at least to an extent parallels in substantive social changes. They remain the latest twist in the long relation and struggle between culturalist and structuralist perspectives.

Alongside this, the sociology of consumption has been something of a growth area, in a way that would have almost been unthinkable even in the 1970s. Both general sociologies of this arena of social life and more particular studies of forms of consumption, such as shopping, food and eating, and tourism, have been produced. These have pointed to new forms of relations between the social and the spatial, for example, in the mixing of uses, activities, signs and symbols in the 'postmodern city'. The overlap between the sociology of consumption and cultural studies, media studies and indeed studies of literary and other texts has become more intense. Arguably, much of this heightened concern with consumption follows from the coming together of feminist-influenced, gendered debates on families, households and the organisation of everyday life, and often much less explicitly gendered debates on late modernity and late modern society. There is also increasing interest in the changing links between consumption, lifestyle, identity and the social construction of the self, and in the elaboration of consumer politics, consumption politics, life politics and body politics (see Roseneil and Seymour, 1999). For all these reasons we may now talk of a revival of interest in the two concepts of culture and consumption.

This is, however, not just another book on consumption or culture. As already discussed, it attempts to put the two approaches together, with their rather different meanings and emphases. More specifically, there is, in keeping the original theme of the 1997 British Sociological Association Conference, a central concern with power and resistance. This combination of consumption/culture with power/resistance is, as far as we know, rather novel. The grand theories of power have generally been formed in relation to community, work, class, state, governance, politics, societal structures and beyond, but less so culture and rarely consumption. When reviewing mainstream theories of power, one can usefully ask: how do they deal with questions of consumption? And just how adequate are these ways of dealing? Sites of consumption and culture are just as much sites of power and resistance as these other arenas. Equally, studies of consumption and culture are enlivened by examining the relevance of power and resistance. This applies, for example, in considering consumption as one of the major ways in which social and societal inequality is experienced, reproduced and represented, by age, class, gender, racialisation, and other social divisions. Power also figures in the micro-processes of consumption, be they selling or shopping or 'surfing the net'. Consumption can be a form of resistance, just as much as consumption can be resisted. Consuming can no longer be innocent.

In a book such as this it would be unreasonable to expect to find agreement on all the issues raised. And thus there are inevitable differences; indeed we see these differences as a strength rather than a weakness. One set of differences is in the range of disciplinary influences. While the book stands at the interface of the sociologies of culture and consumption, and cultural studies, there are also contributions relating to social theory, media and communications studies and social geography. Culture and consumption are examined from sociological, cultural, social psychological, historical and geographical perspectives. Similarly, theoretical and methodological approaches derive from quantitative and qualitative sociologies, feminism, Critical Theory, poststructuralism, postmodernism, and socio-spatial analysis, as well as various permutations thereof. Research methods used include theoretical and empirical reviews, secondary analysis of official statistics, social surveys, interviews of various kinds, participant observation, ethnography, document analysis, discourse analysis, analysis of visual and other texts. Other differences arise simply from the range of substantive sites and forms of consumption, which are explored, and their specific social characteristics. For example, a particular and novel feature in some chapters is the significance of not just consumption, but also what happens afterwards – with waste, rubbish and throwing away. More generally, we may ask to what extent metaphors of consumption and waste are applied to people themselves, as in discussions, whether academic, political or everyday, on the redundancy, marginalisation and exclusion of people from society and social arenas.

On the other hand, despite these differences there are a number of recurring similarities throughout the chapters that should be highlighted. First, many of the chapters deal with contemporary social change and transformation. Second, many also address a variety of social divisions and their interconnections rather than focusing primarily on one particular social division. Third, there is a continuing concern to examine 'consuming cultures' that span macro–micro social relations. Fourth, and linked to this, a theoretical and methodological pluralism is observable in many of the contributions, that, for example, bridges the material and the discursive, rather than arguing that one specific theoretical position fully explains the world. Fifth, there is a strong concern with social theory throughout.

Consuming Cultures addresses some of the variety of ways in which consumption is structured and organised through culture and cultures, and how in turn cultural technologies of consumption construct the person, the senses and the self. It comprises two main sections: Homes and Households, Places and Spaces; and Technologies of Consumption and Waste. Particular attention is given to consumption in families and households, housing, the impact of technology on social life, and changes in contemporary lifestyles.

The first section is introduced by Gill Jones and Chris Martin on 'The Young Consumer at Home: Dependence, Resistance and Autonomy'. Jones and Martin's prime concern is with the interaction between spending patterns and domestic arrangements. Their focus on young consumers is especially interesting as a counterweight to the notion of 'teenage affluence', and with the social changes of the 1980s meaning an increased domestic dependence of young people on their families of origin. Leaving the parental home is becoming more difficult. Through secondary analysis of the Family Expenditure Surveys of 1982, 1987 and 1992, they examine patterns of youth consumption considered in relation to different kinds of family and household organisation. Throughout they stress the complex interactions of household types, spending patterns, class, gender and lifestyle. Consumption, particularly leisure consumption, can in this perspective sometimes be seen as resistance to inequality.

The next two chapters continue the theme of the cultural importance of the home, the first focusing on home ownership, and the second on home decoration. In '"We've Got Friends who Live in Council Houses": Power and Resistance in Home Ownership', Craig Gurney locates home ownership within the sociology of consumption as a form of cultural distinction. The home and housing consumption are also terrains of power and resistance, both within and beyond the individual household. The core of Gurney's chapter is his development of a Foucaultian perspective on power and resistance in home ownership, through the concepts of disciplinary power and normalising judgements. Using both governmental policy documents and in-depth interviews amongst working-class home-owning households, the major discourses in which home ownership is reproduced as 'normal' are described. The case is clear for these debates on home and housing to become a more central aspect of contemporary analyses of culture and consumption, and indeed vice versa.

Some of these concerns are echoed in the Tony Chapman's chapter on 'The Ideal Home Exhibition: an Analysis of Constraints and Conventions in Consumer Choice in British Homes'. Here the focus has moved from housing tenure to the contents of homes and houses.

The Ideal Home Exhibition has, apart from the Second World War years and the immediate aftermath, been an annual London-based display of interior decoration and home furnishings since 1908. It is part exhibition, part shop (window), part entertainment, part day out. Through participant observation and interviews with visitors, Chapman argues that the IHE is a means for capital to successfully present products that confirm the tastes of culturally conservative 'middle England' consumers and so powerfully contribute to a typically constrained presentation of self in the home.

All the first three chapters, in different ways, make complex connections between cultures of consumption inside homes and the social world beyond. The next three chapters in this section all examine such links in terms of the relation of the social and the spatial, through considering guests coming into the home, older people moving (at least partially) from home and into residential homes, day centres and lunch clubs, and consumers organising locally in relation to global change. First, Lydia Martens and Alan Warde discuss 'Power and Resistance around the Dinner Table'. This chapter draws on both a large-scale survey in three cities and more detailed semi-structured interviews. There are clear contrasts in the meanings given to commercial and private hospitality – between eating out at restaurants and eating out at friends' houses – especially in terms of 'informality' and 'relaxation'. The domestic setting and the fact of being a guest are particularly well appreciated. This study raises a great many general issues around changing forms of consumption and service provision. For example, the value given to informalisation and domestication in consumption may itself be reincorporated into commercial consumption, so itself further blurring the boundaries between being and not being at home/not at home.

The themes of space and place are broadened still further in the next two chapters. Mark Thorpe develops a socio-spatial analysis of cultures of marginalisation and resistance in day centres and lunch clubs for post-retirement-aged people, in making sense of his method of 'structured conversations' in these settings. As such, his chapter, 'Marginalisation and Resistance through the Prism of Retirement', exemplifies the growing convergence of interest between social geography and sociology, especially around age, class, gender, sexuality and other social divisions. Thorpe is centrally concerned with the interconnections of space and time in the active construction of local meanings and meanings of locality. At first sight, this may appear to be more about culture and less about consumption. However, it is also about the shifts from being in the home to being in institutionalised or semi-institutionalised social spaces, of constructing meaning in situations of material and consumer marginalisation, and indeed of being older rather than young consumers. His general critical discussion of idealist tendencies in valorising 'resistance' and the 'margins' has applications well beyond the specific concerns of this book.

Jörg Dürrschmidt also examines localisation but through a rather different approach. His chapter on 'The "Local" Versus the "Global"? – "Individualized Milieux" in a Complex "Risk Society"' is an interview-based case study of organic food box schemes in South West England. Dürrschmidt's study thus focuses on the local, collective or semi-collective organisation of consumption. Working within the major contemporary theme of the interplay of the local and the global, he examines to what extent these schemes may be understood as forms of local resistance to globalising forces. Instead he concludes that they are better seen as consumers' active attempts to mediate tensions between people's milieux and risk society through collective 'self'-empowerment. These kinds of question have a much more general relevance to both the analysis of consuming cultures, and wider current social experience. Interestingly, this analysis also highlights how changing patterns of local and global consumption may construct the person and identity in very immediate ways.

The second section of the book, Technologies of Consumption and Waste, deals with the impacts of a range of social technologies upon the construction of the person and the senses in more detail. First, Barbara Harrison and Kay Aranda address historical change in what is perhaps the most important of the modern technologies of communication and consumption, namely photography and camera technology. The creation of new visual technologies in the nineteenth century meant that very substantial change became possible in the constitution of the social world, and specifically the relation of the visual and the social. In 'Photography, Power and Resistance: the Case of Health and Medicine', Harrison and Aranda use the example of health and medicine as ways into the investigation of the operation of consumption within relations of power/resistance. The diverse and changing uses of photography are examined, including clinical photography, institutional or organisational photography, 'publicity' or propaganda photography, and photography as a means of subverting institutional and professional power and constructing new identities. This variety illustrates the multiple social meanings of photography and photographic practices, for example in relation to social divisions. Again the case study focus raises many issues of more general interest, and specifically so in charting the links between representation, social relations of power and inequality, and personal experience.

Some similar questions are considered in Rachel Thomson's chapter: '"It was the Way We were Watching it": Young Men Negotiate Pornography'. This thus addresses a field that has been transformed by the use of photography, as well as, of course, video and film technology. Thomson explains that she aims to move beyond the well-established feminist debates on definition, cause and effect of pornography to a specific concern with the place of pornography within the contexts of everyday cultures of consumption – what might be thought of as pornographic practices. Using young men's accounts of how they use pornography, she examines the processes through which men 'make sense' of pornography and through which pornography 'makes sense' of them. The cultures and technologies of consumption of pornography are one of the ways in which boys create themselves as men. Young men's positioning of themselves in relation to pornography is part of the process of negotiating what kind of man they may be, including their relation to adult men. And while pornography clearly misrepresents and objectifies women, the question remains of how it may control men and young men.

This theme of the relation of the person, technology and social power is elaborated further by Michael Bull in 'The Dialectics of Walking: Walkman Use and the Reconstruction of the Site of Experience'. He asks: are Walkman users empowered or are they the colonised recipients of a sound world produced elsewhere, which gives the illusion of autonomy and control? Drawing on an empirical study of Walkman use in London, Bull interrogates the possible meanings that might be attributed to their use and how they may bring a reorganisation of social space, including what has been constructed as 'public' and 'private'. In locating his analysis in relation to the work of such social theorists as Adorno, Bachelard and Lefebvre, he discusses such issues as the recreation of 'direct experience' by and through technological mediation. This perspective opens up a space to argue against the notions of both free or liberatory experience and colonised experience, and so suggests the need to work beyond this and similar dichotomies.

The general question of technological mediation, and specifically the various forms of electronically mediated communication, is discussed by Shaun Moores in 'The Mediated "Interaction Order"'. Three specific issues are explored: the position of different media in social arrangements of space and time; cultural experiences of modernity; and constructions of self-identity and community. His chapter critically reviews a large body of literature in setting out more clearly than previously the case for a new field of study on electronically mediated communication. This rapidly developing form of communication is of increasing importance in current social changes of culture and consumption. Moores goes on to outline the conceptual and practical implications of so delimiting the field, in terms of: the expansion and more inclusive definition of electronic media; a modified vocabulary of critical terms; research strategies with which to investigate the complex interaction mixes of daily life in modern society; and the examination of the grounding of modernity's mixed or hybrid interactions in ongoing biographical projects.

One particular kind of consumption-related cultural product that has mushroomed as a result of the growth of electronic communication is junk mail. This phenomenon is examined by Gillian Reynolds and Catrina Alferoff in 'Junk Mail and Consumer Freedom: Resistance, Transgression and Reward in the Panoptic Gaze'. Junk mail is both a means of advertising and selling, and a major form of rubbish. Its name says it all. It is sometimes indiscriminate, sometimes locality-based, sometimes highly selective. Reynolds and Alferoff's chapter derives from postal questionnaires and in-depth interviews with receivers of junk mail on what might be called its cultures of consumption. While many people may resist junk mail, some actively encourage the process, engage with it with enthusiasm and provide positive feedback into the system. Others practise various participative transgressions, for example, by returning false information on themselves or others. In this analysis electronic surveillance and the associated panoptic gaze, though extremely far-reaching, are not all-powerful; and thus deterministic, more structuralist arguments need to be seen through a more culturalist lens.

Finally, Martin O'Brien writes on waste and rubbish in 'Rubbish-Power: Towards a Sociology of the Rubbish Society'. Like Moores, he is at pains to delimit a new sociological field. For O'Brien a necessary step in doing this is the consideration of the place, and significantly the neglect, of rubbish as a serious topic in sociology. He continues with an analysis of some of the social processes by which rubbish is organised, distributed and destroyed throughout 'the rubbish society'. Of special interest here are the general relationship of production, consumption and waste, and the specific change in the social organisation of recycling. The latter part of the chapter focuses on the social meanings of junk and other forms of rubbish, drawing on focus group discussions on the subject. He concludes by asking how existing sociological theories address these issues, and how a social theory of wasting might contribute to sociological theories of production and consumption.

One of the excitements and joys of editing this book has been in considering and comparing the various approaches adopted by the contributors. While we have already noted some of these differences, there are also a number of emerging strands of attention that are worth noting and that may become of growing importance in the future studies of consuming cultures. First, we should reiterate the central relation of consuming cultures, power and resistance. These often involve powerful processes of inequality, surveillance and normalisation, as well as continuing resistances. Second, there is the frequently contradictory and dialectical relations between the individual, technology (especially electronic communication) and social structures. Third, these relations are themselves simultaneously social and spatial. Fourth, we may highlight the ways in which consumption is not an end point of production but rather itself a form of further production. Fifth, there is the growing recognition of the social processes of junk, rubbish and waste. We hope you will find some interest and inspiration in these particular offerings from this particular display – look, consume, read, write, shelve, and re-read!

REFERENCES

Foster, Hal (ed.) (1985) *Postmodern Culture* (London: Pluto).

Franklin, Sarah, Celia Lury and Jackie Stacey (eds) (1991) *Off Centre: Feminism and Cultural Studies* (London: Unwin Hyman).

Game, Ann (1991) *Undoing the Social* (Milton Keynes: Open University Press).

Jameson, Frederic (1991) *Postmodernism or the Cultural Logic of Late Capitalism* (London: Verso).

Kroeber, A. L. (1948) *Anthropology* (New York: Harcourt).

Lash, Scott (1988) 'Discourse or Figure? Postmodernism as a Regime of Signification', *Theory, Culture and Society*, 5(2/3), 311–36.

Lash, Scott and John Urry (1994) *Economies of Signs and Spaces* (London: Sage).

Linton, Ralph (1940) *Acculturation in Seven American Indian Tribes* (New York: Appleton-Century).
Moore, Henrietta (1987) *Feminism and Anthropology* (Cambridge: Cambridge University Press).
Morris, Meighan (1988) *The Pirate's Fiancée* (London: Verso).
Mulvey, Laura (1975) 'Visual Pleasure and Narrative Cinema', *Screen*, 16(3), 6–18.
Ortner, Sherry (1974) 'Is Female to Male as Nature is to Culture?', in Michele Z. Rosaldo and Linda Lamphere (eds), *Women, Culture and Society* (Stanford, CA: Stanford University Press), pp. 67–87.
Penley, Constance (ed.), (1988) *Feminism and Film Theory* (New York: Routledge).
Roseneil, Sasha and Julie Seymour (eds), (1999) *Practising Identities: Power and Resistance* (London: Macmillan).
Scott, Alan (1997) *The Limits of Globalization* (London: Routledge).
Swingewood, Alan (1977) *The Myth of Mass Culture* (London: Macmillan).
Tylor, Edward B. (1871) *Primitive Culture* (London: J. Murray).
Williams, Raymond (1976) *Keywords* (Glasgow: Fontana).

Part I

Homes and Households, Places and Spaces

2 The 'Young Consumer' at Home: Dependence, Resistance and Autonomy

GILL JONES and CHRIS D. MARTIN

Patterns of consumption are intimately related to patterns of family and household structure. Young people become increasingly visible as consumers as they emerge, socially, economically and geographically, from their families of origin. But economic emancipation has become more difficult for young people. As a result of an extended period of education and training, and a gradual withdrawal of their rights to incomes at the levels available to adults, many now experience a protracted period of economic dependence on their parents, some of whom cannot or will not provide financial help or a place to live (Jones, 1995). Increasingly, young people in all social classes are using credit and getting into debt (Hutton, 1990). There is continuing concern about social exclusion, poverty and homelessness in youth (e.g., Kirk *et al.*, 1991; Hutson and Liddiard, 1994; Coles, 1995). Surprisingly, although young people are targeted as consumers and appear to have considerable spending power, there have been few attempts to understand their spending patterns (cf. Hutton, 1990). Abrams' (1959) study *The Teenage Consumer*, undertaken at a time of low unemployment, promoted a myth of teenage affluence, and research on consumption in youth has since been dominated by an interest in youth sub-cultures and youth style (Cohen, 1965; Brake, 1980). Though Hebdige (1979) argued that spending on style is part of the process of identity formation and empowerment, and that consumption should be seen as a form of subversion, we are still faced with a public image of young people as a relatively affluent consumer group. This image puts young people at risk. It has been argued, for example, that young people cope with income changes by adjusting their leisure expenditure and that family poverty would thus not be tackled by an increase in youth incomes (Roberts and Parsell, 1991). Such an argument could form a rationale for the reduction of youth incomes. It would be a mistake, however, to equate spending with affluence; instead, all forms of spending and all budgeting decisions should be seen in their domestic context, and some can be seen as strategies of resistance, as this chapter will show.

An emphasis on 'lifestyles' masks the structural inequalities underlying consumption. Postmodernist accounts of cultural consumption have been criticised for failing to recognise exclusion from consumer markets (Warde, 1990), while even studies of inequalities in consumption in youth (Griffin, 1985; Mintel, 1988; Roberts *et al.*, 1991) tend to overlook *processes* of exclusion. Inequalities may not, however, be immediately apparent. The effect of the withdrawal of income opportunities from young people may be masked, since low incomes and unemployment may generally lead to adaptations of the forms of transition to adulthood rather than the postponement of 'adulthood' (Wallace, 1987; Jones, 1995). Hutson and Jenkins (1987) further suggest that young people have been so socialised into 'commitment to the mainstream values of consumerist accumulation' that even the long-term jobless are locked into consumer markets. Thus, activity in the consumer market may not always be a good indicator of wealth and poverty, and issues of power and resistance, manifested through adaptive strategies, are endemic to a study of income and expenditure in youth.

There are also some basic life-course changes. During the transition to economic independence, spending on leisure and style may give way to spending on home-based leisure activities, housing and consumer goods, as domestic responsibilities change (Roberts, 1981; Wallace, 1987). Leaving the parental home and establishing an independent home involve new living costs and new expenditure behaviour (Walker, 1988; Jones, 1995). In their studies of adult consumption of consumer durables, Piachaud (1982) and Dale (1987) have shown the need for a life-course approach. The extension of youth, and the greater complexity of youth transitions, make a longitudinal approach to youth consumption even more necessary.

We draw on a recent empirical study[1] of income and expenditure in youth to show that, as consumers, young people are a very heterogeneous grouping, and that this heterogeneity stems to a great extent from the varying ways in which they become adult citizens. We consider the relationship between increasing economic independence, household responsibility and patterns of consumption. First, we examine the domestic and economic contexts of young people; then we consider consumption on housing and domestic goods, finally moving on to individual spending on day-to-day living. Our particular concerns are with the inequalities revealed between young people in these different modes of consumption (Featherstone, 1990), the extent to which spending represents power in the consumer market, and the various strategies young people may develop to maintain a *semblance* of power in the consumer market in the face of a withdrawal of power and autonomy elsewhere. Do young people seek solace in 'consumer citizenship' (Jones and Wallace, 1992), when their rights as citizens have been threatened in other spheres? Can we distinguish between expenditure on style and expenditure on basic needs in youth, as an aid to understanding the contribution of young people themselves to the 'cost of growing up' in Britain?

HOMES AND HOUSEHOLDS

The research was based on secondary analysis of the Family Expenditure Survey (FES), an annual survey of private households in the UK (HMSO, 1993; Department of Employment, 1985). From the data sets for 1992, 1987 and 1982, subsets were created of all households containing 16–25-year-olds.[2] While the FES is a valuable first port of call for data on youth income and expenditure, it is not without its problems. Firstly, it does not distinguish intra-household financial exchanges, and so we cannot determine who pays household costs, and who subsidises whom. Secondly, it is based on private households: young people in other situations such as student or nurses' accommodation, barracks, hotels or hostels, or who are homeless, are not included in the FES. This problem is off-set in the following analysis by the use of a typology of households (Figure 2.1).

Households provide the domestic context for spending and consumption. The typology of 'household careers' shown in Figure 2.1 was adapted from previous studies of household formation in youth

Figure 2.1 Household typology

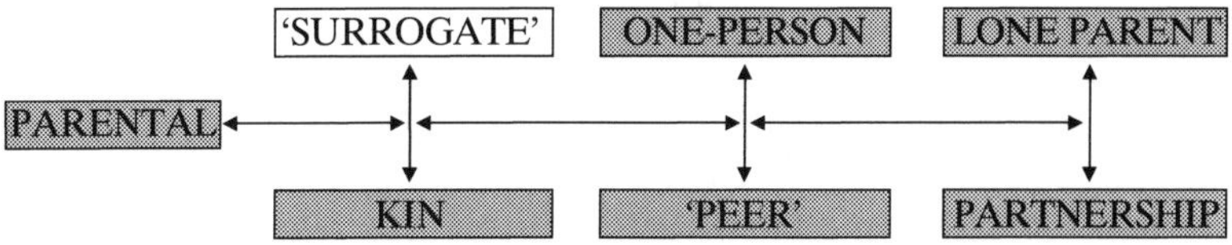

(Jones, 1987, 1995). It identifies various types of household in which young people may live after leaving their parental homes and before setting up more permanent households of their own. The typology describes a process which for some people can be quite extended. We should not assume that all young people move directly from their parental homes into family homes of their own, though some still do. Transitional household statuses[3] increasingly represent varying degrees of social and economic independence and domestic responsibility, revealing the complexity of the transition out of the parental home. Nor is this transition uni-directional: returning to the parental home doubled in the late 1980s among teenage home-leavers (Jones, 1995), while partnership breakdown will lead some out of partnership households and into lone-parent or perhaps one-person households.

The combination of low youth incomes and shortage of suitable affordable housing means that leaving the parental home is becoming more difficult. The housing market caters for families, rather than single young people who leave home to take up jobs, training and courses. Increasingly, young people are being 'encouraged' to remain in the parental home, as 'economic incentives' for them to leave are being removed through negative youth policies such as the withdrawal or reduction of welfare benefits in the 1980s and 1990s (Jones, 1995). Lacking assistance from the state for the establishment of independent homes, young people have to continue to live with their parents, or resort to household and housing 'strategies' (Pickvance and Pickvance, 1994). These may include sharing with peers or partners to reduce housing costs, or taking up employment with housing attached, any of which may be brought into play to ease the transition to independent living in the face of an unwelcoming housing market.

Table 2.1 shows the household typology applied to the FES survey data. In 1992 the majority (58 per cent) of all 16–25-year-olds in the FES were still living in their parental homes and a quarter were in 'family homes' of their own, as lone parents with their children, or in partnerships, with or without children. There remain 16 per cent of the sample who were in 'transitional' household statuses (living with kin, in shared flats, or alone). These are transitional in the sense that the young people concerned have left the parental home but not formed a partnership or family one; they may of course never do so. Household type depends on a number of factors, including economic, marital and parental status, sex, age and income. In general, young men were more likely to be living with parents or kin, while women were more likely to be at a further stage in household and family formation careers, living with partners

Table 2.1 Household type by age and sex (FES, 1982–92; column percentages)

Household type	Males			Females			All
	Age 16–17 (%)	Age 18–20 (%)	Age 21–25 (%)	Age 16–17 (%)	Age 18–20 (%)	Age 21–25 (%)	(%)
1982							
Parental	96	87	45	96	70	25	61
Kin	2	2	1	2	3	1	2
Peer	2	4	5	1	9	5	5
Single person	0	2	7	0	4	4	4
Lone parent	0	0	0	1	1	4	1
Partners	0	3	20	0	9	29	14
Partners + child(ren)	0	2	20	0	4	31	14
All (=100%)	**344**	**432**	**669**	**315**	**414**	**751**	**2925**
1987							
Parental	96	82	44	95	69	25	58
Kin	3	2	1	1	1	1	2
Peer	1	5	6	0	5	8	5
Single person	0	4	10	1	4	7	6
Lone parent	0	0	0	0	4	7	3
Partners	0	3	21	2	10	27	14
Partners + child(ren)	0	3	17	0	7	26	13
All (=100%)	**294**	**353**	**649**	**258**	**399**	**751**	**2704**
1992							
Parental	95	82	46	94	68	28	58
Kin	4	2	1	2	1	1	2
Peer	1	6	8	3	9	9	7
Single person	0	7	11	0	5	6	6
Lone parent	0	0	0	0	2	10	3
Partners	0	2	21	0	10	26	14
Partners + child(ren)	0	2	13	0	5	20	10
All (=100%)	**231**	**301**	**571**	**220**	**284**	**641**	**2248**

and/or children. Those living in the most 'dependent' situations – with parents or kin – tended to be younger single workers: 44 per cent of those in the parental home were in full-time jobs, and 57 per cent were under 20 years of age, while nearly all those on training schemes were living with their parents. Peer-shared accommodation mainly contained students, but also many of those with jobs. One-person households were dominated by young workers (55 per cent), and multivariate analysis showed that living alone rather than with peers was mainly associated with working-class males who could *afford* to live alone. Finally, marital and parental status affected the type of household in which people lived: though some lone parents and young couples lived in other people's households, the majority have formed new households. There is a further economic distinction between childless partnerships (in which 81 per cent of partners were in full-time jobs) and those with children (in which only 31 per cent were, others being in part-time jobs or fully involved with the children). Eighty per cent of the lone mothers in their own homes were doing full-time housework and child care; and 27 per cent were divorced or separated.

Table 2.1 also shows trends over the decade 1982–92. Young people are leaving home earlier: proportions of young people living in their parental homes have decreased from 61 per cent in 1982 to 58 per cent in 1992. There has been an increase between 1982 and 1992 in transitional households: peer households and single-person households (from 5 to 7 per cent, and from 4 to 6 per cent respectively). There have also been changes in patterns of family formation: an increase in lone-parent households from 1 to 3 per cent, and a decrease in partnerships with children from 14 per cent to 10 per cent, while proportions in childless partnerships have remained static at 14 per cent. In other words, household and family formation processes have become more extended and complex. There is a greater separation between leaving home, forming partnerships and having children, and evidence that more young people (not just students) live independently of their parents prior to forming a co-resident partnership.

Closer analysis by age and gender (Table 2.1) shows that while men and women in the younger age groups are more likely to be living independently in 1992 than they were in 1982 or 1987, those aged 21–25 are slightly more likely to be living in the parental home, and this could be because they have left and returned (Jones, 1995). The older age group are also more likely to be living in transitional households in 1992 than they were in 1982, the increase being mainly among men in single-person households (an increase from 2 to 7 per cent among 18–20-year-olds, and from 7 to 11 per cent among 21–25-year-olds). Women are more likely than men to live with their peers, but there have been increases for both sexes in peer-sharing since 1982 (from 4 to 6 per cent for men, and from 5 to 8 per cent among women). Among those who have left their parental homes, there is therefore more diversity in household type.

ECONOMIC CONTEXT

During the period 1982–92 there have been major changes in the labour market and benefit system, as well as an extension of education and training, all of which have affected the economic power of young people, and these are reflected in the FES data (see also Hutton, 1990). There has been a striking decrease in full-time working, from 22 per cent to 9 per cent for women, and from 28 per cent to 16 per cent for men. This is partly because of the increase in numbers staying on longer in education, but is also because of an increase in part-time employment during the decade, to an extent that part-time employment has become more common than full-time employment among under-18s. Though part-time jobs were associated mainly with women, there has been an increase in male part-time working among those aged 16–21 years. The FES thus documents the collapse of the youth labour market and the re-defining of young people (mainly the under-18s) into students or trainees. Those still in the labour market have only a tenuous hold on it.

As a result of these structural changes, there is now greater income disparity between young people. Analysis showed that incomes of 16–25-year-olds in the bottom 20 per cent range were lower in absolute terms in 1992 than in 1987, and also that those under 21 years of age were relatively poorer in 1992 than their age peers in 1982, while the incomes of 21–25-year-olds have remained stable. This would suggest that income is now more structured by age than it was in the early 1980s. At the time of writing, current debate about the minimum wage suggests that the age inequalities in income will extend, with those under 26 years of age lacking the right to an adult minimum wage as they currently lack the right to adult levels of income support. Like the changes in benefit entitlement of young people, particularly during the 1980s and early 1990s, the proposals for excluding young people from an adult minimum wage will increase the social exclusion of the most disadvantaged.

The greater disparity in incomes since 1982 may have affected household formation. While median incomes of young people in their parental homes, kin households and peer households were all broadly similar in 1982, by 1992 there were clear income differences between the three groups, those living alone being the richest and those living with their parents being the poorest. The decisions regarding when and how to leave home may thus be more income-related in 1992 than they were in 1982. It is in these circumstances that housing strategies may come into force: while 'loners' have to be relatively affluent to make a successful break from the parental home, some young people may form partnerships or temporary households and pool their income resources to increase their power in the housing market.

HOUSEHOLD CONSUMPTION

The quality of a young person's home, and the goods in it, may not reflect wealth or poverty at an individual level. Attributing household-level data to individuals is problematic because of the different models of internal equity which may apply: because of age or generation (when young people are living in their parental homes) or gender (in the case of marital and partnership households), or social class (where young people share flats with age peers). Just because a household contains a television set or a washing machine it does not necessarily mean that an individual in the household has contributed to its cost or benefits from its presence.

Housing

If young people leaving home are more likely than before to live in transitional households before forming partnerships and having children, this means that the housing demand from *single* people has increased. Analysis of the FES confirms that the demand side of the 'youth housing market' (Jones, 1995) is defined by the transitional nature of youth. Young single people may need to be geographically mobile in order to chase courses and jobs, and need housing which offers flexibility; the private rented sector has tended to offer this, though not without risk. As they form partnerships and start families, they increasingly need stability and home comforts instead. By this stage in a 'housing career' (Ineichen, 1981; Jones, 1987) there has been a split between home ownership for wealthier groups, and social housing for the poor, as they enter the adult housing market. Stratification in youth housing ('housing classes') should be viewed on two dimensions: ownership versus renting reflecting conventional measures, but also impermanence versus permanence reflecting youth transitions.

The tenure in parental households, and to some extent that in 'destination households', provides a benchmark indication of trends overall. The increase in home ownership (from 59 per cent to 75 per cent) and the loss of public sector rented housing (from 36 per cent to 21 per cent) during the 1980s are clear in parental households (Table 2.2). For young people who have left the parental home, the private rented

Table 2.2 Tenure by household type (FES, 1982–92; row percentages)

Household type	Public rented (%)	Private rented (%)	Owner-occupied (%)	Rent-free (%)
1982				
Parental	36	3	59	2
Kin	40	4	47	9
Peer	24	41	29	6
One-person	16	62	16	6
Lone parent	97	0	3	0
Partners	16	19	62	4
Partners + child(ren)	52	8	38	3
All households	**35**	**10**	**53**	**3**
1987				
Parental	27	2	69	2
Kin	43	5	50	2
Peer	19	41	37	3
One-person	20	49	27	3
Lone parent	84	6	9	1
Partners	12	20	66	3
Partners + child(ren)	43	9	44	4
All households	**28**	**10**	**59**	**3**
1992				
Parental	21	3	75	2
Kin	32	6	59	3
Peer	13	52	33	3
One person	18	53	26	3
Lone parent	86	9	4	1
Partners	10	23	65	3
Partners + child(ren)	54	12	33	1
All households	**24**	**13**	**61**	**2**

sector also comes into play. Partnerships, with and without children, and peer households show the loss of the public rented sector, but suggest that housing demand was increasingly met in the private rented sector after a peak in home ownership in the late 1980s. Lone parents' housing also increasingly occupied the private rental sector (from 0 to 9 per cent). One-person households, like peer households, are mainly found in the private rented sector, but again there have been fluctuations, with home ownership peaking in 1987 and the private rented sector rallying thereafter.

We seem to be seeing here the effects of a variety of changes in the supply side of the housing market: firstly, the government incentives to increase home ownership, and the depletion of council housing stocks; secondly, the boost given to the private rented sector with the removal of controls; thirdly, the effects of the housing recession which occurred at the end of the 1980s and particularly affected young home-buyers, many of whom were saddled with negative equity. The findings suggest that some young people may have flirted with the idea of home ownership at the peak of the housing boom only to get their fingers burnt. The picture is not of a healthy youth housing market which caters for housing demand. Invisible in these data are young people who increasingly became homeless during the latter part of the decade (Hutson and Liddiard, 1994).

Domestic Goods

If consumption and spending become more home-based as individual household careers and domestic responsibilities develop, then we can expect a relationship between the type of household and the presence of consumer goods in it. The transitory nature of some households may, however, affect goods 'ownership'.

There is wide variation between household types in terms of 'goods-wealth', with parental households and childless partnerships being relatively goods-rich, while transitional households are goods-poor (Table 2.3). The standard of living of the parental home is lost to most when they leave, particularly if they live in transitional households before establishing more permanent homes where they can begin to accumulate household goods of their own. Clearly, some household goods reflect need – parents need washing machines, while others may manage without. For young people living in shared accommodation or bedsits, goods may be an encumbrance rather than a help. We must therefore beware of over-simplification. Even where both need and opportunities exist, strategies other than buying consumer goods may be brought into play. Those without freezers may eat out or get take-aways; those without washing machines may use launderettes (or take their washing 'home' to their parents), and those without television sets may spend their leisure in other ways: and all of these 'strategies' could reflect consumer choice rather than constraint. There appears to be little doubt, though, that childless couples form the wealthiest group of young people in terms of household goods.

Table 2.3 Proportion of households containing domestic goods (FES, 1982–92)

Household type	Freezer or fridge-freezer			Washing machine			Telephone			Television			Video		Computer	
	1982 (%)	1987 (%)	1992 (%)	1982 (%)	1987 (%)	1992 (%)	1982 (%)	1987 (%)	1992 (%)	1982 (%)	1987 (%)	1992 (%)	1987 (%)	1992 (%)	1987 (%)	1992 (%)
Parental	69	85	96	94	97	98	84	89	92	99	100	100	67	92	32	36
Kin	53	78	96	87	91	92	70	78	88	97	100	100	65	88	9	8
Peer	38	69	74	53	69	70	66	71	80	93	96	98	52	69	18	26
Single	12	38	60	29	38	53	38	47	64	69	84	87	28	53	6	10
Lone Parent	24	41	80	68	84	93	24	30	45	100	96	99	19	66	3	6
Partners	54	73	82	82	88	89	72	75	84	97	98	98	56	87	14	20
Partners + child(ren)	54	79	90	92	96	93	60	59	65	99	100	98	58	81	12	18
All households	**60**	**77**	**89**	**87**	**89**	**91**	**75**	**78**	**84**	**97**	**98**	**98**	**59**	**84**	**23**	**28**

There have been countervailing trends: the first towards the acquisition of consumer goods, in an increasingly consumption-oriented society (at least until the recession), and the second the increasing social division between the rich and the poor, with young people as a social group being over-represented among the latter, and divisions among young people increasing (as we have seen in other respects). With increased availability and visibility of goods, there may be among young people both an increased wish to own goods and a decreased capacity to do so. Goods ownership has changed dramatically over the decade and new goods such as videos and computers have come onto the market. Parental households again provide a base line for comparison in the following analysis, and also provide an indicator of what young people might have left behind in the parental home, and what they might aspire for in their own new homes. Table 2.3 shows more homes with freezers, telephones (though note the continuing low proportion of lone parents with telephones), and washing machines in 1992 than in 1982. Television ownership remained high, mainly increasing in single-person households. These findings may reflect changes in attitude in an age of consumerism (Warde, 1990) – television sets, for example, now being seen as a necessity rather than a luxury.

Judging from the consumer goods they contain, the households in which young people live have become more affluent. The transitional households in which more now live are less sparsely equipped than they were a decade before. Leaving home and entering a transitional household rather than a partnership home involved less material deprivation in 1992 than it did in 1982. Nevertheless, those living in one-person households and peer-shared households still have less access to household goods than those in other household situations, and lone parents are clearly disadvantaged compared with other family types. Still, we should wonder whether, if transitional households are becoming more comfortable, they are also becoming less transitional and whether people will opt to live in them for longer.

INDIVIDUAL CONSUMPTION

We now move from household consumption to individual spending, but retain the household typology as an aid to understanding the domestic context of spending. This has been observed to be crucial in research on adults. Research on expenditure among couples (Morris,

1990; Pahl, 1990) suggests a gendered division of labour within which (for example) women typically buy the food, while their male partners typically pay the costs of the car, and meals away from home. In many cases this means that women tend to buy on behalf of others while men benefit more directly from their spending (for example, women buy clothes for themselves and others, while men tend to buy clothes for themselves). This gendered division of labour suggests that the household is operating as a unit of consumption, within which individual inequality is in danger of becoming invisible. According to Jan Pahl (1983), individual spending is not necessarily a reflection of economic autonomy; nor, in many cases, will it fluctuate with individual (rather than household) income; instead, she suggests (Pahl, 1990) that household expenditure can be fully understood only in the context of the control of money within households. Though she is commenting on adults in couples, the same issues, of management and control, autonomy and responsibility, apply to young people's spending. Not all are researchable with the FES. Our intention is to explore the differences between 'consumer groups', defined by gender and household type, in their spending behaviour. The analysis of individual expenditure covered a wide range of expenditure categories. Here we focus on food, alcohol, clothing and footwear, and leisure. Analysis is of the 1992 data set unless otherwise stated. Rates of 'average weekly expenditure' are derived from the 14-day expenditure diaries and represent the average among the whole subgroup including those who spent nothing on a particular category during the diary period.

Food

Nearly everyone in the sample bought food. Figure 2.2 shows average weekly food expenditure for men and women in different household types. Food expenditure reflects domestic responsibility, and so spending on food increases when young people leave home. Young people living alone spend twice as much on food as those living with their parents (averaging £20.59 for men and £22.25 for women, compared with under £10), but sharing with peers keeps the costs down to under £18, supporting the value of this household strategy for those trying to leave home cheaply. Gender differences in food expenditure increase with family rather than household formation, women living in partnerships with or without children spend considerably more on food than their male partners, and further analysis indicated that this applied particularly where the latter were in manual work.

Figure 2.2 Spending on food (FES, 1992)

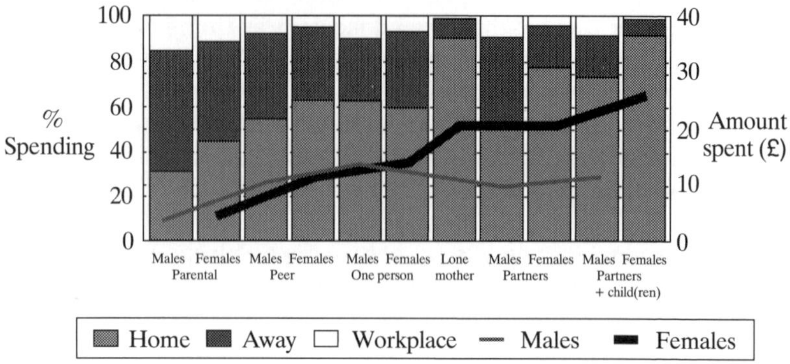

The FES data set distinguishes between the purchase of food for eating at home, for eating away from home, and for eating at the workplace, with 83 per cent, 79 per cent, and 47 per cent of the 16–25 subset spending in each category. These categories give some purchase on the distinction between eating out and eating at home, the former becoming more popular especially among the young with the increase in fast-food outlets in the last two decades (though see Beardsworth and Keil, 1997, for a critique). It is also tempting to distinguish between food as need and food as leisure, but this distinction immediately runs into difficulties. As the vertical bars in Figure 2.2 show, men are more likely than women to spend on eating out in all groups, but gender differences are weaker in transitional households than in partnership homes. Though men in partnerships or 'courting' may pay for their partners' meals, individuals in transitional households may have more autonomy. Only in one-person households do women spend a greater proportion of their food budget than men on eating out. The relative poverty of lone mothers is indicated: they are the most tied to eating at home and, though providing for their children as well as themselves, have similar levels of spending on food (£22.82) to women in one-person households. Men living in the parental home tend to buy food for eating out rather than at home, when they do buy food, and are the group most likely to allocate their food budget – as reflected in their expenditure – to eating out. Eating out is not necessarily, however, an indicator of wealth, even if eating in may in some cases be an indicator of poverty: young people living in the parental home may eat out as a form of escape, as a social activity, or as an assertion of independence from their parents; people living alone or with their peers may eat out because they do not know how to cook, because they lack cooking facilities, or because they like company; conversely parents may eat at home to save money, to be with the children, or because they enjoy it. For some, eating out is a form of leisure, but for others it might be a strategy for survival.

Drink

At all ages, men spend considerably more than women on alcohol (and may be buying for women, just as women appear to buy food for men), with a growing gender gap until both sexes reach their spending peak at around 21 years, after which the gender difference is maintained. The gender difference is in buying alcohol to drink away from home, rather than at home. For both sexes, drinking out appears to decrease, and the purchase of alcohol for drinking at home increases, as family formation begins. Across households, women spend less than men on drinking out, even those in single-person households and peer households spend less than men in the same household types. Women with children spend least of all. The biggest spenders on drinking out were 21–25-year-old men living in the parental home, who spent an average of £13.91 on drinking out, and were the group most likely to buy alcohol for drinking away from home (79 per cent did so). As with eating out, going out for a drink may be seen to fulfil an important function for those still living with their parents when many of their friends may have left home; through their social lives, if not their housing, they can perhaps define themselves as independent.

Clothes

Clothes and footwear represent another major expense, whether for style or need or a complex mixture of the two, and further reveals the increasingly gendered nature of buying. Women are almost twice as likely as men to buy clothes (69 per cent compared with 36 per cent), and thus spend more: the average weekly expenditure among women was £11.93 compared with £6.28 for men. The amounts spent and the likelihood of spending increase with age and household/family formation for both sexes. As with food expenditure, the greatest gender similarity is in peer households, while in contrast women living alone spend more than twice as much as men living alone. Buying for others is also gendered: even in households which do not contain children, such as peer households, women are more likely than men to buy children's clothing. There is, however, more variation among women than among men, ranging from women living alone, who spend an average £15 a week on clothing, and women in childless partnerships, who spend £13.23, to lone mothers, spending only £6.88 on clothing for their children as well as themselves. The high level of expenditure on clothes among young women living alone begins to identify this as a relatively new and interesting consumer group.

Leisure

The problem of distinguishing need from style or 'luxury' in young people's spending is highlighted in the analysis of leisure expenditure, which may represent a very real need for an age group where the main dynamic is emancipation from the family of origin, and where an important locus of this transition is in leisure activity.

With age, more people spend on leisure, and they also spend more. Average expenditure on leisure doubles for both men and women during the 16–25 age period, but men tend to spend more than women at all ages. Patterns are similar for men and women up to the 18–20 age group, when a distinct gender gap appears, with women's expenditure levelling and even falling, while that of men continues to increase. It appears to be children rather than partnership formation which suppress spending on leisure. Women living alone spend most on leisure: an average £14.84 a week, and as much as £16.15 in the 21–25 age group; next are men in peer households and in partnership households without children. Women living alone appear once again to be emerging as a distinct consumer group of women unencumbered by family responsibility.

The leisure categories analysed varied in the extent to which they represented passive or active leisure, the extent to which they were home-based, and their cost. Multivariate analysis showed that on the whole, age is not a good indicator of leisure spending. Gender affected whether leisure was active (men), and home-based (women), while income affected spending on more expensive leisure items. Even when these and other variables were included in the model, however, household type had a statistically significant effect on leisure spending. Table 2.4 shows leisure expenditure according to household type.

Table 2.4 Spending on leisure (FES, 1992). Percentage spending and mean weekly expenditure (£) among all, including non-spenders

	Entertainment		Sport		Electrical goods		Hobbies and games		Reading materials	
Household type	%	£	%	£	%	£	%	£	%	£
Parental										
Male	38	1.45	37	1.72	38	2.88	10	0.56	54	1.21
Female	35	1.32	21	0.73	29	2.05	18	0.61	56	1.11
Kin										
Male	22	1.55	44	5.82	33	1.59	22	0.52	56	1.11
Female	19	1.19	19	1.33	19	1.12	19	0.67	62	1.10
Peer										
Male	42	1.97	46	1.96	36	3.58	12	2.20	65	1.43
Female	49	1.67	23	0.56	34	1.08	19	1.07	61	1.26
One-person										
Male	33	1.04	31	1.28	42	2.48	11	1.20	82	1.66
Female	30	1.02	40	1.74	30	2.33	17	1.73	77	1.29
Lone parent										
Female	15	0.31	4	0.21	23	4.01	35	1.24	72	1.08
Partners										
Male	24	0.97	45	2.10	36	4.52	11	0.44	70	1.55
Female	16	0.59	24	0.87	22	1.21	17	0.59	77	1.53
Partners + child(ren)										
Male	18	1.39	29	0.71	39	1.96	22	1.25	70	1.13
Female	16	0.33	17	0.47	18	1.02	42	2.65	70	1.26
All males	**35**	**1.40**	**38**	**1.74**	**38**	**2.99**	**11**	**0.99**	**60**	**1.29**
All females	**29**	**1.03**	**21**	**0.73**	**27**	**1.82**	**22**	**0.99**	**64**	**1.22**

Entertainment and sport relate to leisure *outside* the home. In all, 32 per cent spent on entertainment, ranging from young people at the start of their household careers, in peer households (46 per cent), parental households (37 per cent) or living alone (32 per cent), down to those with family responsibilities (only 15 per cent of lone parents and 17 per cent of couples with children). Men were more likely than women to have spent on entertainment in all except peer households.

The greatest gender difference was between men and women in childless partnerships, where men may have been paying for both. Cutting across the normative gender pattern, however, were women in peer households, who were more likely (at 49 per cent) than any other group to spend on entertainment. Sport shows a similar picture, with men more likely to spend on sport and tending to spend more, except in one-person households, where women spenders spent an average £4.40 and men £4.15. These findings suggest that women living in transitional households may be less subject to gender constraints with regard to leisure outside the home.

Other leisure categories are more associated with domesticity – electrical leisure goods (mainly bought by men, especially those living alone), games and hobbies (mainly women living with partners and children), and reading materials (mainly those living alone or living with a partner and/or child). Young people living in the parental home were least likely to spend on reading materials, and (along with those living alone, or living in a childless partnership), were least likely to spend on hobbies and games – as with eating and drinking, they tend to be the least home-based consumer group.

ALLOCATION OF SPENDING

In all, we examined expenditure within seven different categories: food, clothing and footwear, personal goods and services, leisure, cigarettes and alcohol, motoring and transport, and household goods and services. Within each of these categories we identified changes in spending patterns as young people become adult, and considered how and why spending is differentiated, particularly by gender, economic status and household type. These seven categories are now combined into total individual expenditure (excluding housing costs) to explore how spending is allocated to different categories, and how this varies with age, gender and stage in household formation. The analysis of the 1992 data shows the shift from expenditure on leisure and 'style' to expenditure on domestic costs in the course of a household 'career' (Figure 2.3). This is clearer for women than for men, mainly because of the increased emphasis on food spending in the course of a household career. Women living in the parental home allocated only 22 per cent of their spending to food, compared with around 36 per cent for women with children; conversely, leisure spending similarly decreased from 14 per cent to 8 per cent respectively,

Figure 2.3 Allocation of expenditure (1992)

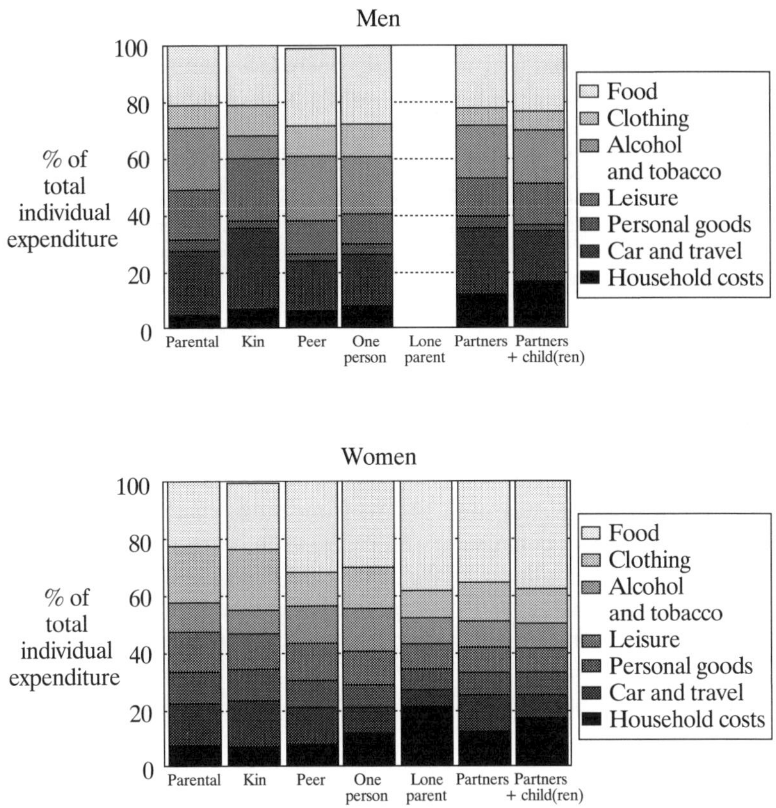

and clothing also tends to decrease in 'significance'. On the other hand, women's expenditure on alcohol and tobacco peaks in transitional households, then falls again.

Among men, the proportion of total expenditure spent on food, clothing and alcohol and tobacco products increases from living in the parental home to living in transitional households, and then decreases again with entry into partnership households, where, as we found, female partners shop for others. Thus, food represents 21 per cent of expenditure among men in the parental home, rises to around 30 per cent among men living with peers or alone, but decreases again to around 23 per cent for men in partnerships. Clothing has the greatest 'significance' for men, in terms of their own spending, in kin and peer households. Spending on tobacco and alcohol increases slightly in transitional households, but decreases again in partnership households (to around 17 per cent), while household and travel costs increase with domestic responsibility.

Over the 1982–92 period there have been changes in the overall allocation of spending (Figure 2.4). Men's spending on tobacco and alcohol has reduced in relative terms from 24 to 20 per cent, while their expenditure on travel has increased from 19 to 22 per cent. In contrast, women allocate more to tobacco and alcohol (up from 8 to 11 per cent), and more to leisure and travel, but considerably less to food (down from 41 to 28 per cent – Figure 2.5). The change among 25-year-old women was marked: in 1982, 56 per cent of their expenditure was on food, while by 1982 this was down to one-third. Between 1982 and 1992 the amounts men spent on food nearly trebled, while that of women in 1992 was less than double its level in 1982, indicating that men are bearing more of the food costs. This may be partly because of the increase in 'eating out' over the decade, or it may reflect a real difference in patterns of food shopping. Whatever the cause, this dramatic decrease in the dominance of food buying among women means that women's spending has become more varied.

Figure 2.4 The changing allocation of expenditure (FES, 1982–92)

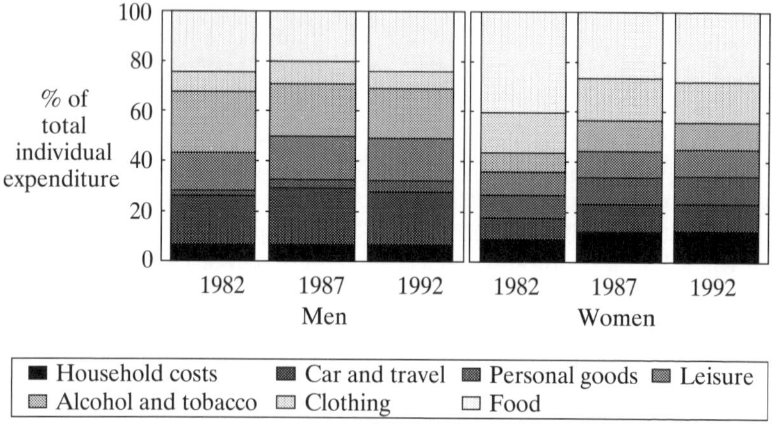

Figure 2.5 Changing expenditure among women (FES, 1982–92)

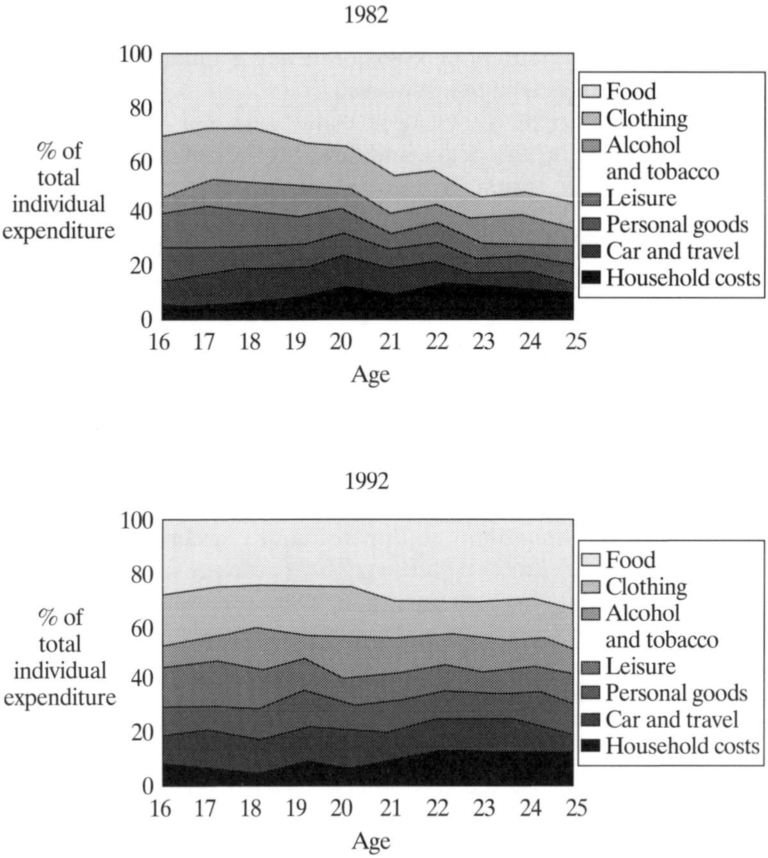

DISCUSSION

In many ways this research raises more questions than it answers. A survey designed for the study of consumption and spending in households has limited value for the study of consumption in youth. In many respects our findings are tentative and simply raise research questions for closer study. Nevertheless, there are some issues on which we are clear. Spending patterns among young people can best be understood in relation to their household context, which changes as they leave home. As patterns of household formation become more extended and more complex, this leads to changes in patterns of consumption. New household forms offer opportunities for patterns of expenditure to become less gendered.

More young people are living in transitional (or 'non-familial') households, alone or with peers, and these present an interesting phenomenon for study. It may be argued that they are ephemeral: their temporary nature is reflected in their tenure and lack of consumer goods, and their 'undomesticated' spending patterns. Yet we do not know how long such households last. Despite Diana Leonard's (1980) observation that to set up 'home' alone or with peers was 'a contradiction in folk terms', attitudes may be changing. Transitional households may thus become less transitional and more 'home-like'. Compared with other household types they may not be particularly comfortable, though they increasingly do contain consumer goods, yet they may fulfil a need for young people seeking independence. They appear to offer a period of relative autonomy to young people – especially women – leaving home on one dimension of consumption at least. Expenditure on leisure and style may be a strategy for coping with material deprivation in the home, or an assertion of new-found independence from parents – both a political statement and a 'lifestyle choice'.

The circumstances of young people living in their parental homes is somewhat different. Here they are more likely to be surrounded with domestic goods and 'home comforts', but they are more dependent on their parents. They may be wishing to set up independent homes but be unable to afford to do so. The strategy of finding a job with accommodation provided, or of sharing with peers may not be available to them. Can they assert their independence from their parents through their consumption? The findings have suggested that those living at home try to live a life away from their parents, eating and drinking out, and are unlikely to spend on domesticity. Through their consumption they may be able to define themselves (to their peers) as emancipated from their parents. This may be crucial to those living in the parental home, and it could be seen as a strategy through which they are resisting the economic and social dependency imposed on them by government policies which have made independent living more difficult to achieve. However, this strategy may result in 'conspicuous consumption' at a superficial level but which may be misleading. It may in practice indicate poverty rather than wealth.

As young people take on more domestic responsibility, their spending shifts from leisure spending to expenditure on the home. Gender differences in spending patterns increase with household and family formation, as young women begin to buy food or clothing or leisure goods for others rather than themselves. Women are more likely than men at all stages in a 'household career' to spend on home-based consumption. Family formation and responsibility for children makes women more home-centred, and their patterns of expenditure more differentiated from those of men. However, the analysis has shown that spending patterns in transitional households indicate a domestic division of labour which is less gendered. Women living in peer households or living alone thus appear to have far greater autonomy and power in the consumer market than they do when living with parents or partners and children. They are spending more on themselves, on clothing and leisure, and less on others, and their spending patterns are more similar to those of men. With the development of transitional households, and with changes in leisure (especially 'eating out'), gender differences in spending patterns appear to have decreased over the decade studied.

This research has shown not only the extent of inequalities among young people, but also the inadequacy of one-dimensional measures of consumption. Nevertheless there are two main points we would like to stress. The first is the importance of household status as an indicator of spending patterns. While the state welfare system tends to rely heavily on age as a criterion of need, and apportions income accordingly, this research confirms the importance of taking account of young people's changing domestic circumstances when assessing needs and the social adequacy of incomes. The second (related) point is that there is a danger of gaining a false impression of wealth from 'conspicuous consumption' in youth if the domestic context of spending is not taken into account. There is a growing wealth divide among young people. Some may be using short-term consumption strategies to cope with their lack of power in other spheres of their lives, but this does not make them 'consumer citizens', with real economic power in the consumer markets. Spending on 'style' and leisure may, for example, make life more bearable for those forced into extended dependence on their parents, but it may also be a trap, making it even more difficult for them to set up an independent home of their own.

NOTES

1. The project, *Changing Patterns of Income and Expenditure in Youth*, was funded by the ESRC (R000235393). Material from the Family Expenditure Survey is Crown Copyright, has been made available by the Central Statistical Office through the ESRC Data Archive and has been used by permission. Neither the CSO nor the ESRC Data Archive bear any responsibility for the analysis or interpretation of the data reported here. The views expressed here are those of the authors alone.
2. FES data are held at individual and household level. The *individual-level* data include an expenditure diary over the last 14 days. The *household-level* data, mainly collected from designated 'heads of households', allowed us to construct the household typology, and examine domestic goods, tenure and housing costs at household level.
3. The concept of transitional household statuses may itself become more complex and even more problematic, with the increasing number of one-person households, and increasing impermanance of households generally. Alternatively, it could be argued that households are generally becoming transitional.

REFERENCES

Abrams, M. (1959) *The Teenage Consumer*, LPE Chapter 5 (London: Routledge and Kegan Paul).

Beardsworth, A. and Keil, T. (1997) *Sociology on the Menu* (London: Routledge).

Brake, M. (1980) *The Sociology of Youth Cultures and Youth Subcultures* (London: Routledge and Kegan Paul).

Cohen, A. K. (1965) 'The Sociology of the Deviant Act: Anomie and Beyond', *American Sociological Review*, 30, 1–14.

Coles, B. (1995) *Youth and Social Policy: Youth Citizenship and Young Careers* (London: UCL Press).

Dale, A. (1987) 'The Effect of Life Cycle on Three Dimensions of Stratification', in A. Bryman, B. Bytheway, P. Allatt and T. Keil (eds), *Rethinking the Life Cycle* (Basingstoke: Macmillan).

Department of Employment (1985) *Family Expenditure Survey Report* (London: DOE).

Featherstone, M. (1990) 'Perspectives on Consumer Culture', *Sociology*, 24(1), 5–22.

Griffin, C. (1985) *Typical Girls?* (London: Routledge and Kegan Paul).

Hebdige, D. (1979) *Subculture: The Meaning of Style* (London: Methuen).

HMSO (1993) *Family Spending: A Report on the 1992 Family Expenditure Survey* (London: HMSO).

Hutson, S. and Jenkins, R. (1987) 'Coming of Age in South Wales', in D. Ashton and P. Brown (eds), *Education and Economic Life* (Brighton: Falmer Press).
Hutson, S. and Liddiard, M. (1994) *Youth Homelessness: The Construction of a Social Issue* (London: Macmillan).
Hutton, S. (1990) 'Comparison between Cohorts', SPRU Working Chapter 756, University of York.
Ineichen, B. (1981) 'The Housing Decisions of Young People', *British Journal of Sociology*, 32(2), 252–8.
Jones, G. (1987) 'Leaving the Parental Home: an Analysis of Early Housing Careers', *Journal of Social Policy*, 16(1), 49–74.
Jones, G. (1995) *Leaving Home* (Milton Keynes: Open University Press).
Jones, G. and Wallace, C. (1992) *Youth, Family and Citizenship* (Milton Keynes: Open University Press).
Kirk, D., Nelson, S., Sinfield, A. and Sinfield, D. (1991) *Excluding Youth: Poverty among Young People Living Away from Home* (Edinburgh: Centre for Social Welfare Research, University of Edinburgh).
Leonard, D. (1980), *Sex and Generation: A Study of Courtship and Marriage* (London: Tavistock).
Mintel (1988) *Special Report: British Lifestyles* (London: Mintel).
Morris, L. (1990) *The Workings of the Household* (Cambridge: Polity).
Pahl, J. (1983) 'The Allocation of Money and the Structuring of Inequality within Marriage', *Sociological Review*, 31, 237–62.
Pahl, J. (1990) 'Household Spending, Personal Spending and the Control of Money in Marriage', *Sociology*, 24(1), 119–138.
Piachaud, D. (1982) 'Patterns of Income and Expenditure within Families', *Journal of Social Policy*, 2 (4), 469–82.
Pickvance, C. and Pickvance, K. (1994) 'Towards a Strategic Approach to Housing Behaviour: a Study of Young People's Housing Strategies in South-East England', *Sociology*, 28(3), 657–77.
Roberts, K. (1981) *Leisure*, 2nd edn (London: Longman).
Roberts, K. and Parsell, G. (1991) 'Young People's Sources and Levels of Income, and Patterns of Consumption, in Britain in the late 1980s', *Youth and Policy*, 35, 20–5.
Roberts, K., Parsell, G. and Furlong, A. (1991) 'Class and Gender Divisions among Young Adults at Leisure', in C. Wallace and M. Cross (eds), *Youth in Transition* (Basingstoke: Falmer).
Walker, R. (1988) 'The Costs of Household Formation', in R. Walker and G. Parker (eds), *Money Matters: Income, Wealth and Financial Welfare* (London: Sage).
Wallace, C. (1987) *For Richer, For Poorer: Growing up in and out of Work* (London: Tavistock).
Warde, A. (1990) 'Introduction to the Sociology of Consumption', *Sociology*, 24(1), 1–4.

3 'We've Got Friends who Live in Council Houses': Power and Resistance in Home Ownership

CRAIG M. GURNEY

INTRODUCTION

The dramatic growth of home ownership in Great Britain during the second half of the twentieth century has created new processes of power and resistance around the consumption of housing. Drawing on a reading of Foucault's work on *disciplinary power* and the *normalising judgement*, this chapter argues that home owners are both the objects and the subjects of power and resistance. The results of intensive research from two sources is reported; first, an analysis of transcripts generated from in-depth interviews with home owners in St George, Bristol; second, a discursive analysis of the language of landmark housing policy documents. The diversity of these data sources is significant as it enables a focus on the exercise and experience of processes of power and resistance which reinforce pervasive cultural stereotypes of owners and tenants at a local and a national level. The first part of the chapter outlines the inter-relationships between consumption, culture and housing. It argues that a specific set of taken-for-granted ideas and attitudes about home owners and tenants is deeply embedded in contemporary British culture. The chapter then goes on to present a Foucaultian perspective on power and resistance in home ownership. The third part of the chapter draws upon qualitative data to explore power and resistance in discourses which construct owners as 'normal' and tenants as 'abnormal'. The chapter concludes by locating the consumption of housing within a cultural studies perspective.

WE ARE WHERE WE LIVE: CONSUMPTION, CULTURE AND HOUSING

In this section I argue that homes and households represent key sites in the exercise of power and resistance and, consequently, that *we are where we live*. First, I draw upon the sociology of consumption literature to show how the privatised consumption of housing through home ownership has been used to suggest the emergence of consumption sector cleavages in contemporary British society. Second, I argue that cultural distinctiveness has been neglected at the expense of economic and political distinctions in this debate. Finally, I outline questions about the power and resistance inherent in the consuming cultures of homes and households. These questions are addressed in the remainder of this chapter in relation to home ownership, and in subsequent chapters in relation to home decoration, the dinner party, the use of space in retirement, and in local versus global emancipatory practices in the environmental movement.

The Sociology of Consumption and the Growth of Home Ownership

The emergence of the so-called *sociology of consumption* has been well documented elsewhere (Saunders, 1986; Otnes, 1988; *Sociology*, 1990; Campbell, 1995; Urry, 1995; Corrigan, 1997). Although this tradition has a rather fragmented lineage the work of Peter Saunders is influential. His work in urban sociology identified the emergence of new divisions of inequality which, he argued, were based upon access to the means of *consumption* and that these divisions cut across traditional class divisions based upon access to the means of *production*. He argued that divisions between owners and non-owners of consumption goods and services represented a 'new and crucial aspect of stratification', and that their effects might be seen in 'patterns of political alignment' and in 'patterns of economic privilege and cultural advantage' (Saunders, 1986: 162). Saunders went on to argue that these divisions were most clearly visible in the consumption of housing.

Table 3.1 demonstrates the growth of home ownership in Great Britain from less than one-third of all dwellings in 1950 to more than two-thirds of all dwellings at the end of the century. This trend has attracted considerable research interest, but whilst there has been extensive work on the relationship between class dealignment and

Table 3.1 The growth of home ownership in Great Britain (1950–95)

Tenure	Percentage stock of all dwellings at end of year					
	1950	1960	1970	1980	1990	1995
Owner occupied	29.5	42.0	49.5	55.0	65.8	66.8
Rented from local authority or new town	18.0	26.6	30.5	31.1	21.9	18.9
Private renting	44.6	25.7	14.9	13.7	9.2	9.9
Other tenures, including housing associations	7.9	5.7	5.1		3.1	4.3

Sources: Figures for 1950 and 1960 from Central Statistical Office (1970: 137). Figures for 1970 from Central Statistical Office (1971: 125). Figures for 1980 from Department of the Environment *et al.* (1990: 27). Figures for 1990 from Department of the Environment *et al.* (1994: 129). Figures for 1995 from Department of the Environment *et al.* (1997: 33).

housing consumption (Dunleavy, 1986; Byrne, 1989; Sullivan, 1989), patterns of housing wealth accumulation and inheritance (Forrest and Murie, 1989, 1994; Hamnett *et al.*, 1991) and the relative costs to the consumer of owning or renting (Kemeny, 1981; Saunders and Harris, 1988; Duncan, 1990), little attention has been paid to what Saunders called the *cultural advantage* of home ownership. Apart from some diversionary discussions about whether home owners might derive a sense of 'ontological security' from their dwellings (Harloe, 1984; Franklin, 1986) questions about cultural distinctiveness have been simply ignored or dismissed as maverick within the dominant 'economic or material perspective' (Campbell, 1995: 97) on consumption and social stratification within urban sociology. Nor has housing consumption featured in the 'cultural and psychological perspective' on consumption, identity and postmodernity which grew out of the popular culture and critical theory literature (Campbell, 1995: 97–8). There is an irony here, in that a set of deeply ingrained attitudes about owners and tenants seems to have accompanied the dramatic postwar growth of home ownership with the result that the cultural distinctiveness of housing tenure is now as well established in popular culture as it is under-researched. Below I briefly review these attitudes and raise a number of broader questions of relevance to power and resistance in housing consumption.

The Cultural Distinctiveness of Home Ownership

Housing tenure is much more than a socially and legally constructed set of consumption rights. It also functions as a shorthand for the cultural attributes of particular social groups. Surprisingly little research has been carried out on this topic, but the work of Collison and Saunders merits special attention.

Collison's (1963) *The Cutteslowe Walls* is a case study in social class, housing tenure and the appropriation of space on a housing estate in Oxford. Two 3-metre walls 'topped by a set of formidable revolving iron spikes' (Collison, 1963: 13) were erected across existing roads in 1934 by a private company who had developed an estate of predominantly owner-occupied, semi-detached dwellings. On the other side of the walls was a 'corporation estate' of predominantly local authority rented, terraced dwellings. The dispute about the walls, which lasted until their eventual demolition in 1959, revealed deep-seated suspicion, mistrust and hostility between middle-class and working-class residents in the area. The implied status of home owners and local authority tenants was undeniably at the crux of this dispute. Whilst the growth of home ownership suggests that the tenure no longer represents a relatively scarce 'positional good' (Hirsch, 1977), Collison's study reminds us of the ways in which housing tenure has been used as a label denoting a particular set of social attitudes, characteristics or status.

More recently, Saunders (1990) has drawn on the results of research in Burnley, Slough and Derby to argue that important cultural differences between owners and renters persist. In simple terms he suggests that the meaning of home, attachment to dwelling and neighbourhood and the desire to personalise the dwelling all exhibit variations based on whether people own or rent their accommodation.

> Owners associate home more strongly with values such as personal autonomy and they are more likely to see home as a place where they can relax and 'be themselves'. Owners experience greater freedom in expressing choice over where they live and they experience greater control over their living space. In many cases they derive a high level of satisfaction from working on their homes, whereas many tenants feel unwilling or unable to perform such labour on a house which they constantly remember is not their own.
>
> (Saunders, 1990: 302)

Saunders' findings have been subject to considerable scrutiny (Forrest *et al.*, 1990; Gurney, 1990, 1997; Gurney and Means, 1993; Mandic and Clapham, 1996). A common counter-argument is that attitudes towards housing tenure and housing consumers are socially constructed and thus are liable to change over time and place according to prevailing conditions in the housing market. This means that any cultural advantages inherent in home ownership will, at any time, reflect the currency of some attitudes over others.

Because they are so deeply embedded in contemporary culture these socially constructed attitudes are difficult to refute empirically or liable to be easily changed. Table 3.2 reports national survey data to illustrate this. Despite an increase in the perceived risks associated with the tenure between 1986 and 1997, a commitment to home ownership as the preferred choice remains strong even amongst households with mortgage arrears or in negative equity (Kempson and Ford, 1995; Forrest *et al.*, 1997). The persistence of 'common-sense' assertions that owning is cheaper than renting in the long run appear to have been largely unaffected by the housing market slump of the 1990s.

Similarly, 'common-sense' assertions which characterise council or housing association tenants as 'problem' families, petty criminals, scroungers, drug and alcohol abusers, rioters or common people lacking taste and decency are both easy to make and difficult to resist. Every time a taxi-driver refuses to take passengers to a part of a town or city, or vandalism is blamed upon children living on a particular estate, or someone is refused financial credit because of their

Table 3.2 Trends in attitudes towards home ownership in Great Britain (1986–97; percentages in each year)

	1986	1989	1991	1996	1997
Over time it is cheaper than renting	83	81	76	82	82
It is something to leave to your family	80	85	83	76	76
Buying is too risky for couples without secure jobs	59	58	68	69	65
It is a big financial burden to repair and maintain	50	54	57	55	55
It can be a risky investment	20	20	32	50	44
It makes it easier to move when you want	64	65	54	34	44

Source: Office of National Statistics (1998: 176).

address, deeply pervasive cultural stereotypes about housing tenures are reproduced. The association of cultural attributes with particular parts of towns and cities is a long-established one but, in Britain, at the turn of the twenty-first century, housing tenure has become a convenient label behind which to mobilise suspicion or fear of minority groups. Housing tenures must therefore be understood as labels which enable cultural stereotypes of 'owners' and 'renters' to be deployed.

Power and Resistance in Housing Consumption

Students of cultural studies may have found the preceding discussion of housing tenure a distraction. Indeed, a major criticism of much contemporary housing research is its 'tenure fetishism' (Barlow and Duncan, 1988). The final part of this section temporarily puts discussions of owning and renting aside to consider broader issues of power and resistance in housing consumption.

> Throughout our lives, whether we our conscious of it or not, our home and its contents are very potent statements about who we are.
>
> (Cooper Marcus, 1995: 12)

Housing is a consumption good like any other, and the argument that identity is either affirmed or contested through consumption of the 'home and its contents' is by no means new (Becker, 1977; Csikszentmihalyi and Rochberg-Halton, 1981; Duncan, 1981). Consequently, we are, in a very real sense, where we live. Cooper Marcus's distinction between the dwelling and its contents is a useful one and is used below.

Dwelling exteriors represent an effective and visually striking site for the transmission of complex and contradictory messages (Preziosi, 1979). In Britain these are typically manifested in dwelling type (terraced house, bungalow, starter home, etc.) and in dwelling and garden furniture (lucky horseshoes, stone-cladding, garden gnomes, etc.). The transmission of these housing messages raises a whole host of questions about taste, aesthetics and cultural practices, but they also raise questions about the degree of choice which different housing consumers may exercise, and questions about the search behaviour people use when exercising that choice. Crucial to these is the idea that the consumption of housing satisfies more than the basic human need for shelter. As Corrigan observes:

> [C]onsumption communicates social meaning, and is the site of struggles over social distinction. The fulfilling of more concrete needs arising from, say, individual feelings of cold or hunger seems almost an accidental by-product.
>
> (Corrigan, 1997: 32)

The problem is, of course, in unravelling precisely what these social meanings are. Do the messages mean the same things to different people? Are they about keeping up with the Joneses or about people differentiating themselves from the Joneses? (Jackson and Thrift, 1995: 227). Are they ironic or serious? Do they affirm a message from all the inhabitants or are they contested within households? Questions such as these form an important part of the way in which analyses of housing consumption could incorporate issues of power and resistance.

The home is a crucial location for the consumption of goods and services in contemporary British society. As such it is also a crucial location wherein power and resistance in consumption can be studied. Although this is the basic premise of a number of other chapters in this book, it is worth briefly considering the forms this power and resistance might take. Csikszentmihalyi and Rochberg-Halton (1981: 17) have argued that domestic interiors constitute a 'complex ecology of signs'. This may include, for example, soft and hard furnishings; ornaments; the display of CD, record and book collections, posters or photographs; and tidiness or disorder. In relation to decoration and decor, Madigan and Munro (1996: 44) suggest that such consumption patterns may reveal deliberate choices to convey preferences for four distinct styles of *traditional cottagey, country house, modern hi-tech*, or *postmodern*. In practice, of course, such styles can seldom be identified in the purest sense because people tend not to buy all their furniture at the same time from the same retail outlets. Nevertheless, the consumption of decor can reveal important relations of power and resistance between household members (meticulous parents and untidy or rebellious children, for instance). Madigan and Munro go on to argue that consumption in/for the home carries a 'heavy burden of ideological conformity' (1996: 41). This can be revealed in power and resistance relations between household members and their guests when differing expectations of taste and etiquette can be observed. These might include, for instance, the presentation of self and of intimate relationships, or the consumption of food, spare bedroom spaces, or the strategic removal or addition of certain artefacts. Mike Leigh's film *Abigail's Party* provides overdrawn but accurate representations of these processes of power and resistance. Finally, there are issues of power and resistance between individual household members and others. Postmodern discussions of consumption which suggest that there is 'no essential correspondence between particular commodities and particular identities' (Jackson and Thrift, 1995: 227) enable consumption for/in home to take the form of a complex code which is indecipherable to all but the visitor who has the cultural capital to crack it. Two examples illustrate the argument that some people are able to exert power and resistance through home-based consumption patterns. The first is the growth of a self-consciously ironic *loungecore* consumption culture associated with easy-listening music and a postmodern reworking of the excesses of 1970s fashion and design. This trend can be identified amongst people in the late 1990s who 'wear ironic flares, position their irony coffee tables next to their ironic brown couches and, amazingly, [are] not ... dismissed as tasteless morons' (Rumbold, 1998: 70). The second is the use of domestic symbols in gay and lesbian households to establish a sense of identity and to construct home as 'the place they [*sic*] can forget the habit of self-concealment and constant vigilance which spring from having a "secret" self' (Egerton, 1990: 76). Johnston and Valentine suggest that in heterosexual households lesbian identity is subverted by 'hiding pictures of lesbian icon kd lang under the mattress and gay fiction behind the bookcase' (Johnston and Valentine, 1995: 102), or is 'discreetly performed so that it is not read by other family members' (*ibid.*: 103). Even when lesbians leave the parental home, and can create and manage their own domestic space, visits from guests to whom they are not 'out' can necessitate changing the performance of home by removing posters, books or photographs to 'de-dyke' the house (*ibid.*: 106–7).

This section has illustrated how housing tenure constitutes an important variable in economic and material discussions on the sociology of consumption. It argued that cultural discussions concerning housing tenures have been neglected in this debate. Finally, a number of broader questions about power and resistance in the consuming cultures of homes and households were raised. The neglect of cultural discussions concerning housing tenure are addressed in the remainder of this chapter through a selected reading of Foucault's work on power and resistance.

POWER AND RESISTANCE IN HOME OWNERSHIP: A FOUCAULTIAN PERSPECTIVE

> An all pervasive, subtle and discrete 'power' obsesses Foucault ... for example, he points out that the minute operations of power are often not perceived in the daily routine of modern lives ... [t]he disciplining which Foucault finds everywhere in our society is ... largely unseen ... [The mechanisms] so successfully representing themselves as 'natural' and so effectively disseminate themselves that they remain anonymous and unexplained.
>
> (Bové, 1994: 318)

In this section I outline a theoretical framework for the study of home ownership derived from Foucault's work on power. I argue that home owners are both the object and subject of disciplinary power and that the precise nature of this power remains unexplicated within the contemporary literature on housing consumption. In Bové's terms this power has gone unnoticed because it is regarded either as natural or is simply unseen. This section challenges the invisibility of housing tenure in three ways. The first part of this section draws on a reading of Foucault to introduce the idea that a particular kind of power is embodied in home ownership. It then goes on to consider Foucault's *normalising judgement*, and applies this to an understanding of home ownership. The section concludes by making some observations on the links between power and discourse as a framework for data presented in the rest of the chapter.

The Disciplinary Power of Home Ownership

Because debates within the economic and material perspective on consumption have remained largely untouched by the influence of Foucault's work, the debate about the power relations of tenure change has been characterised by a somewhat restricted, bipolar definition of power. Thus, home owners *derive* economic power from the value of their dwellings, whilst local authority tenants become *disempowered* through processes of social exclusion. Foucault's notion of power, on the other hand, is constituted in quite a different way. The extracts below emphasise this;

> We must cease once and for all to describe the effects of power in negative terms; it 'excludes', it 'represses', it 'censors', it 'abstracts',

> it 'marks', it 'conceals'. In fact, power produces; it produces reality; it produces domains of objects and rituals of truth.
>
> (Foucault, 1977: 194)

> Power ... must be understood ... as the multiplicity of force relations immanent in the sphere in which they operate ... power is everywhere, not because it embraces everything but because it comes from everywhere.
>
> (Foucault, 1979: 92)

> Power must be analysed as something which circulates, or rather as something which only functions in the form of a chain. It is never localised here or there, never in anybody's hands, never appropriated as a commodity or a piece of wealth. Power is employed and exercised through a net-like organisation. And not only do individuals circulate between its threads; they are always in the position of simultaneously undergoing and exercising this power. ... In other words, individuals are the vehicles of power, not its points of application.
>
> (Foucault, 1980a: 98)

These extracts from Foucault's work clarify the purpose of this chapter. The intention is to focus not on the source of power, nor upon who exercises it but, rather, the processes and outcomes of power and resistance inherent in home ownership. Thus, power is understood here as the forces and tactics which socially construct home ownership as the *normal* way to consume housing. This argument suggests that the tenure is imbued with a disciplinary power which normalises home owners in the same way that Foucault's inmates, orphans and soldiers are normalised. The mechanisms, processes and outcomes of power are, of course, different in this analogy but home owners nevertheless are simultaneously undergoing and exercising disciplinary power.

The Normalising Judgement

In *Discipline and Punish* Foucault uses historical case study evidence to identify disciplinary power in 'a policy of coercions that act upon the [physical and social] body' (Foucault, 1977: 138). Arguably, the most important of these is the *normalising judgement*. Foucault operationalises this term in his description of the orphanage of Chevalier Paulet where, around the turn of the nineteenth century, a series of *infra-penalties* governed the conforming/non-conforming practices of the children living there. He describes them thus;

> The workshop, the school, the army were subject to a whole micro-penalty of time (lateness, absences, interruptions of tasks), of activity (inattention, negligence, lack of zeal), of behaviour (impoliteness, disobedience), of speech (idle chatter, insolence), of the body ('incorrect' attitudes, irregular gestures, lack of cleanliness), of sexuality (impurity, indecency) ... by way of punishment a whole series of subtle procedures was used from light physical punishment to minor deprivations and petty humiliations.
>
> (Foucault, 1977: 178)

The 'normal' order was laid down by a set of regulations based on repetitive observations of the children's activities. Foucault argues that these observations have a number of profoundly important implications. First, they allow the comparison of individuals by assessing the degree of normalcy of their various actions. It follows from this that an individual's skills, attitudes or attributes are demonstrable and quantifiable and that these can be used to quantifiably (re)define what constitutes normalcy or conformity. Finally, that these processes allow the identification of a frontier of abnormal behaviour at which point infra-penalties are applied. Foucault goes on to describe how young people who failed to conform to these expectations were punished as a 'shameful class' at the École Militaire (*ibid.*: 182). In Foucault's words, where this kind of normalising power exists it 'compares, differentiates, hierarchizes, homogonizes, [and] excludes' (*ibid.*: 183). But what relevance have these accounts of normalising judgements got for an understanding of home ownership in contemporary British society?

It has certainly been established in this chapter and elsewhere that home ownership is, in numerical terms, now 'normal' in Great Britain. Seven out of every ten households in Britain are home owners, whilst eight out of ten of all households want to be home owners (Pannel, 1997). The marketing strategies of mortgage companies reflect this in their conflation of the words *home* and *ownership* in selling mortgages as the natural prerequisite to *a home of one's own*. A home-improvement industry centred around DIY, decoration and taste has grown up in response to the assumption that home ownership denotes a certain success and buying into a certain lifestyle package. This, in turn, has meant that home owners constitute a specific marketing target for companies which sell double glazing, or equity release schemes, for example. Conversely renters may encounter difficulties in hiring electronic equipment or in securing personal loans. These trends provide some evidence to suggest that home owners are normalised through comparisons and measurements, but is there any evidence to suggest that Foucault's infra-penalties can also be identified in patterns of housing consumption?

Perhaps the most effective infra-penalty is exclusion. The measurement and comparison of normal behaviour and the identification of a frontier of abnormal behaviour has become a natural and inevitable part of moving house in Great Britain. A number of normalising practices which constitute effective barriers of entry to social rented housing,[1] private rented housing and home ownership currently exist. In the social rented sector, many local authorities and housing associations refuse to accommodate people convicted of certain crimes. In the private rented sector, potential tenants are routinely expected to provide references from former landlords, employers and a bank or building society. An examination of earnings, marital status, sexuality, health and indebtedness are routinely part of the process of entering home ownership or moving within the tenure. This process enables mortgage applicants to be categorised as either quality borrowers or a high risk. The extract below demonstrates this. It is a personal correspondence from the senior underwriter of a life assurance company seeking to insure my life as a mortgage applicant. The letter is a response to an earlier letter in which I queried the homophobic assumptions revealed in the design and contents of a *supplementary health and lifestyle questionnaire*.

> I do not concur with your statement that most homosexuals are only at a similar risk of HIV infection as heterosexuals. *It has been proven statistically*, that in the United Kingdom that [sic] the male homosexual community are more at risk than the heterosexuals of a similar age and social group. ... Obtaining the information you talk about such as number of partners, frequency and nature of sexual acts and whether appropriate precautions are taken is extremely difficult and obviously impossible to validate in the unfortunate event of an AIDS related claim. In view of the restrictions placed upon us as detailed above, we are left with little option but to attempt to *place individuals in more easily identifiable groups* and then underwrite each accordingly. Obviously each case is different ... but the system does give us a place to start the risk assessment. An example of this may

> be a monogamous homosexual who would receive better terms than an obviously promiscuous heterosexual with a history of sexually transmitted disease, the latter being very likely to be refused terms altogether.
>
> (Correspondence to the author, 25 July 1994; emphasis added)[2]

The consanguinity of *normal* sexuality and *normal* housing consumption is striking in this account and suggests opportunities for further research which assesses the extent and nature of resistance to disciplinary power for borrowers outside the *normal* range of lifestyles. Normalising judgements which equate *normal* home ownership with a *normal* heterosexual family or *normal* household have profoundly important implications for housing access and affordability amongst lesbian and gay couples, single parent households and single person households (Watson, 1986; Gilroy, 1994; Smailes, 1994).

Making the Disciplinary Power of Home Ownership Visible

In this final part of the section I outline a framework for the analysis of data which focuses on the relationships between power and discourse by asking: what empirical evidence can be drawn upon to demonstrate the normalisation of home ownership?

We have already seen that to demonstrate normalisation is more complex than simply identifying a numerical superiority. Instead, it necessitates collecting, studying, foregrounding and deconstructing the ideas produced by the disciplinary power created through the processes of normalisation. Foucault explains the reasons for this:

> What makes power hold good, what makes it accepted is simply the fact that it doesn't only weigh upon us a force that says no, but that it traverses and produces things.
>
> (Foucault, 1980b: 119)

One of the things produced in this way is discourse. Foucault's contribution to an understanding of discourse, language, truth and knowledge is well documented elsewhere (Foucault, 1972a,b, 1980b; Guédon, 1994; Said, 1994) whilst the precise link between power and discourse is revealed in Cavallari's assessment of Foucault's (1972a,b) theory of discursive practice:

> Power and order is put into play both *by* and *in* 'the fundamental codes of a culture ... those governing its language, its schemas, its exchanges, its techniques, its values, the hierarchy of its practices'.
>
> (Cavallari, 1994: 212, citing Foucault, 1970: xx–xxii; emphasis in original)

Power and discourse become intimately linked in this theoretical framework, as the final two extracts illustrate:

> I am supposing that in every society the production of discourse is at once controlled, selected, organised and redistributed according to a set of *procedures*.
>
> (Foucault, 1972b: 216; emphasis added)

> Foucault is proposing a method for understanding social behaviour as *what it is that people must do in order to speak and write* as contributors to an on-going system of the values, discoveries, errors and institutions that we call knowledge. Since knowledge is neither a mysterious jumble of ideas nor a fact of nature, and since it is not something that one has but something that one does, it is best conceived of initially as occupying a group of *hypothetical spaces*.
>
> (Said, 1994: 79; emphasis added)

Two further questions remain. What are the *spaces*; and what are the *procedures* which constitute home ownership knowledge? It should be clear by now that this is not an easy question to formulate or to answer. The remainder of this chapter attempts to provide some answers through an analysis of normalising discourses of home ownership.

NORMALISING DISCOURSES OF HOME OWNERSHIP

This section considers empirical evidence from two sources: first, a reading of a number of landmark policy documents; second, in-depth interview transcripts generated as part of ethnographic research amongst working-class home owner households in St George, East Bristol.[3] These data reveal three normalising discourses of home ownership; first, *new forms of homelessness*; the distinctive use of the word *home* to differentiate between owners and tenants; second, *being good citizens*; the association of home ownership with a set of desirable values; third, *being natural*; the association between normal and natural behaviour embodied in home ownership.

New Forms of Homelessness?

The word *home* weighs heavily under a range of highly selective[4] emotional, existential, phenomenological and natal ideas (Rybczynski, 1986; Somerville, 1992; Bowlby *et al.*, 1997). A reading of landmark housing policy documents and selected in-depth interview transcripts suggests that the word *home* is crucial in normalising discourses of home ownership. Data presented below illustrate how the selective use of the word is used to differentiate between the *dwellings* of householders in owner-occupation and those in rented accommodation and the *experiences* implied by ownership of a home compared to tenancy in a home. This discourse enables a normalising judgement to be cast over home owners and tenants which underpins expectations of home improvement and maintenance to create *a new form of homelessness* for those outside of the 'external frontier of the abnormal' (Foucault, 1977: 183).

A linguistic analysis of the 1995 White Paper, *Our Future Homes* (Department of the Environment and Welsh Office, 1995) demonstrates this. A comparison of the three chapters of the document which deal with the three main housing tenures instantly reveals a normalising judgement in the way the word *home* is used. This judgement does not suggest that home, with all the significance this word implies, *only* exists for home owners, but it does seem to suggest that home exists in a much more meaningful way for those in home ownership. A close textual reading of these chapters reveals *home* is used not only more frequently but more evocatively and more emotionally in relation to home ownership than to private and social renting. A count was made of the number of times *home* was used in the three chapters. This count excluded its use in specific terms such as home ownership, home owner(s), homeless(ness), and homesteading and its use in the proliferation of section headings, graphs, diagrams and key point panels. The results of this simple count are dramatic, and are presented in Table 3.3. To enable comparison a crude but effective measure – the density of home index – is employed. This can be expressed as $d = l \div h$ (where d is the density of home index, h is the number of occurrences of the word *home* in the document and l is the number of lines in the document).

Table 3.3 The selective and normalising use of '*home*' in the 1995 White Paper

	Chapter 2: *Promoting sustainable home ownership*	Chapter 3: *Sustaining the revival of private renting*	Chapter 4: *A new framework for social renting*
home (h); n =	35	10	7
Lines of text (l)	373	309	315
Density of home ($d = l \div h$)	10.7	30.9	45.0

Home is, on average, mentioned once every 11 lines in chapter 2, compared with once every 31 lines in chapter 3 and once every 45 lines in chapter 4. This compares with an average of once every 107 lines of the 1971 White Paper (Department of the Environment and Welsh Office, 1971) and once every 234 lines of the 1967 White Paper (Ministry of Housing and Local Government and Welsh Office, 1968). These findings on their own reveal little, not least because of the crude and simplistic methodology which has been used. They do, however, provide a starting point for a more detailed analysis of the text. Extracts from the opening paragraphs of each chapter illustrate important tenure-specific differences in the use of the word *home*:

> 80% of people favour home ownership over other forms of tenure. they value independence and control over their own home.
> (Department of the Environment and Welsh Office, 1995: 12)

> A healthy private rented sector can provide an essential first stage for young people leaving home, including students and those saving for a deposit to buy their own home.
> (*ibid*.: 20)

> For people who are likely to have low incomes in the long term, social housing is the most cost effective way to ensure they have access to a decent home.
> (*ibid*.: 26).

The particular use of the word associates housing consumers in different tenures with different sets of values and experiences. For renters in the private sector the discourse has a particular 'temporal salience'

(Werner *et al.*, 1985). It exists as a departure point in their parental home and as a destination in home ownership. For renters in the social sector the discourse is about access to a home which is 'decent'. Owners have indistinguishable homes and values. Renters are offered access to decency implying, perhaps, that their values are indistinguishable from indecency. The power of this normalising discourse is embedded in the suggestion that the evocative images of home are those of the *normal* housing consumer. However, a Foucaultian perspective does not imply that the abnormal housing consumer is a passive recipient of others' judgements. Instead, as the following data illustrate, all housing consumers are simultaneously undergoing and exercising power and resistance.

The power of, and resistance to, the tenure-specific use of *home* as a normalising discourse is clearly visible in the following extracts from the St George Surveys:

> All our families own our own *homes*, all our grand-parents they owned their *homes*, so we don't really know how non home-owners feel. We have got friends who live in council though. We're not, um against people who live in council *houses*, we've got friends who live in council *houses* but we don't really know how they feel about their *houses*.
>
> (Mr Guthrie,[5] emphasis added)

In this extract owners are normal and normalised and live in homes, renters are neither and live in houses. The normalising discourse has here created a tenure prejudice. Expressions such as 'we have got friends' or 'we're not ... against' could easily be found in equally prejudicial discourses of racism or homophobia.

The most significant resistance to the normalising discourse of *home* is revealed in three extracts from women who made a distinction between the pride derived from domestic labour and the implication that an owner-occupied home is 'more loving' or more 'home like':

> If you were in any house it's your home and it's what you make it, so if we lived in a council home I'd still want it to look nice and as good as we could make it. I just know that my parents just did the best they could even though it was a council house it was a happy loving home. I think we would be the same.
>
> (Mrs Ramsey)

> I don't like it when people say; 'I own my own home', like you (to husband) were saying the other day that they always have to say that they've bought their own home, they think it's so important but it's not, it doesn't really matter, but people always emphasise that don't they?
>
> (Mrs Carter)

> I think a home is more important to the wife insofar as you feel it reflects either good or bad things about you. ... I feel somehow responsible that I haven't done enough to keep it tidy. ... You can have a home anywhere it's not necessarily a house. A house is a thing, when you talk about a home, to me it conjures up a completely different thing. It's more to do with how you feel emotionally, how supportive your family is. It's more to do with feelings.
>
> (Mrs Quinn)

There are important forces of resistance at work here. First, Mrs Ramsey uses the word *home* across tenures, and not as a normalising discourse to define council tenants as abnormal. Second, for Mrs Carter the normalising discourse of home was both visible and contested. Her resistance is an articulate and direct challenge to the normalising judgement. Third, Mrs Quinn seeks to preserve the value of her own emotion work (Duncombe and Marsden, 1993) by resisting the emotional association of home with ownership. Since the normalising judgement is intimately tied up with Mrs Quinn's observation that 'home reflects either good or bad things about you', the highly gendered infra-penalty of falling short of achieving a loving, caring, tidy and tastefully decorated home may suggest a failure for some women. Such an argument is not, as Darke (1994, 1996) has pointed out, incompatible with a feminist perspective on domestic labour, thus:

> Most women who have ever run a home will recall some embarrassing incident where someone found out that our standards fell short of a norm.
>
> (Darke, 1996: 63)

The evidence from St George suggests that the values which some women attached to their domestic labour constituted a strategy to separate pride in their home from pride in home ownership. Such resistance operated within the context of two other normalising discourses described below.

Being Good Citizens

The second normalising discourse of home ownership concerns a raft of specific values of pride, self-esteem, responsibility and citizenship. The following extracts from Command Papers published ten years apart illustrate this:

> It is scarcely surprising, therefore, that home ownership should have gained to much ground in the last half century. ... this trend is a sign of *social advance*. The Government shares this view. ... experience shows that the owner occupied home is visibly *better maintained* and at less cost in real resources than the rented one.
>
> (Department of the Environment and Welsh Office 1971: 4; emphasis added)

> There is in this country a deeply ingrained desire for home ownership. The Government believe that this spirit should be fostered. It reflects the wishes of the people, ensures the spread of wealth through society, encourages a personal desire to *improve and modernise* one's own home, enables *parents to accrue wealth for their children* and stimulates the attitudes of *independence and self-reliance* that are the bedrock of a free society.
>
> (Department of the Environment, 1981: 11; emphasis added)

This discourse carries with it an expectation that home owners are good citizens, good parents and good caretakers. To admit failure in any of these areas is to expose oneself, as in the École Militaire (Foucault, 1977: 182) to the infra-penalty of falling into a *shameful* housing class. The normalising judgement sustains discourses of an abnormal outgroup characterised thus;

> I've got relations who've got council houses, and they couldn't care tuppence about them, do you know what I mean? They say 'well the council will see to it.'
>
> (Mrs Lewis)

> Working on different council estates, I get to see a lot, some people don't seem to take that much care of the place, *they're just not bothered, got no self respect*, there's dogs running about, rubbish in the gardens, whole families ripping off the social and that.
>
> (Mr Williams; emphasis added)

> People who own or who are buying have that sense of pride, and those that are renting do not. *They let that sense of pride slip*. It's very very noticeable on large council estates where you can pick out the ones that have been bought from the ones that haven't. They're not necessarily of a higher standard, but they are a little cleaner, a little more tendered [tended], a little more tidy, the gates are shut, there isn't quite so much rubbish on the front lawn, the hedges are cut.
>
> (Mr Rowland; emphasis added)

In these extracts abnormality is constructed as a lack of pride and self-esteem, laziness and fecklessness. The gendered resistance of Mrs Carter and others to a tenure-specific *home* should not be forgotten, but the infra-penalty of comparison with a stigmatised stereotyped outgroup is an important and powerfully normalising discourse.

Being Natural

The third discourse which normalises home ownership is tied up with ideas of natural and instinctual drives. The well-documented American and Australian dreams of home ownership provide an example of the pervasiveness of this idea. The 'dreams' have been sustained by the stoking up of emotional energy behind moral tales of yeoman farmers and wild west pioneers who battled against the elements (Kemeny, 1983; De Neufville and Barton, 1987). The alleged relationship between home and instinctual drives is crucial in these tales, and reminds us how frequently heart and home are juxtaposed in discourses about the natural desire to mark out and defend your own territory. These ideas are best illustrated in Saunders' use of ethological evidence to support a natural desire for home ownership (Saunders, 1990: 72–84). The consequences of this association of nature with home is that any rejection of what home variously stands for can be constructed as unnatural – perhaps the most damning *infra-penalty* of all. The following extracts from policy documents illustrate the disciplinary power of this discourse. They all, in emphasising the 'natural' basis of home ownership and a set of values embedded in the *being good citizens* discourse simultaneously, create an 'unnatural' group. Who, given a choice, would want to be perceived thus?

> Home ownership is the most *rewarding* form of housing tenure. It satisfies a *deep and natural desire* on the part of the houseowner to

> have *independent control* of the home that shelters him and his family.
>
> (Department of the Environment and Welsh Office 1971: 4; emphasis added)

> A preference for home ownership is sometimes explained on the grounds that potential home owners believe that it will bring them financial advantage. A far more likely reason for the secular trend towards home ownership is the sense of greater *personal independence* that it brings. For most people owning one's home is a *basic and natural desire*.
>
> (Department of Environment and Welsh Office 1977: 50; emphasis added)

These extracts demonstrate the power of natural behaviour as a normalising discourse of home ownership. They suggest that not only is home ownership natural but the values of pride and esteem associated with it are natural too. Extracts from interview transcripts illustrate how individual home owners are simultaneously undergoing and exercising this power.

> When you own your own home you feel different. It's difficult to put into words, but it's probably more of a home you know you're doing it for yourself. It's the old *nesting instinct*; you're putting down roots, you're building your own security, your future.
>
> (Mr Rowland; emphasis added)

> I think that it is just a fact of *human nature*, that if it's something that belongs to you, you look after it better than what you'd do if it belongs to someone else.
>
> (Mr Moss; emphasis added)

There is no denying that words like *instinct* and *human nature* are emotive. They frequently provoke a knee-jerk reaction from social scientists. Such a reaction is wholly inappropriate for this chapter, however. The important thing here is that home ownership is so frequently characterised as natural. The implications of this for a study of power relations have typically been either that home owners are being duped, or that they are satisfying a deep-seated desire. A Foucaultian analysis of power, however, suggests that this characterisation, precisely because it is 'natural' and inevitable, is a *process of power relations* rather than an explanation of power relations.

Drawing on an analysis of discourses of housing consumption, this section has argued that relations of power and resistance are revealed in discursive practices which produce a socially constructed housing reality based upon a socially constructed stock of housing knowledge. In these discourses it becomes *normal* for the majority of householders in Great Britain to aspire to home ownership, it becomes *normal* for home ownership to be associated more closely than any other form of housing consumption with evocative and emotional ideas of home, it becomes *normal* for home owners to be represented as good citizens and good parents, and it becomes *normal* for a preference for home ownership to be constructed as a fact of human nature.

CONCLUSION: DISCIPLINE AND FURNISH? CONSUMING CULTURES OF HOUSING AND HOUSEHOLDS

Housing tenure is a socially constructed collection of consumption rights which has been appropriated as a convenient label of status and behaviour by some commentators. Important economic, political and cultural differences undoubtedly do exist between owners and tenants in contemporary British society, and it may well be the case that the source of these distinctions comes, in part, from the way in which they consume housing. But this chapter has demonstrated that there are dangers in using housing tenure as a proxy in broader arguments about social life. An understanding of the cultural significance of housing tenure must, therefore, recognise that it is also tied up with a complex network of power and resistance relations. Contemporary analyses of housing consumption have tended to ignore these complex processes of power and resistance with the result that we know very little about the role that housing consumption plays in struggles over social meanings and identities. We know very little, for instance, about the way in which consumption cultures *in the home* have a role to play in constructing a stock of 'common-sense' knowledge about housing tenures. Similarly, the lack of a cultural studies tradition in housing research has led to a neglect of the way in which people furnish their homes to sustain complex meanings and identities, or the way in which they use domestic space as strategies of power or resistance. When housing research has addressed issues surrounding the consumption of housing it has tended to focus on the economic or material perspective. The neglect of the cultural perspective has hampered our understanding of the profound ways in which the growth of home ownership has transformed British society.

Work elsewhere on discourses of power and resistance has failed to come to terms with the 'praxical paralysis' that a Foucaultian conception of power implies. If power is everywhere and possessed by all people, argues Porter (1996: 76), how do we go about changing the world? I would argue that in the field of housing consumption we must become more aware of *how* housing tenure is used to make normalising judgements about people in contemporary British society. The first steps in this praxis must be to recognise the power and resistance tied up in discourses of home owners as *good citizens* and local authority tenants as *feckless scroungers*. This task, I would suggest, is too important to be left to a handful of researchers with an interest in the sociology of housing. Instead, these questions should be incorporated into contemporary accounts of culture and consumption.

The way in which people consume housing may or may not reveal important representations of their status or identity. Similarly, they may or may not convince us that a particular view which we hold of the world is correct. In the absence of answers to these kinds of questions we must rely on our existing stock of 'common-sense' knowledge about home owners and local authority tenants. This chapter has illustrated that this knowledge is at best partial and at worst prejudicial.

ACKNOWLEDGEMENTS

Table 3.3 and parts of this chapter originally appeared in 'Pride and Prejudice: Discourses of Normalisation in Public and Private Accounts of Home Ownership', *Housing Studies,* 14 (2) (1999). The author and editors acknowledge the kind permission of Carfax Publishing Company to reproduce these extracts here. The chapter has benefited from the comments of Chris Allen, Lisa Doyle, Jim Kemeny, David Knight and Pauline Papps. The fieldwork data presented was funded by the ESRC.

NOTES

1. Renting from a local authority, new town, or housing association.
2. For reasons of confidentiality the company concerned cannot be named and therefore this letter is not referenced in the bibliography.

3. *The St George Surveys* were conducted between July 1990 and July 1991. The research included (1) *a postal survey* (*n*=115 households); (2) *a semi-structured interview questionnaire survey* (*n*=54 people); and (3) *an unstructured in-depth interview survey* (n=8 people). The three surveys were administered to a purposive sample of home-owner households. The fieldwork data reported in this chapter were drawn from surveys 2 and 3, and funded by the ESRC.
4. The use of the word is selective because home is also a locale where the absence of safety and comfort is most acutely experienced by some women, children and older people (Gurney and Means, 1993; Malos and Hague, 1997).
5. The names of all respondents are pseudonyms.

REFERENCES

Barlow, J. and Duncan, S. (1988) 'The Use and Abuse of Housing Tenure', *Housing Studies,* 3: 219–31.

Becker, F. (1977) *Housing Messages* (Stroudsburg, PA: Dowden Hutchinson and Ross).

Bové, P. (1994) 'The End of Humanism: Michel Foucault and the Power of Disciplines', in B. Smart (ed.), *Michel Foucault: Critical Assessments*, vol. 2 (London: Routledge) pp. 313–28 (originally published in *Humanities in Society,* 1980; 3: 23–40).

Bowlby, S., Gregory, S. and McKie, L. (1997) '"Doing Home"; Patriarchy, Caring and Space', *Women's Studies International Forum,* 20: 343–50.

Byrne, D. (1989) 'Sociotenurial Polarization – Issues of Production and Consumption in a Locality', *International Journal of Urban and Regional Research,* 13: 339–64.

Campbell, C. (1995) 'The Sociology of Consumption', in D. Miller (ed.), *Acknowledging Consumption: A Review of New Studies* (London: Routledge), pp. 96–126.

Cavallari, H. (1994) '*Savoir and Pouvoir:* Michel Foucault's Theory of Discursive Practice', in B. Smart (ed.), *Michel Foucault: Critical Assessments,* vol. 2 (London: Routledge), pp. 209–23 (originally published in *Humanities in Society,* 1980; 3: 55–72).

Central Statistical Office (1970) *Social Trends* 1 (London: HMSO).

Central Statistical Office (1971) *Social Trends* 2 (London: HMSO).

Collison, P. (1963) *The Cutteslowe Walls: A Study in Social Class* (London: Faber and Faber).

Cooper Marcus, C. (1995) *House as Mirror of the Self: Exploring the Deeper Meaning of Home* (Berkeley, CA: Conari Press).

Corrigan, P. (1997) *The Sociology of Consumption: An Introduction* (London: Sage).

Csikszentmihalyi, M. and Rochberg-Halton, E. (1981) *The Meaning of Things: Domestic Symbols and the Self* (Cambridge: Cambridge University Press).

Darke, J. (1994) 'Women and the Meaning of Home', in R. Gilroy and R. Woods (eds), *Housing Women* (London: Routledge), 11–30.

Darke, J. (1996) 'The Englishwoman's Castle; or Don't You Just Love Being in Control?', in C. Booth, J. Darke and S. Yeandle (eds), *Changing Places: Women's Lives in the City* (London: Paul Chapman), pp. 61–71.

De Neufville, J. and Barton, S. (1987) 'Myths and the Definition of Policy Problems: An Exploration of Home-Ownership and Public–Private Partnerships', *Policy Sciences,* 20: 181–206.

Department of the Environment (1981) *Council House Sales: The Government's Reply to the Second Report from the Environment Committee: Session 1980–1; HC366*, Command Paper 8377 (London: HMSO).

Department of the Environment and Welsh Office (1971) *Fair Deal for Housing*, Command Paper 4728 (London: HMSO).

Department of the Environment and Welsh Office (1977) *Housing Policy: A Consultative Document*, Command Paper 6851 (London: HMSO).

Department of the Environment and Welsh Office (1995) *Our Future Homes: Opportunities, Choice, Responsibility,* Command Paper 2901 (London: HMSO).

Department of the Environment, Scottish Office Environment Department, Welsh Office (1990) *Housing and Construction Statistics Quarterly,* June quarter 1990, Part 2 (London: HMSO).

Department of the Environment, Scottish Office Environment Department, Welsh Office (1994) *Housing and Construction Statistics, 1983–1993: Great Britain* (London: HMSO).

Department of the Environment, Scottish Office Environment Department, Welsh Office (1997) *Housing and Construction Statistics Quarterly* December quarter 1996, Part 2 (London: HMSO).

Duncan, J. (ed.) (1981) *Housing and Identity: Cross Cultural Perspectives* (London: Croom Helm).

Duncan, S. (1990) 'Do House Prices Rise That Much? A Dissenting View', *Housing Studies,* 5: 195–208.

Duncombe, J. and Marsden, D. (1993) 'Love and Intimacy: the Gender Division of Emotion and Emotion Work', *Sociology,* 27: 231–42.

Dunleavy, P. (1986) 'The Growth of Sectoral Cleavages and the Stabilization of State Expenditures', *Environment and Planning D: Society and Space,* 4: 129–44.

Egerton, J. (1990) 'Out But Not Down: Lesbians' Experience of Housing', *Feminist Review,* 36: 75–88.

Forrest, R. and Murie, A. (1989) 'Differential Accumulation: Wealth, Inheritance and Housing Policy Reconsidered', *Policy and Politics,* 17: 25–39.

Forrest, R. and Murie, A. (1994) 'Home Ownership in Recession', *Housing Studies,* 9: 55–74.

Forrest, R., Kennett, T. and Leather, P. (1997) *Home Owners on New Estates in the 1990s: New Problems on the Periphery?* (Bristol: Policy Press).

Forrest, R., Murie, A. and Williams, P. (1990) *Home Ownership: Differentiation and Fragmentation* (London: Unwin Hyman).

Foucault, M. (1970) *The Order of Things: An Archaeology of the Human Sciences* (New York: Pantheon).

Foucault, M. (1972a) *The Archaeology of Knowledge* (New York: Pantheon).
Foucault, M. (1972b) 'The Discourse on Language', in Appendix to M. Foucault, *The Archaeology of Knowledge* (New York: Pantheon), pp. 215–38.
Foucault, M. (1977) *Discipline and Punish: The Birth of the Prison* (London: Allen Lane).
Foucault, M. (1979) *The History of Sexuality*, vol. 1: *An Introduction* (London: Allen Lane).
Foucault, M. (1980a) 'Two Lectures', in C. Gordon (ed.), *Power/Knowledge: Selected Interviews and other Writings, 1972–1977* (Brighton: Harvester Wheatsheaf), pp. 78–108.
Foucault, M. (1980b) 'Truth and Power', in C. Gordon (ed.), *Power/Knowledge: Selected Interviews and other Writings, 1972–1977* (Brighton: Harvester Wheatsheaf), pp. 109–133.
Franklin, A. (1986) *Owner Occupation, Privatism and Ontological Security: A Critical Reformulation*, SAUS Working Paper 62 (Bristol: School for Advanced Urban Studies).
Gilroy, R. (1994) 'Women and Owner Occupation in Britain: First the Prince, then the Palace?', in R. Gilroy and R. Woods (eds), *Housing Women* (London: Routledge), pp. 31–57.
Guédon, J.-C. (1994) 'Michel Foucault: the Knowledge of Power and the Power of Knowledge', in B. Smart (ed.), *Michel Foucault: Critical Assessments*, vol. 2 (London: Routledge), pp. 124–50 (originally published in *Bulletin of the History of Medicine* (1977) 51: 245–77).
Gurney, C. (1990) *The Meaning of Home in the Decade of Owner Occupation: Towards an Experiential Research Agenda*, SAUS Working Paper 88 (Bristol: School for Advanced Urban Studies).
Gurney, C. (1997) '"... Half of Me was Satisfied": Making Sense of Home through Episodic Ethnographies', *Women's Studies International Forum,* 20: 373–86.
Gurney, C. and Means, R. (1993) 'The Meaning of Home in Later Life', in S. Arber and M. Evandrou (eds), *Ageing, Independence and the Life Course* (London: Jessica Kingsley), 119–31.
Hamnett, C., Harmer, M. and Williams, P. (1991) *Safe as Houses: Housing Inheritance in Britain* (London: Paul Chapman).
Harloe, M. (1984) 'Sector and Class: a Critical Comment', *International Journal of Urban and Regional Research,* 8: 228–37.
Hirsch, F. (1977) *Social Limits to Growth* (London: Routledge and Kegan Paul).
Jackson, P. and Thrift, N. (1995) 'Geographies of Consumption', in D. Miller (ed.), *Acknowledging Consumption: A Review of New Studies* (London: Routledge), pp. 204–37.
Johnston, L. and Valentine, G. (1995) 'Wherever I Lay my Girlfriend That's my Home: the Performance and Surveillance of Lesbian Identities in Domestic Environments', in D. Bell and G. Valentine (eds), *Mapping Desire: Geographies of Sexuality* (London: Routledge), pp. 99–113.
Kemeny, J. (1981) *The Myth of Home Ownership: Private versus Public Choices in Housing Tenure* (London: Routledge and Kegan Paul).
Kemeny, J. (1983) *The Great Australian Nightmare: A Critique of the Home Ownership Ideology* (Melbourne: Georgian House).

Kempson, E. and Ford, J. (1995) *Attitudes, Belief and Confidence: Consumer Views of the Housing Market in the 1990s* (London: Council for Mortgage Lenders).
Madigan, R. and Munro, M. (1996) '"House Beautiful": Style and Consumption in the Home', *Sociology*, 30: 41–57.
Malos, E. and Hague, G. (1997) 'Women, Housing, Homelessness and Domestic Violence', *Women's Studies International Forum,* 20: 397–410.
Mandic, S. and Clapham, D. (1996) 'The Meaning of Home Ownership in the Transition from Socialism: the Example of Slovenia', *Urban Studies,* 33: 83–97.
Ministry of Housing and Local Government and Welsh Office (1968) *Old Houses into New Homes,* Command Paper 3602 (London: HMSO).
Office of National Statistics (1998) *Social Trends 28* (London: HMSO).
Otnes, P. (ed.) (1988) *The Sociology of Consumption: An Anthology* (Atlantic Heights, NJ: Humanities Press International).
Pannel, B. (1997) 'Tenure Choice and Mortgage Decisions: 1996 Market Research Findings', *Housing Finance,* 33: 9–13.
Porter, S. (1996) 'Contra-Foucault: Soldiers, Nurses and Power', *Sociology,* 30: 59–78.
Preziosi, D. (1979) *The Semiotics of the Built Environment* (Bloomington, IN: Indiana University Press).
Rumbold, J. (1998) 'Disco Fever', *The Observer: Life,* 1 February 1998: 70.
Rybczynski, W. (1986) *Home: A Short History of an Idea* (New York: Viking Penguin).
Said, E. (1994) 'An Ethics of Language: Review of Michel Foucault's *The Archaeology of Knowledge and the Discourse on Language*', in B. Smart (ed.), *Michel Foucault: Critical Assessments,* vol. 2 (London: Routledge), pp. 69–87 (originally published in *Diacritics* (1974) 4: 28–37).
Saunders, P. (1986) 'Comment on Dunleavy and Preteceille', *Environment and Planning D: Society and Space,* 4: 155–63.
Saunders, P. (1990) *A Nation of Home Owners* (London: Unwin-Hyman).
Saunders, P. and Harris, C. (1988) *Home Ownership and Capital Gains,* Urban and Regional Studies Working Paper 64 (Brighton: University of Sussex).
Smailes, J. (1994) '"The Struggle has Never Simply Been About Bricks and Mortar": Lesbians' Experience of Housing', in R. Gilroy and R. Woods (eds), *Housing Women* (London: Routledge), pp. 152–172.
Sociology (1990) 'Special Issue: the Sociology of Consumption', *Sociology*, 24 (1).
Somerville, P. (1992) 'Homelessness and the Meaning of Home: Rooflessness or Rootlessness?', *International Journal of Urban and Regional Research,* 16: 529–39.
Sullivan, O. (1989) 'Housing Tenure as a Consumption-sector Divide: a Critical Perspective', *International Journal of Urban and Regional Research,* 13: 183–200.
Urry, J. (1995) *Consuming Places* (London: Routledge).
Watson, S. (1986) 'Housing and the Family: the Marginalization of Non-family Households in Britain', *International Journal of Urban and Regional Research,* 10: 8–28.
Werner, C., Altman, I. and Oxley, D. (1985) 'Temporal Aspects of Homes: a Transactional Perspective', in I. Altman and C. Werner (eds), *Home Environments* (New York: Plenum Press), pp. 1–32.

4 The Ideal Home Exhibition: an Analysis of Constraints and Conventions in Consumer Choice in British Homes

TONY CHAPMAN

INTRODUCTION

In Terry Gilliam's film *Baron Munchausen* there is a classic scene in which the Baron, together with his band of followers, drop through a time warp into Hell. Amidst the flames they find the Devil and his wife, who takes an immediate shine to the Baron. Consumed by jealousy, the Devil (played by Oliver Reed) manages to keep up appearances and spreads his arms to show Munchausen his home. In a northern brogue, he booms, 'We've just had it done.'

People from different social situations, whether they are defined as classes, socioeconomic groups, or *niche markets*, must be able to empathise with the Devil's predicament. But it is not just being under the pressure of a spouse courting the attentions of a philanderer that makes us want to draw attention to our houses rather than our inner turmoil. On the contrary, almost every time somebody significant to us comes into the house, we need to make a show of it. In making a show, householders tend to decorate and furnish their homes in such as way as to reflect their current status or future aspirations.

Paying attention to the impact of people's tendency to want to impress (or sometimes conceal from) significant others is particularly important when patterns of domestic consumption are considered. And yet this line of analysis has received little attention over the years by sociologists. One reason for this omission is the current popularity of the view that under *postmodernity*, capitalism has produced new social relationships where people's personal identities are not so much shaped by their family origins, neighbourhood, friends and local culture, or the work they do, but by *what they choose to buy*. While many sociologists now believe that people are relatively unconstrained in their lifestyle options, these transformations have not been universally applauded. Some writers fear the impact upon society of the excessively selfish form of individualism that postmodernism is claimed to produce. Others celebrate the carnival of consumption, the crazy cultural juxtapositions and the opportunities to choose who you want to be.[1] Featherstone has characterised the more optimistic brand of the postmodernist view when he states that:

> This is the world of men and women who quest for the new and the latest in relationships and experiences, who have a sense of adventure and take risks to explore life's options to the full, who are conscious they have only one life to live and must work hard to enjoy, experience and express it
>
> (1991: 86)

Featherstone may be correct in asserting that there is a much wider range of options available to a larger number of consumers in the late twentieth century. While it is accepted here that patterns of consumption are important in defining and identifying lifestyles of groups, the availability of goods and services does not necessarily mean that individuals can resist the substantial social pressures imposed upon them by family, neighbours and friends to conform to established patterns of domestic life. It needs to be recognised, then, that gaining access to and maintaining a position in a social group requires much more than the wherewithal to buy the relevant couture.

To gain a subscription to a group, people must acquire the right credentials – the most important of which is the right kind of *know-how*. Robert Ezra Park (1950) acutely observed that the propensity of individuals to play out roles is an enduring and universal feature of society, and that people realise their self (or selves) through the execution of this complex social drama.

> It is probably no mere historical accident that the word person, in its first meaning, is a mask. It is rather a recognition of the fact that everyone is always and everywhere, more or less consciously, playing a role … . It is in these roles that we know each other, it is in these roles that we know ourselves.
>
> (Goffman 1969: 30)

In the process of acting out social roles, Goffman argues that people use 'fronts' as a 'part of the individual's performance which regularly functions in a general and fixed fashion to define the situation for those who observe the performance' (1969: 32). The front is an important idea because it exposes several layers of social behaviour, from that of the physical 'stage set' where the performance takes place to that of the deeply embedded spoken and unspoken behaviour patterns of the actors.

In The *Presentation of Self in Everyday Life*, Goffman (1969) re-introduces the idea that people set the scene for social encounters with the express intention of letting other people see them in their best light. It is not always possible to present the stage set appropriately. Many households adopt emergency procedures to create the right impression for people they seek to impress, or in order to avoid the prospect of being 'stigmatised' for their unruly lifestyle. A classic example is the doctor's home visit to a sickly child, where, in spite of the parents, obvious concern for the child, they tidy up madly to the point at which the doctor's car door bangs outside. How many times must doctors have witnessed people shoving toys or clothes under a child's bed with the side of the foot? The necessity of keeping up a front like this is obviously connected to the need to give an impression of respectability, from which the doctor may impute a sense of care for the child's welfare and environment. The doctor may not see it this way, and may believe that chaotic households may well be amongst the happiest ones, for the house is always in a comfortable state of disorder where there is a symbiotic relationship between people and things.

It is not just the level of organisation and cleanliness of homes that is important in maintaining a sense of self-respect in the eyes of families, friends and neighbours. The home is not, in this sense, an entirely private place; on the contrary, it is the stage upon which people project the most intimate image of their 'selves' to the world (Allan and Crow, 1989; Chapman and Hockey, 1998). The fact that they can 'control' this image to a certain extent is important – but their control is mediated by expectations from family, neighbours and friends about acceptable forms of decoration, furnishing, service and order.

One potential consequence of long-term membership of a social group is that people become culturally conservative – that is, they may lose the ability to take risks and try new things. This is not to say that the rules of the social group are frozen in aspic or that membership of a social group is permanent. Most people do play different roles in a number of social groups: the extended family, the workplace, the neighbourhood, the sports club. But our principal location, for example, metropolitan intellectual, rude rustic, eco-warrior or biker, requires such an effort of will to join, and shapes our options to such an extent that we are precluded from unstitching ourselves from its constraints.

Of course people do change their attitudes and behaviour as they move through the life course – although they may do so in a broadly predictable way – depending on, for example, their luck economically, or upon the long-term reliability of their body. People are faced with a serious dilemma – they do not want to offend others by being too outlandish, ostentatious or vulgar, but neither do they dare to leave things entirely as they are for fear of being left behind. Although cultural conservatism of this kind can easily be observed, there will usually be the odd one out; like Alan Bennett who allowed an old woman to live, and ultimately die, in a stinking van on his driveway (Bennett, 1994).

Because cultural conservatism is shaped by the expectations of family, friends and neighbours (who are extremely effective in containing Bohemian outbursts) this provides a major challenge to manufacturers and retailers who face the task of persuading a potentially recalcitrant population to take radical action in the way they organise, use and spend money on their homes.

Although designers, marketing directors, retail psychologists, advertisers and commercial exhibition organisers have considerable power of persuasion at their disposal,[2] it is recognised that they must tread a fine line between, on the one hand, consumers' fear of ridicule for being out of fashion and, on the other, being too far out of the ordinary. This chapter will demonstrate how carefully capital treads in attempting to break down consumers' resistance to change their ways by marshalling a range of *promises* that buying their goods will improve the consumers' lives, while also *threatening* consumers with the risk of leaving things as they are.

THE IDEAL HOME EXHIBITION

If cultural conservatism can result in consumer resistance to change, then it is useful to examine how capital persuades people to buy its products and services. To do this, I will present a study of the Ideal Home Exhibition (IHE) which serves the *popular Middle England* market in domestic architecture, interior design and furnishings. Commercial shows like the IHE serve to reinforce a view, in the minds of culturally conservative consumers, that their products are appropriate for their target audience. This chapter will show that getting that message across requires that the show organisers produce a subtle blend of *aesthetic reassurance*, *celebrity association and expert help*, *financial incentives and prizes* and *warnings about the risks of leaving things as they are*.

London hosted the first IHE in 1908. Since then, with the exception of the Second World War years and its immediate aftermath, *the Daily Mail* has sponsored this (mainly) annual jamboree to persuade people to buy the best new labour-saving gadgets, popular styles of interior decoration and home furnishings. This study is based on the observation of the 1995, 1996 and 1997 IHE which takes place in March and April at Earl's Court, London. The six-acre indoor show space is taken up by 650 commercial exhibitors divided into three main areas. The most expensive rentable floor space for exhibitors is set in two vast ground-floor galleries. Most of the commercial stands in this area exhibit goods and services associated with home 'improvement', furnishing and decoration of houses – together with a large number of stands displaying leisure goods, finance and gardening.

A considerable effort is made in the presentation of goods and services in order to attract the attention and favourably impress visitors. On the press and preview day the stands were staffed by colour-coordinated teams of public relations (PR) personnel – comprising mainly conventionally pretty, slim young women in short skirts and sometimes hats, who were eager to pass leaflets to the press and refer more detailed enquiries to (mainly men) company representatives.

The first-floor exhibition space housed a very large number of smaller stands. This area was less well maintained than the ground floor. Its carpets were badly worn and stained. The 'international food court' was situated here, comprising 31 outlets. The other stands, selling relatively low-cost products – including, for example, clothes, housewares, 'craft' ware and gifts – resembled small shops in an indoor town market.

Only about 15 per cent of the floor space was taken up by 'formal' exhibits. In all cases, these formal exhibits were sponsored by individuals or a range of companies – which blurs the line between commercial stands and exhibition features. In the 1995 exhibition, for example, the main displays included a 'fabulous show house village and gardens' produced by Bellway Homes. The village comprised four show homes – each of which was sponsored by one or more large companies, including the 'Direct Line Insurance' home, which was accessible only though an embarrassingly large shiny red telephone.

Table 4.1 Floor space usage at the 1995 Ideal Home Exhibition

Exhibition themes	Number of stands	Percentage of floor space	Main exhibition area
Home improvements	73	18%	A
Furniture	56	19%	A
Leisure and finance	76	14%	B
Lighting	19	3%	B
Art	23	3%	B
Gardening	30	3%	B
House wares	64	8%	C
International food court	31	6%	C
Crafts and gifts	71	4%	C
Babies and children	50	3%	C
DIY	23	2%	C
Clothes	37	3%	C
Home furnishings	12	2%	C

Notes
1. The percentages given are relatively crude estimates of exhibition space for illustrative purposes. They are derived from graphic floor plans produced for visitors in the exhibition *Show Guide*.
2. The exhibition areas can be roughly categorised as follows: **A** – principal exhibition space surrounding main exhibits – Earl's Court 1; **B** – secondary exhibition space with main exhibits – Earl's Court 2; and **C** – upstairs exhibition space with most expensive stands set around a balcony overlooking main exhibit.

The IHE generally attracts in the region of 550,000 visitors for three weeks in March and April. Some 70 per cent of the visitors were aged between 18 and 50 years, and 70 per cent of all visitors were women. The show targets *Daily Mail* readers, composed mainly of people situated in the Registrar General's social class categories B, C1 and C2; that is, semi-professionals, clerical and technical workers, and skilled manual workers. The audience is also targeted through other magazines with readers who broadly match this marketing profile; this includes, for example, similarly geared women's magazines and home-style and home-improvement magazines such as *Home Flair*, *Home Style*, *Good Housekeeping* and so on. A number of magazines in this range included special show ticket concessions for their readers.

Up-market magazines such as *Home and Garden*, *House and Gardens and Elle Decoration* do not generally carry advertisements in the editions preceding the show.

The organisers attempt to reassure visitors that this is a 'safe' place to buy through a number of marketing strategies, as described below.

Aesthetic Reassurance

A general analysis of the products on show demonstrates that the visiting public are not at the forefront of fashion, but tend to follow broad trends. Companies offer goods and services that are generally available in the high street or out-of-town shopping centres, and are careful not to exhibit goods that are too far out of the ordinary. There are some exceptions in the smaller stands – for example, one company that makes bulky furniture from railway sleepers – but nothing has come to my attention at the show between 1995 and 1997 that might be described as avant-garde.

This aesthetic conservatism is illustrated when stands which display 'fine art' are observed. The pictures on display tend to be highly representational – depicting, for example, vaguely impressionistic landscapes or portraiture of people or animals, often in romantic historical settings. Sculpture or porcelain figurines, similarly, tend not just to be figurative, but to carry easily readable messages – with, perhaps, wheelbarrows overflowing with flowers, a carpenter working at his craft, or a ballet dancer at full stretch.

Similarly, furniture manufacturers make no pretence about the authenticity of their products. Manufacturers recognise that visitors prefer to have something *new* which 'looks like' antique furniture. Manufacturers are certainly not embarrassed to recognise this. One company described its range of products as 'a fabulous French Louis Phillippe *style* cabinet range', 'Chelsea is a brilliant *interpretation* of the wonderful loose cover', 'a supremely elegant, *classic* design'. To reinforce the credibility of its 'traditional' furniture, the company made claim to 'some pretty impressive contracts for some pretty important clients: a Czar's Palace in St Petersburg; a royal palace in Bangkok, not to mention Balmoral Castle' (Maples, Press Information, IHE 1995; my emphases).

A constant theme of the show, then, is to provide people with new products that appear to be of traditional design (as might have been seen on days out at, say, National Trust homes) rather than adopt modern designs which are currently regarded as unfashionable by the visitors.

Celebrity Associations and Expert Help

The role of the celebrities is to add legitimacy to the status of the exhibition. In 1995 about 100 celebrities took their turn on the National Children's Homes stand. They included actors from well-known drama or soap series such as *Home and Away*, *The Bill*, *Peak Practice*, or *Heart Beat*; quiz shows like *The Generation Game* and *Blockbusters*; and from situation comedies like *Birds of a Feather*. Comedians, agony aunts, an 'ex-Goodie' and a number of Independent Television News readers also attended the stand, together with daytime television presenters.

One of the show's main exhibits in 1995 displayed *'personal places for famous faces'* which gave some clue about the assumed design preferences of a group of celebrities. Here, room sets were decorated and furnished by several designers from the KLC School of Interior Design with television celebrities in mind, including Jane Asher, 'known for her thriving party cake business', Anne Diamond, a daytime television presenter, and Derek Evans, 'Mr Motivator'.

The absence of 'authoritative expert' celebrities is particularly revealing. Well-known architects and interior designers were conspicuous by their absence at the exhibition, as were academics, artists and politicians who have set out their stalls as experts on the home and family life. In the early years of the show there was no such reticence on the part of the show organisers. As the editor of the Ideal Homes Book said, in her introduction of 1947: 'The Ideal Home Exhibition is ... the finest medium through which *the people can learn* what architects, scientists, artists and artisans are doing to give us homes worthy of our heritage' (Sherman, 1947: 3; my emphasis). The absence of architects, designers and artists may also reflect the fact that the show does not display the kinds of products that such designers could easily associate themselves with. This is not to say that the manufactured products displayed at the IHE are of poor quality – but it does suggest that they lack the distinctive, individualistic, hand-crafted quality of products which are displayed at, say, the Chelsea Design Week.

Financial Incentives and Prizes

IHE visitors are constantly bombarded with financial incentives to buy goods and services. At the 1995 show all visitors were invited to enter into a prize draw to win one of ten Bellway houses, a Volvo 440 and 'a luxury weekend in a country retreat'. Visitors were issued with a 'cheque book' of offers worth £1000 which were 'redeemable' on goods exhibited at the show, together with promises of 'on-the-spot' prizes in a 'cash bonanza'. One lucky visitor could win a £5000 patterned brick driveway for their home by guessing correctly the hand prints of 'famous Radio DJ's such as Terry Wogan and Gloria Hunniford' (*Show Guide,* 1995).

Individual companies also offered special 'unrepeatable' discounts and interest-free credit arrangements for show visitors which were 'not available' in the shops together with 'free advice' to guide you through the choices available.

The up-beat language of the IHE, with its offers of advice, bargains and prizes – together with implied association with famous celebrities – do not, by themselves, sell goods and services on offer. In fact the jolly language of the show, and its 'you don't have to spend a fortune to be ...' theme is underscored by a range of prompts to promote a real sense of insecurity amongst the visitors. These prompts highlight the risks people face unless they take their cue from the show and do something about it.

The Risks of Leaving Things as They Are

The principal exhibition feature at the 1995 IHE provides a useful example of the way in which visitors were encouraged to believe that their current home was in some sense sub-standard. This was achieved by presenting to the public a mock-up terrace of 'Yesterday's Houses'. Four houses were constructed to depict the changing design of housing across the century (Chapman, 1995).

The inside of the exhibit was reached via a small darkened doorway leading visitors through a long corridor in cohorts of about 20 at a time to view the bathroom, bedroom, sitting room and kitchen of each house. Although the official *Show Guide* hoped that 'you enjoy it, and that many of you will indulge yourselves in a bit of good, old fashioned nostalgia' (1995: 33), it was made plain that the nostalgia people might feel should be tempered.

> Our memory tends to be selective, and we often look back through rose-tinted spectacles. We may remember our first 1920's-built house as being 'solid' and having 'character', while forgetting that it was cold, draughty and cost us an arm and a leg to run! Sunny days spent relaxing in our gardens are more easily remembered than the

> amount of time we had to put in painting window sills, repairing broken gutters or fixing roof tiles … . We also forget that we could hear our next door neighbour sneeze because sound-proofing was non-existent at the time, and we may look back fondly at the amount of time it took us to save for a new cooker.
>
> (*Show Guide,* 1995: 34)

As the show visitors left the darkened terrace, they emerged on the patterned brick driveway of a brand new show home – the so-called 'House of Tomorrow'. The *Show Guide* reinforced the visitor's obvious sense of relief at the sight of a fashionably painted and decorated house that was fitted with a gleaming new hi-tech kitchen, and a bathroom with a jacuzzi, and was furnished with the best new furniture and fabric British Homes Stores could muster.

> The reality is that housebuiling has come a long way this century, and the owner of a brand new home will never have to put up with these and the many other easily forgotten problems associated with older properties ... should a similar feature ever be staged at the Ideal Home Exhibition in 2095, the equivalent turn-of-the-millennium house's imaginary family won't be prompting memories of cold bathrooms, damp walls, broken gutters and heating bills that break the bank.
>
> (*Show Guide,* 1995: 34)

The interwoven messages that the organisers of the IHE want to press upon visitors is clear enough – they want to assure consumers that it is *safe* to buy, but *risky* to leave things as they are.

How Do Visitors 'Consume' the IHE?

This chapter has shown that capital goes to considerable lengths to sell the goods and services on show at the IHE. Their marketing strategies are sophisticated and appear to be well matched to its target audience of *middle England*. But how do visitors actually *receive* the messages the show organisers wish them to?

Two research techniques were adopted: first, a participant observation of the show, and second, a series of interviews. The observations were undertaken on Easter Saturday in 1996 at eight locations – seven of which were planned, and one unplanned. One hour was spent at each location. These included: the threshold of the exhibition; the main exhibition feature (a giant bathroom); mock-up of a terrace house make-over; the show house village; people taking part on stands offering health promotion (20 minutes on each stand); the international food court; inside one of the show homes; and finally, an unplanned observation of a people jam on the balcony area of the first floor. With the exception of the unplanned observation, all observations were noted discreetly on paper, and written up fully afterwards.

The interviews took place at the 1997 IHE Press and Preview Day outside two of the four show homes in a fenced paddock through which the visitors were constrained to travel. Respondents were chosen randomly and a taped semi-structured interview was undertaken. All of the visitors approached were willing to be interviewed, and talked to me for five minutes at most. Sixty people were interviewed: 52 respondents were women. All the men respondents were accompanying women.

Observing the Show

The majority of visitors to the show came via Earl's Court underground station and then walked in silence through the long subterranean low-ceilinged bare concrete tunnel that runs underneath the main show space until they reached the main entrance. At the entrance of the show, people were handed their IHE official carrier bags. At this point visitors emanated a full sense of anticipation for the event. Although people did not necessarily talk to other members of their party at this point, they did make a good deal of eye contact, smiled at each other and had something of a spring in their step as they crossed the threshold of the show space. From my observation of the show, this was the only point in the entire exhibition space where such a jaunty attitude was so openly expressed.

In spite of the organisers' claim that the 1996 IHE main theme was centred upon 'having fun', observation of visitors' behaviour suggested that if they were having fun, they were reluctant to show it publicly by, for example, smiling, laughing, touching each other, or engaging in humorous interchanges with their own visiting party when confronted with amusing scenes or activities. Where fun opportunities were offered (for example, the central feature of the 1996 show depicted an outsized bathroom with two canal boats floating in an enormous sunken bath with very high running hot and cold taps), most visitors did smile briefly at the amusing spectacle.

But the impact of this feature quickly subsided as visitors began to queue up to see inside the canal boats. Interestingly, the street theatre performers on the adjacent stage seemed to produce little response from the visitors. Indeed, even those people who were self-evidently bored as they queued to see the canal boats paid scant attention to the circus troupe of jugglers and clowns.[3] While queueing to see the boats the vast majority of visitors did not converse with their party, nor did they read the show guide or other brochures, features, free gifts or information on prize draws and so forth included in the official carrier bag which every visitor is given on entry into the show. This is perhaps surprising, because the bathroom scene was the first major exhibit the visitors were likely to see on entering the show. The relatively passive response to the feature, or the process of waiting to see inside the canal boats, set a pattern of behaviour for most people throughout the day.

Where street theatre troupes were more pro-active in entertaining the visitors, the visitors' response was again generally passive. This may be explained partly by the quality of some of the acts which patrolled key show areas such as the large bathroom or the show house village. In the show house village, one street theatre act involved a man in an official tee-shirt waving a set of car keys close to the faces of women visitors whilst pulling a silly face. His clownish behaviour did not amuse the vast majority of people he approached – instead, they tended to walk on past him or backed off nervously. When he patrolled the long (30–45-minute) queues to the show homes, people either ignored him, as they might ignore a menace on a tube train, or simply turned around to avoid his manic stare. Had the actor been dressed in a clownish costume, his reception may have been greeted with some amusement – for his fancy dress would, at least, have symbolised that a funny experience was about to take place.

At the show house village, where visitors could expect to wait as much as two hours if they wished to see all four houses, they did not appear to complain while in the queue, nor did they engage in conversation with their party.[4] In the show homes themselves, people moved through relatively quickly in cohorts of about six or eight at a time. Visitors rarely engaged in conversation about the houses or the interior design except, and usually in whispered tones, to comment briefly on what they saw. Comments included, for example, 'there's not much cupboard space', 'Look, there's a fireplace like ours' or 'I couldn't live with that'. This pattern of observation suggests that visitors were checking to see that the exhibition met with their existing taste rather than to seek out ways of transforming it.

This general theme of passive assimilation of the messages of the show can also be illustrated by my observations of visitor responses to a series of room 'make-overs' from a traditional terraced house. The room 'make-overs' feature comprised seven rooms, including hallway, sitting room, dining room, kitchen, two bedrooms and bathroom, and provided before-and-after photographs of previously dilapidated 1970s decoration. This emphasis on before and after made the feature interesting as it encouraged visitors to imagine how they might 'makeover' their own homes. The level of engagement with the feature by visitors was, however, surprisingly low. The majority of visitors only spent between 50 seconds and 1 1/2 minutes viewing this exhibit. A minority stopped at the looped scarlet rope barriers which cordoned them off from the room sets to look in more detail, or pointed at a particular feature of a room to draw attention to it, but would rarely comment. The majority of visitors spent only about a third of their time actually looking at this exhibit. The rest of the time was spent looking at and picking up brochures in the central area.

The process of brochure hunting at this exhibit was interesting in itself, as if the exhibit was less important than reading about the products being marketed at a later date. Thin brochures were picked up readily and placed in the IHE carrier bag. Visitors were much more reticent about picking up the thicker magazine-like brochures, and went through an extraordinarily common procedure of flicking the first few pages of the brochure, then turning it over to look at the back before straightening it up and leaving it alone. In a show which emphasises the theme of 'something for nothing' so strongly, it is perhaps surprising that these magazines were not just taken away without worry. That reticence did not ultimately dissuade some people from taking the magazine away. In the period of observation, four half-metre-high piles of magazines were taken away and quickly replenished by the exhibit staff who spent most of their time unpacking parcels of brochures.

While the passive reception of the spectacle of the IHE is observable, it should also be stated that this passive involvement was not accompanied by strong gestures of irritation. This is perhaps surprising because the extent to which visitors consigned themselves to long queues may well have tested people's patience to the limit. I certainly felt a sense of personal discomfort as I became caught up in a tightly packed traffic jam of bodies making their way around the balcony area, where I spent three quarters of an hour in an *inescapable* crush of visitors.

The response of visitors to this crush of strangers was to maintain their personal space through the maintenance of 'polite inattention' to the plight of all the people around them. This polite inattention was maintained by avoiding eye contact, bodily contact and again, an almost complete suspension of conversation – or complaint. The only audible speech came from the keepers of small stalls which surrounded the balcony, as they attempted to hawk their products.

The quiescence of visitors at the exhibition is perhaps surprising because, unlike a traditional non-interactive or non-activity-based museum or art gallery, the show gives people plenty of opportunities to interact with each other or with the show stand personnel, or actively to take part in events. There were partial exceptions to this observation. For example, on a number of stands visitors were offered the opportunity of trying out new things, including ergonomic chairs, vibrating and uplifting beds, electrical pain-reduction devices, aromatherapy, face make-up, hair styling, manicures and foot massage. With the exception of trying out electronically controlled beds and chairs which changed their shapes, which produced a degree of amusement or embarrassment, the visitors were the passive recipients of treatments. At one stand as many as 20 women sat in a long row, with vibrating chair cushions behind them to relieve stress. All 20 faced in the same direction at a mass of milling visitors – each sporting a vacant expression. Perhaps this is proof positive that the stress-relieving treatment they were undergoing was actually working? More than likely, they were just exhausted having nearly completed a tour of six acres of show space, and were thankful for a brief respite.

Interviewing Visitors

Making observations about consumer behaviour throws some light on the way that visitors received the messages of the show. Observations alone may not provide a full enough understanding of this process of passive assimilation of the messages the show intends to put across. The interviews undertaken at the 1997 IHE Preview Day demonstrate the level of engagement with the show, and also reveal some insights into visitors' motivations for being there.

At the start of each interview I asked the same question. The following exchange represents a fairly typical response:

TC	Why are you here? What are you looking for?
Man	Er …
Woman	For different ideas
Man	Ideas, really. You get a lot of people here exhibiting stuff you wouldn't find elsewhere. Products, really.
TC	So have you got any ideas, then? [*all laughing*]
Woman	Yeah, we have, haven't we?
Man	Yeah.
Woman	Vinyl,
Man	Yeah.
Woman	Lemon vinyl.
Man	Yeah.
TC	And you think that you will make some changes, then?
Man	Oh yeah.
Woman	Yeah.
Man	Yeah, it gives us ideas. I think one of the main reasons we came here for was looking at the furniture. You know, the furniture makers. That's what we're looking forward to, isn't it? Plus the food hall, gadgetry in there as well.
TC	Will you buy anything?.
Man	If we see something really different, you know, some thing you don't see elsewhere, then we'll go for it.

Relatively few people seem go to the IHE with the intention of seeking out ideas or practical advice on home decoration in a focused way. When I pursued the point, one visitor commented:

> We like the same colours, don't we? I don't like the new apple and purple look, which is very modern, and I can't see that lasting. I can't see it particularly taking off, unless you're a bit Art-Deco yourself. But I do like the warm pastels where they've used the oranges and the peaches. I think that looks nice. I'm that sort of person, I like to go into a room and feel that I'm home.
>
> (Woman in late 20s)

A second example shows a less definite view on what they were looking for:

1st Woman The particular thing I'm looking for is colours.
2nd Woman We are very much into colours.
1st Woman We love colours.
2nd Woman I come round here and I thought I'd pick their brains on colours and see what they got.

(Two women in mid 30s)

It is indicative of the lack of close attention visitors paid to detail that several people did not necessarily notice which house they had just been in, and seemed to be quite vague about what they had seen or liked.

Daughter We've not been in the one with the thatch yet.
TC (I direct their attention to the roof of the house they've just been in)
Mother Oh, we have been in!
TC What are your impressions?
Mother Ideas, lovely ideas.
Daughter The more, er, darker.
Mother Dark and light mixture.
Daughter Rather than just light colours.
TC What ideas have you got, that you didn't have before?
Mother There were the curtains (daughter laughs)
Daughter Ideas with the, er, decorating that were so simple. That it's a creative idea, isn't it. And also ideas with flowers.
Mother Things you can repeat at home.
TC What about the zig-zaggy wallpaper upstairs, did you like that?
Daughter Yes, that. In one of the bedrooms. Yes that's quite good. And no coving, on the ceilings, that going, you know. Lines going on the ceiling (from the walls) that's er.
TC Would you do that?
Daughter Definitely for a children's room and things like that, yes.
Mother I quite like coving.
Daughter But I possibly wouldn't do that in my room, I don't think.
TC What is your house like?
Daughter We've just finished building. It'd be a kind of farm-housey type of house … Er …
Mother Got beams on the outside, hasn't it. Oak beams.
Daughter We've used a lot of natural colours, you know, and things. You know, like wood, and natural things.

(Daughter in late 30s, mother late 60s/early 70s)

Generalised questions about what ideas visitors were receiving from the show revealed few insights. This may not be surprising because visitors did not expect to be asked about their views – the show is billed, after all, as an enjoyable day out rather than an educational visit. When attention was turned to personal notions of an ideal home, respondents produced insights on aesthetic preference. This line of enquiry revealed a strikingly uniform set of values that centred upon the popular notion of buying an older (or, more often than not, *old-looking*) house.

> I would like to have a Georgian windows theme, more arched windows. And a conservatory. I'd like older, well, new-built, old style. Because I'm getting to the stage where I haven't got enough character to play with in a seventies house.
>
> (Woman in 40s with husband)

In another interview, this point was mirrored quite closely.

> **Woman** In an ideal world I'd choose a very very old house. A seventeenth-century farmhouse, basically, [*laughs*] it's a private fantasy.
> **TC** And why would you like that?
> **Woman** Er, because it's got old original features. I'm not too keen on new houses. I find them a bit cold. I like something with a bit of character about it.
>
> (Woman in her 40s with woman friend of same age)

Conscious of these popular preferences, the 1997 exhibition had a real thatched roof that looked, on the surface at least, a little bit cottagey. Visitors showed considerable interest in this show home

> **1st Woman** I don't know what the thatched roof one's like. Is it very cottagey?
> **TC** I haven't been in yet [not true].
> **2nd Woman** Well, that's the one that I, er…
> **1st Woman** We're going to go in that one.
> **2nd Woman** I thought that one's really lovely.
> **1st Woman** The quaintness of it. And I think it's dateless. You know, it's been around for years, that look, and it'll be around for many many years, guaranteed.
> **2nd Woman** We [the woman and her husband] bought three months ago, and you know, we would have loved a

cottage. But we're very inexperienced, we don't know what we're looking for. We don't know if it's a good or bad buy, so we went safe and went for a new one. But ideally that would be my dream ideal house. And have your beams and your inglenook fireplace and you know, an Aga. It's brilliant.

While some visitors were critical of the fact that the show was aesthetically quite so safe, and that it changed little from year to year, most people enjoyed the show as a 'good day out' and an excuse to indulge themselves in some shopping. In the mix of shopping opportunities, in the context of a show that celebrates notions of the ideal home, it is hardly surprising that about 70 per cent of visitors were women. Neither is it surprising, then, that some women purposefully left their husbands at home.[5]

TC Will you buy things while you are here?
1st Woman Oh yes.
2nd Woman We're suckers.
TC What will you buy?
1st Woman Pictures.
2nd Woman But last year we both came away with vibrating cushions.
1st Woman Colour changing lipstick. Massage oils.
2nd Woman Loads of aromatherapy stuff.
1st Woman But pictures, I came home with pictures.
TC How many did you buy?
1st Woman Fifteen.
TC My God, How did you carry them home?
1st Woman With difficulty [*both laugh*].
TC Would you bring your husbands?
1st Woman No.
2nd Woman No, I wouldn't.
1st Woman No, because, our two husbands are very good friends. We do go out together as couples a lot, as families.
2nd Woman And as soon as you get anywhere, they want to know where they can go and eat.
1st Woman And when they've eaten they want to know where they can go and eat again.
2nd Woman And it just wouldn't interest them.

1st Woman	They'd be useful for carrying the bags – but I wouldn't want them anywhere near really.
TC	Cramps your style?
Together	Absolutely! [*both laugh*]

This interview reflects a general impression that women at the show were there for a good day out to do some shopping, and perhaps be a little extravagant by buying goods that they would not normally buy – particularly so if their husbands had been with them. The interchange between the two women and me also shows the extent to which rapport could be achieved in a relatively short period of time. My interview style was purposefully informal, chatty even, in order to elicit a response from respondents. This was necessary because respondents were ill-prepared for an interview – they were, quite literally, caught 'on the hop'. Other more formal methods of interviewing were attempted at shows in previous years, but these tended to make the respondents suspicious of me, and elicited little in the way of insightful or spontaneous comment – often they thought I was trying to sell them something. Of course, there may also be some kind of gender effect coming into play here – and the mainly women respondents might have said different things to a woman interviewer. I doubt this, however, judging from the speed at which rapport was achieved. Indeed, it was the men respondents with whom I had the most difficulty in eliciting opinions and reactions to the show. Men seemed to be embarrassed by my questions, and to some extent by their own presence at the show. On almost all occasions, when asked to comment on what they had seen, they referred to 'manly' artefacts like interesting radiators, new technology and the like. Had I been a woman interviewer these men may, perhaps, have been more open in their responses.

CONCLUSIONS

In this chapter I have argued that the way that people spend money on their home life is important for their projection of self-identity to families, friends and neighbours. Drawing upon the work of Erving Goffman, I have argued that the presentation of self in the home is anything but unconstrained and that, as a consequence of this, capital must proceed very carefully in its methods of marketing products for consumption in the domestic sphere.

While capitalism exercises considerable power in affecting consumer attitudes and behaviour through the sophisticated media of advertising, retail psychology and marketing which has been identified at an event such as the IHE, its influence is mediated by a strong sense of cultural conservatism. If, as I have argued, consumers anticipate the reaction of family, friends and neighbours, then it seems obvious to me that changing things, or leaving things as they are both carry the perceived risk of stigmatisation. Consequently, consumers tread very carefully when they buy goods and services for their homes, and are resistant to radical change.

This chapter has demonstrated that the IHE is a venue where capital successfully presents products in a way that will not offend the relatively conservative taste of *Middle England* consumers. Indeed, the observations and interviews seem to demonstrate that the messages are so subtle that visitors participate in a process of passive assimilation of these idealised images of home. Indeed, the show's success seems to be its avoidance of radical new ideas – but instead, the presentation of safe images that do not openly challenge established popular fashions in domestic architecture and interior design.

The organisers get the message across that it is safe to buy the products by producing a subtle blend of *aesthetic reassurance, celebrity association and expert help, financial incentives and prizes,* together with *warnings about the risks of leaving things as they are*. This analysis strongly suggests, then, that the IHE is a place where culturally conservative *Middle Englanders* can *assure* themselves that their taste is along the right lines: to *check* that they are broadly up to date with fashions, but not too far out of the ordinary. The IHE is, then, a location within which capital attempts to shape consumers' attitudes and desires through a subtle blend of promises and threats, and it owes its longevity to the ability of the organisers to successfully *reflect* the needs and wants of a culturally conservative audience.

ACKNOWLEDGEMENTS

Thanks are due to Jenny Hockey and Rosemary J. Lucas, who made valuable comments on an earlier version of this paper.

NOTES

1. There is no space here to stage a critique of the notion of excessive individualism that is claimed to exist under postmodernity. For a brief and incisive introduction see Warde (1994) or Jenkins (1996); more detailed analyses can be found in Bauman (1988, 1991); Beck (1992); Featherstone (1991); Giddens (1991, 1993).
2. There is a substantial literature dealing with the power of persuasion capital can marshal in selling its goods and services. Useful recent overviews of theoretical and empirical material include Bocock (1993), Corrigan (1997), Dittmar (1992), Falk and Campbell (1997), and Gabriel and Lang (1997).
3. Visitors on the Press and Preview Days in 1995 and 1997 tended to display through their deportment a more animated engagement with the show, which was perhaps due to the carnival atmosphere created by the presence of a number of celebrities, the press and the major influx of PR personnel who were not present at the rest of the show. Nevertheless, the street theatre troupes at the Press and Preview Day of the 1997 show were largely ignored. It was difficult not to feel sorry for a group of very competent men and women soul singers in the show house village who received no applause, nor even an audience for most of their performance.
4. There was apparently one exception to this, which I learned from a PR assistant at the 1997 show. The story went that a number of visitors at the 1996 show were issued special vouchers by Laura Ashley PLC that allowed them into the show houses ahead of the rest of the visitors who had been queueing for a considerable time. The ensuing pandemonium led to the abandonment of this practice in the 1997 show.
5. There is a growing literature on gendered aspects of shopping. Useful overviews of research can be found in Campbell (1997), Falk and Campbell (1997), Lunt and Livingstone (1992).

REFERENCES

Allan, G. and Crow, G. (1989) *Home and Family: Creating the Domestic Sphere* (London: Macmillan).
Bauman, Z. (1988) *Freedom* (Milton Keynes: Open University Press).
Bauman, Z. (1990) 'Modernity and Ambivalence', in M. Featherstone (ed.), *Global Culture: Nationalism, Globalization and Modernity* (London: Sage).
Beck, U. (1992) *Risk Society: Towards a New Modernity* (London: Sage).
Bennett, A. (1994) *Writing Home* (London: Faber and Faber).
Bocock, R. (1993) *Consumption* (London: Routledge).
Campbell, C. (1997) 'Shopping, Leisure and the Sex War', in P. Falk and C. Campbell (eds), *The Shopping Experience* (London: Sage).
Chapman, T. (1995) 'Stage Sets for Ideal Lives', *New Statesman and Society*, 7 April.

Chapman, T. and Hockey, J. (eds) (1998) *Ideal Homes? Social Change and Domestic Life* (London: Routledge).
Corrigan, P. (1997) *The Sociology of Consumption* (London: Sage).
Dittmar, H. (1992) *The Social Psychology of Material Possessions: To Have is to Be* (Hemel Hempstead: Harvester/Wheatsheaf).
Douglas, M. (1977) 'In Defence of Shopping', in P. Falk and C. Campbell (eds), *The Shopping Experience* (London: Sage).
Falk, P. and Campbell, C. (eds) (1997) *The Shopping Experience* (London: Sage).
Featherstone, M. (1991) *Consumer Culture and Postmodernism* (London: Sage).
Gabriel, Y. and Lang, T. (1997) *The Unmanageable Consumer* (London: Sage).
Giddens, A. (1991) *Modernity and Self Identity: Self and Society in the Late Modern Age* (Oxford: Polity).
Giddens, A. (1993) *The Transformation of Intimacy: Sexuality, Love and Eroticism in Modern Societies* (Oxford: Polity).
Goffman, E. (1963) *Stigma: Notes on the Management of a Spoiled Personality* (Harmondsworth: Penguin).
Goffman, E. (1969) *The Presentation of Self in Everyday Life* (Harmondsworth: Penguin).
Jenkins, R. (1996) *Social Identity* (London: Routledge).
Lunt, P. and Livingstone, S. (1992) *Mass Consumption and Personal Identity: Everyday Economic Experience* (Buckingham: Open University Press).
Park, R. E. (1950) *Race and Culture* (Glencoe, Illinois: Free Press).
Sherman, M. (1947) *Daily Mail Ideal Home Book, 1947-48* (London: Daily Mail Publications).
Show Guide (1995) (Ruislip, Middlesex: DMG Home Interest Magazines).
Warde, A. (1994) 'Consumption, Identity Formation and Uncertainty', *Sociology,* 28(4): 877–98.

5 Power and Resistance around the Dinner Table

LYDIA MARTENS and ALAN WARDE

INTRODUCTION

The dinner table, whether situated in a domestic home or in a commercial establishment, is a site for the enactment of social relations of power and resistance. 'Family meals' (which, of course, do not always happen around a dinner table) are characterised by diverse power relations: between adults and children, between husbands and wives or men and women, as well as between the 'family unit' and the 'world outside', as cultural expectations of appropriate domestic relations (Murcott, 1982, 1983; Charles and Kerr, 1988; DeVault 1991). These power relations have so far received most scholarly attention. Those operating around the dinner tables of commercial establishments have received considerably less attention, whilst a sociology of dining at the homes of friends or extended families is currently non-existent.

Several commentators have regarded the restaurant and the hotel dining room as sites of social control and discipline. Mostly this has been a matter of the strategies that staff or management use to obtain maximum desired compliance from clientele, it being not enough for customers to spend money, for they must also behave in an acceptable fashion. Contrary to any presumption of consumer sovereignty, some accounts (Whyte, 1948; Mars and Nicod, 1984) suggest that waiters are adept at manipulating their customers, and that there are some unpleasant punishments for those who resist. Finkelstein (1989) implies that control is built into the design of a restaurant, such that its 'diorama', or ambience, serves to prescribe customer behaviour. Wood (1994), probably more sanguine than Finkelstein, observes that there is a genuine problem of appropriate interaction between providers and consumers of commercial hospitality services. Elsewhere he notes that the restaurant is a masculine environment, implying that male managers, serving staff and diners exercise some degree of power and control over women (Wood, 1990).

In this chapter we explore these propositions regarding the operation of power around dinner tables outside the home, examining whether people feel restrained, constrained and repressed; and if so, by what or by whom. We do this by comparing dining out in public, in a commercial establishment, with being entertained in a private house, where a host(ess)–guest relationship still exists.[1] This comparison is used to indicate some features of the nature of public behaviour in places of entertainment, particularly trends of informalisation and domestication. Is there a tendency for restaurant meals to become more like domestic ones? Is there a process of informalisation? What do these activities indicate about attitudes to strangers and decorous behaviour in public places? The comparison is based on research conducted in 1994–5. We start by briefly outlining the methods of our empirical investigation. Two sections follow which compare the experience of being a client in a restaurant and a guest in someone else's home. The experience of eating out is used to speculate about relationships of reciprocity and commodification.

METHODS OF INVESTIGATION

Our investigation has two components. In the first instance we conducted in-depth interviews with principal food provider(s) in households in diverse circumstances. Interviews were conducted in the autumn of 1994, were in Preston and the surrounding area, and each lasted between one and two hours. Interviewees, 27 women and 6 men, were asked a number of questions relating to aspects of eating at home and eating out. These included questions exploring the understanding of the term eating out, the frequency with which interviewees ate out in various places, detail about three recent eating out experiences, and how interviewees felt about eating out. The interviews were of a semi-structured type and discussion was wide-ranging around the key topics.

In addition, 1001 people were surveyed, a third each in three cities in England – London, Bristol and Preston. A quota sample matched respondents to the overall population of diverse local wards by age, sex, class and ethnic group. The survey was undertaken in April 1995 and questions were asked about frequency of eating out, types of outlet visited in the previous 12 months, attitudes to eating out and detail about the most recent meal eaten away from home. The answers were analysed to explore social variations in eating out by class, income, age, gender, education, place of residence, and so forth.[2]

SERVICE AND FORMALITY IN THE RESTAURANT

Eating out involves service delivery and reception, and as such brings together customers, waiters and waitresses, as well as proprietors and managers. This has generated some sociological interest. Some work has been done to understand the face-to-face relationship between the service deliverer and recipient in air travel (Hochschild, 1983) as well as in restaurants (Whyte, 1948; Mars and Nicod, 1984), in the past. As suggested above, Whyte, and Mars and Nicod conclude that waiters wield a great deal of power over customers; but one might speculate whether this has been subject to change. One reason for doing so is Finkelstein's insistence that the restaurant is a site designed to create a particular kind of social order which is orchestrated by the restaurant owner, who thereby exercises control over customers. By contrast, there has also been recent speculation in the sociology of consumption about shifts in power relationships from producer to consumer (Keat *et al.*, 1994).

A principal reason for speculating about power relationships between actors involved in service is the apparent change in the character of service delivery itself. The contemporary trend is probably towards the greater use of self-service. Self-service means a different role for the waiter/waitress compared to more extensive types of service, which offer greater opportunity for the direct persuasion of customers. Are such shifts in the character of service delivery related to the power the consumer wields to shape commercial meal provision in ways that accord with their sensibilities, or is it a reflection of market strategies?

In order to throw light on these issues, we explore how contemporary customers of commercial food establishments feel about the process of delivery. The nature of their judgements and concerns is illustrated by our qualitative interviews. Our interviewees gave us many reasons why they went where they did, why they enjoyed meals, and why they liked particular venues. In the course of this we discovered a good deal about how they evaluated service, which was in an important degree related to an overriding notion of formality.

Descriptions of the encounter between customer and serving staff revolve around three themes; time, style of personal interaction, and the nature of the establishment regime.[3]

The majority of interviewees made reference to time when asked about the quality of service. Concern with time was sometimes expressed in minutes: the delays between arrival, having an order taken, and the appearance of the first part of the meal on the table, were measured. Besides the absolute times involved, there was also a more subjective sense of acceptable tempo. The goal was to avoid either feeling rushed or being kept waiting too long. Quite a number of people said that they did not mind even quite long intervals before ordering or between courses. But they were susceptible to feeling unduly hurried; it was even more widely observed that staff might hover around, waiting to take your plate away and hoping that you will vacate your table soon so that other customers can be accommodated.

Judgements of service suggest the existence of other polarities, satisfaction being expressed when the event falls acceptably in the middle of a continuum. The quality of the customer/staff relationship was seen to lie somewhere on a continuum between intrusive and inattentive. The word intrusive was used by several interviewees and this was clearly something reprehensible. The character of the dilemma was succinctly expressed by Rose, 'You want your waiting staff to be attentive, you know, make sure everything's all right, but you don't particularly want to be pestered every two minutes.'

Our interviewees used two other contrasts, between enthusiastic and indifferent, and between friendly and impersonal. There was a certain ambivalence about over-enthusiasm. An occasion in an Italian restaurant where the waiters 'were crazy rather than anything else' was enjoyed as a performance but tinged with reservation because 'I think one of them liked my little sister'. Staff who, it appeared 'couldn't care less', were disparaged. But if staff might be over-enthusiastic, it seemed that they could hardly be too friendly. Being 'welcoming', 'smiling and you know very courteous', 'I like people to be friendly and smile when they bring your food, and ask if everything is all right', were forms of recommendation. The opposite attitude was condemned: 'if the waitresses are not pleasant … that's not good'. This view found its extension in a comment from Sheila, who described the service during a meal at The Golf Club as 'efficient but cool and detached, nothing personal about it'. She continued by saying:

> you know I probably wouldn't go again. Not because the food wasn't nice but I don't know, it's not a place I would choose to go, it's not a homely place. I like to go to homely places like the pub down the road, they have a log fire and you know, you know the landlord and landlady. Yeah, that's more impersonal, you never saw the same waitress twice, they had a lot of staff on.

So, the terminology used to commend good service included not just friendliness but also homeliness.

One theme that came up repeatedly in the interviews was formality. References to formality often related to particular institutional aspects of the meal experience, like dress rules, rules on bodily posture, the timing of the meal, where and with whom an order was placed and the bill-paying regime. As such, formality indicates an awareness by the customer of establishment regime. It is also a means of evaluation of these regimes: references to formal aspects of the eating out experience were always accompanied by an evaluation as to whether these were considered good or bad, liked or disliked.

One of the strongest expressions of aversion to formal places came from Anne (a housewife in her 20s, with husband and two children) who dwelt upon the topic at length. In short, she had a great dislike for anything that was formal.

> I don't like going anywhere that's formal. I can't stand anything formal. I had to go to a wedding on Friday, it's just an absolute nightmare for me.

She held the view that, in order for her to enjoy eating out, the experience had to be free from stress and pressure. And this could only be so if the situation was informal. To 'dress-up' for eating out, for instance, was a source of displeasure. Other elements of Anne's dislike of restaurants included the timing of the meal, not knowing in advance how much the bill would be, and tipping. Overall, she preferred the self-service associated with bar meals, partly because of discomfort with conventions regarding tipping and payment, and partly to avoid surveillance.

Other (though not all) respondents thought about different venue types as residing somewhere on a *scale* of formality, some being more formal than others. The significance of formality for respondents was evident in commentaries about various public eating places. John (a married lawyer in his 20s) was very explicit about different types of commercial venues and their different levels of formality.

> obviously if you go to somewhere like a Wotsit's or Pizza Chain it will be obviously far less regimented than if you go to a Classic's or a Gourmet's or somewhere like that, equally the people in there will tend to be different types of people and the dress would tend to be different. If we went to Wotsit's in the evening I could probably feel

> I could get away with a pair of jeans, where if we went in an evening to one of the other places I mentioned I would go in a suit or a jacket and trousers, invariably a suit. So that in itself tends to put things on a different level of formality in any event.

In sum, service is largely taken for granted, providing it doesn't draw attention to itself, and interviewees were mostly satisfied with service. The overwhelming impression from the interviews was that people were aware that they might be made to feel uncomfortable if they went to certain types of restaurant, particularly to ones whose regimes were considered excessively formal. The threshold of formality, however, varied between interviewees, with younger working-class people most likely to have low tolerance. It seemed that most people simply avoided those places which they considered too formal. Feeling comfortable, avoiding embarrassment, acting appropriately were all important, but there was little sense that our interviewees felt they were being pushed around by the waiting staff, as might have been the case in the establishments described by Whyte, or Mars and Nicod. The courteousness, politeness and friendliness of waiting staff were taken entirely at face value. It was the restaurant regime, its organisation and time scheduling, perceived as means to increasing profits, which was most usually condemned. In the light of the fears inspired by waiters in the past this may be one of the most important signs of a shift to more informal and acceptable types of service delivery.

THE COMPARISON OF PRIVATE AND COMMERCIAL HOSPITALITY

All interviewees agreed that there was a difference between eating in 'private homes' compared with 'public establishments', though they differed as to which they preferred. Formality was mentioned by almost every respondent in comparing commercial with private hospitality, and dislike of formality was clearly communicated. A preference to eat at the home of friends and family was related to the pleasure of relaxation, and its antithesis, the restriction entailed in observing formal rules of appropriate public conduct. Expressions of preference for 'home entertainment' were also related to an awareness and appreciation of the work this entailed for the host(s). Not surprisingly, the degree of satisfaction derived from eating in 'private homes' and eating in 'public establishments' differed, and we shall finish this section with an attempt to explain this.

Relaxation was mentioned only once (negatively) in discussions of restaurant service, but was a much-vaunted reason for liking private hospitality. Two specific themes were isolated in making comparison between public and private sites – presentation of self and time-pressure – and both were referred to in terms of the greater opportunity for relaxation in a friend's home.

The first theme, presentation of the self, reflected awareness of the 'demands' that restaurant regimes make on 'the self', but also included commentaries on the implications for personal behaviour when strangers are present. The general feeling this generated was expressed by Sheila, who preferred eating at the home of friends to eating in a public venue because it is 'more relaxed, you're not on show'. Pressures to 'dress up', something which may relate to establishment regime as well as the presence of strangers, were felt not to be as pressing when eating at the home of friends. For Debby, this was one aspect which contributed to her greater enjoyment of eating at friends'.

Debby	Well it's just relaxed, you just sit round or have a chat and ...
Interviewer	You find that more relaxing than going to a restaurant?
Debby	Well it's not so formal, no. You don't get really dressed for going round to a friend's house than when you go to a restaurant ... .'

Other comments specifically reflected the different degrees of freedom respondents felt they had in different sets of company. Eating in commercial venues inevitably meant eating in the company of strangers as well as people one knew better, whereas this was not the case in someone's home. This consideration made John feel more on guard in a restaurant:

> at the end of the day you are going out to you know this is your leisure time and you are endeavouring to relax, and I think a little bit when you are out you do tend to be on show a little bit. I am a person who is in general what you see is what you get. So I have a very high embarrassment threshold and that it just doesn't bother me, and I will say things in public that possibly you shouldn't say, that would embarrass other people. Well I'll say ... I'm not never offensive, but they will say

> you can't say that somebody might have heard you, you know, and that possibly is a little bit, makes one guarded a little bit, can't relax in the way that you would be able to do with friends.

Eating in public stipulates control of bodily demeanour. Yet certain bodily postures, like 'slobbing out', putting your feet up, and taking your shoes off, were seen as enhancing efforts to relax and were all considered permissible when eating at the home of friends. Trisha was able to relax more at a friend's house by lounging in front of the television.

> Sometimes it's nice to go to a friends because you don't have to make as much of an effort as if you were going to a restaurant so, and erm you can lounge around in front of the tele and erm you know chat and really just relax and sit and chat about things.

This indicates that eating in public places entailed some level of undesirable self-constraint.

The second aspect of comparison associated with judgements about formality was the experience of the passage of time. In Sheila's case, eating at a friends' home was more relaxed because 'you can take as long as you like, sit at the table for as long as you like. I like that.' Other interviewees also said they enjoyed eating out best when they did not feel rushed in any sense, and for them, this was more likely to be found in the home of friends or family. Indeed, for guests in a private house, the longer the event lasted the more enjoyable it was proclaimed. Thirty-seven per cent of respondents spent more than three hours on their last occasion. It seems that people eat at a more leisurely rate when in someone else's home and there is plenty of time on such social occasions to take off one's shoes.

Another aspect which played a role in the evaluation of 'private' and 'public' dining, was an awareness that 'entertaining' involved work for the hosts. The work of entertaining and routine domestic cooking are similar in some respects. For instance, knowing about and accommodating guests' tastes was a common topic of discussion amongst our respondents, in the same way that catering for the tastes of individual household members was prominent in the discussions of DeVault's (1991) respondents. The distribution of the work also reflected that of everyday cooking; female respondents who did most of the everyday domestic cooking also did most of the work of entertaining. In those households men did tasks traditionally associated with the male host, like cooking barbecued meats, taking care of the alcoholic drinks, washing dishes and helping with serving guests. This type of male involvement meant that the work of entertaining was portrayed as team-work, even though women did the lion's share of the work, and in particular that which occurred behind the scenes. In those households where men contributed more towards everyday cooking, their involvement in entertaining work was also more extensive.

The work of entertaining differs from everyday cooking in some important ways too. Unlike everyday cooking, dinner parties often included various courses, and dishes prepared especially for such occasions, and the latter were seen to take more time and effort. A conversation between Sally, Peter and the interviewer illustrates this point well.

Interviewer	So does that mean that when you cook for friends, you cook differently than when you cook for the family?
Sally	We take more time, it can take hours and hours and hours.
Peter	I suppose that's because you are doing more than one course.
Sally	That could have something to do with it. Yeah we usually have soup and a main course and well sometimes we have the lot but. I think you take more trouble.
Peter	Well we tend to be a bit more perhaps not adventurous but most people seem to enjoy the food so perhaps we are doing something that you can't just throw together and takes a lot of preparation.
Interviewer	So there's more fuss when people come?
Peter	I think so.

The work of entertaining can be complex and hence anxiety-provoking. Respondents were anxious about getting dishes right, and consequently tried new dishes out beforehand, used favourite recipes more than once, or 'just hoped for the best'. Managing time and sociability were other concerns which made the work of entertaining potentially more stressful, and respondents talked about using the oven and doing a lot of the work prior to the event as ways of coping.

Awareness about the character of entertaining work generated feelings of ambivalence, particularly amongst some female interviewees, which became evident in the comparison of commercial and communal meals. For some, like Trisha, this meant that they preferred eating in a commercial establishment because it meant that no-one in the company had to do any work, so that everyone could relax and enjoy the occasion more. For others, it meant that they preferred eating at the home of friends or family more. Jean and David, for instance, enjoyed eating at friends' best for several reasons. But the overriding concern in their evaluation was the idea that friends 'gave' their time, and put in a lot of effort, to provide them with a good evening.

David You obviously appreciate, not because you're not paying for it, but you appreciate the time and effort that your friends have put into the meal that you're having.

Jean And you see when we eat out at friends' they usually really go to town.

The appreciation Jean and David had for non-commercial eating was further reflected in their concern about not being able to return the gift of being cooked for. Two occasions where reciprocity had been uneven were talked about at great length. These concerned two holidays which they had had at the home of friends and family. Here, a difference of observation between the two was evident, which related to Jean's identification with the pressure on women who do feeding work. So, when they had been guests at the home of friends on their holiday to the West Indies, Jean had felt very awkward about the fact that her friend Janis had done all the cooking. Particularly when they had been holidaying all day, whilst Janis had been at work. David had been more conscious of this same issue when they had been at the home of family on a subsequent holiday in Canada, because on that occasion they had sat in the kitchen whilst food preparation was in progress.

One of the outstanding findings of our study was the very high degree of satisfaction with eating out recorded by interviewees and respondents. Table 5.1 indicates answers to questions about how much various aspects of the last main meal eaten away from home were liked by respondents to the survey, distinguishing between those meals eaten on commercial premises and those in somebody else's home. In every instance a larger proportion of people were likely to prefer the various elements of the experience in the domestic than in the restaurant setting, though clearly the pleasures of restaurants are not much inferior in terms of their capacity to deliver satisfactions. For instance, no-one disliked the company when eating in a domestic setting, and only two respondents in a public venue said that they disliked the company 'a little'. That 'privately' served food was appreciated more than commercially served food is also a point worth noting.

Table 5.1 Satisfaction expressed with various aspects of the last meal eaten on commercial premises or in the home of another person (percentages by row)

	Liked a lot	Liked a little	Neither liked nor disliked	Disliked a little	Disliked a lot	Don't know or no answer
How much did you enjoy the food?						
Commercial	80	13	3	2	1	–
Private	85	10	2	–	0	3
How much did you enjoy the company?						
Commercial	89	6	3	–	0	2
Private	92	5	1	0	0	3
How much did you enjoy the decor?						
Commercial	56	24	15	2	1	1
Private	68	16	10	1	1	4
How much did you enjoy the service?						
Commercial	65	22	6	4	2	1
Private	78	8	7	0	0	7
How much did you enjoy the conversation?						
Commercial	80	14	4	–	–	2
Private	86	9	2	–	0	3
How much did you enjoy the atmosphere?						
Commercial	72	18	6	2	1	1
Private	89	6	2	1	–	3
How did the place rate as value for money?						
Commercial	67	17	6	5	2	4
How much did you enjoy, overall, the total occasion?						
Commercial	81	14	3	2	–	1
Private	90	6	1	1	0	3

n: commercial = 585; private = 351.
Note: – indicates less than 0.5 per cent, 0 means no response in the category.

It is unclear whether it is the domestic setting, or the fact of being a guest, which is the primary basis for these levels of satisfaction. The difference in satisfaction with the atmosphere between commercial and domestic modes might perhaps indicate a continued preference for privacy, and some ambivalence about eating in public. The atmosphere in the home is, after all, created and supplied entirely by the host(ess) and selected guests, who will normally be expected to value each other's company. There can be no intrusion, or effect upon the proceedings by pure strangers. At the same time, the lack of much-registered distaste for commercial atmospheres suggests that diners are not much distressed by fellow customers nor by the trappings of the aura created by restaurant owners.

Another issue of interest and possible explanation for the different levels of satisfaction found is whether gifts of labour and money are imbued with equal levels of satisfaction? If you are someone's guest in a restaurant, does the level of satisfaction rise to the same levels as if you are a guest in someone else's home? Survey analysis suggests that being someone's guest in a restaurant resulted in higher recorded satisfaction levels than if the costs are shared, or footed by the respondent. Being in receipt of a gift is valued most highly, even in a restaurant. However, since recordings of 'liking the overall occasion a lot' were 85 per cent for guests in restaurants and 90 per cent for guests in homes, levels of enjoyment in a private home still surpassed those in restaurants. This suggests that a gift of labour is valued more than a gift of money.

DISCUSSION

Service and Power in the Restaurant

The concepts used to evaluate service in commercial establishments are time (potentially wasted, lost or incapable of being filled, or being rushed), attitude of staff (friendly or over-friendly, personal or detached, intrusive and casual), efficiency (lack of skill or knowledge), and aspects of regime (dress codes, rituals of ordering and payment). This vocabulary and its application support several conclusions. People recognise differences between types of place and associate them with different regimes, often ranking according to degree of formality and often talking about them in class discriminating fashion. Many have a particular preference for some types of regime, there being systematic variation in thresholds of formality (as well as in other dimensions of quality). Preferences are also to some degree situational. For instance, some interviewees said that they liked getting dressed up and going to a smart restaurant sometimes, perhaps on a special occasion, while at other times they might prefer something less demanding.

There is little evidence that customers are intimidated by waiting staff. When reference was made to aspects of social hierarchy, for instance, it was usually in reference either to the regime and its organisation, or to other diners, rather than to waiting staff. So several interviewees referred to places as 'posh', as 'lah-di-dah', and one described a group at another table as 'toffee-nosed' and used them to sum up the character of the restaurant. But it seemed that generally the structural relationships with waiting staff were not particularly problematic. This might be in part because eating out has become a much more informal activity than it once was. Not only is there a wide variety of establishments with different levels of formality, but the staff themselves are increasingly less likely to be full-time professionals with sufficient social gravitas to manipulate their clients. In fact, the overall evidence shows little consciousness of the exercise of power in commercial eating out situations. Not only did we fail to find power of staff over customers, we found little evidence of the reverse either. The type of scenario where diners are said to be beginning to rile the staff (Fattorini, 1994) was not one that emerged from our interviews. Nor, as Martens (1997) has reported elsewhere, did we find much evidence of the restaurant having a masculine ambience or being a strongly patriarchal form. Conscious appreciation of inequalities of power in the contemporary restaurant was uncommon.

Even so, the existence of appropriate codes of conduct in restaurants was acknowledged. There is potential for embarrassment, as some of our interviewees observed, and there may therefore be some support for Wouters' (1986) claim that informalisation requires simultaneously, as part of the civilising process, greater self-discipline. Certainly, with one exception, people seemed concerned that they should always behave appropriately, including being suitably quiet, fittingly dressed, physically restrained, and so forth. There are codes of conduct which constrain people, but these seem to be largely self-imposed and self-policed. Perhaps this supports Beck's (1992) observation that traditionally mediating agents, in this instance waiters, are becoming increasingly irrelevant as individuals negotiate and regulate their behaviour directly in view of larger and shared cultural understandings about appropriate behaviour. In any case, one important mechanism for avoiding social embarrassment is, as we have shown, that people simply avoid places that they consider too formal. There is a process of self-selection in operation governed by people's wish not to feel 'uncomfortable'.

Private Hospitality as a Mode of Provision

Our finding that the majority of respondents and interviewees valued domestic hospitality offered by a friend more highly than its commercial equivalent is perhaps surprising. The field of food, like many others, is continuously subjected to ever greater commodification. Very little food is grown by the person who finally eats it; ever more of the preparation of raw materials is completed by an industrial manufacturing process; more meals are eaten which require no personal or domestic intervention. The merits of commodification are subject to theoretical and moral debate, but the process seems inexorable. During this process, one would expect the consumer attitude to become more entrenched, the value of consumer choice to be more and more vaunted, and the value of that which is home-made to become more dubious, rather than more appreciated, as appears to be the case. Furthermore, there are several features of the receipt of hospitality that might in principle be unappealing. Obligation to reciprocate is incurred, and that can involve considerable labour; the value of the gift is not precisely measurable and the nature of the incurred obligation uncertain; it is not possible to complain or get another dish if the food is disliked for whatever reason; and there is no choice about what shall be eaten. So, despite the fact that most key features of the state of consumer sovereignty are absent, people claim to be better pleased than in a restaurant.

There probably is a micro-physics of power involved in entertaining, but almost no-one seemed to notice or to speak about these power dynamics. Two potential relations of power can be distinguished within the practice of entertaining; between hosts and guests, and between the members of the household where the event is hosted. The dinner party *appears* to be a model for egalitarian social relations of production. In terms of the relations between hosts and guests this appearance may precisely be because of obligations of reciprocity: one expects to be servant one month and honoured guest the next. The lack of commentary related to power, resistance and the nature of relations between those who host the event, is more surprising. The literature on routine food preparation and domestic politics clearly illustrates the operation of power and resistance in this area of everyday life (Murcott, 1982, 1983; Charles and Kerr, 1988; DeVault, 1991). Reports about the distribution of the work involved while entertaining seemed to reflect everyday patterns. In households where everyday contribution by male partners was negligible, there was some evidence of male involvement in visible aspects of the event, as well as a tendency to construct the work of entertaining as a team effort. One possible explanation for such 'egalitarian' constructions of hospitality work may be the rising prominence of the ideology of greater egalitarianism in households, and the fact that the presence of guests increases the potential for surveillance. Alternatively, given the time-consuming nature of some dinner parties, such constructions may be part of the management of pleasure on the occasion. Whatever is the case, there are significant differences between the social relations of provision and delivery under modes of commercial provision and those of private hospitality, the latter probably retaining greater kudos and commanding more gratitude.

Informalisation and Domestication

Wood (1994) argues that, during the twentieth century, hotels have become increasingly like homes, evidenced, for instance, by the provision of tea- and coffee-making 'facilities', a television for private use, a drinks cabinet, and a private bathroom. However, is there any general trend, from the point of view of consumers, to want more private and quasi-domestic provision? We have seen that standards of service in restaurants are quite often measured against the criterion of friendliness and homeliness. Clients in restaurants, in explaining their discontent with formality, tend to look for domestic virtues. Chris's ideas about good service in restaurants rested on a direct comparison between eating out and home entertaining in which she expressed her view that service in restaurants should approximate the hospitality she gave her guests when she entertained.

> I have to say that the things that I don't like about eating out, is if you're treated, if the waitresses are not pleasant, or ... I do like if I go out I like people to be friendly and smile when they bring your food, and ask if everything is all right, and ask if you need relishes and things like that. Without you having to ask them. I think that's quite important. Cos if you were at home you would go round is everything all right for you, is there anything else you want, do you actually need you know. You do that don't you, make sure your guests are all happy. I think it's important for them to do that to you as well.

This raises the question of the extent to which commercial establishments are setting the pace as regards defining the appropriate standards of service (whether in hotels or restaurants) or whether they are being propelled by changing ways of organising households to offer new and different forms and levels of service.

The two sites for eating out permit reflection on whether these are separate spheres, whether the public event is governed by the same, or by a different, set of rules. Sennett (1978) thought there was considerable virtue to there being different codes of conduct for private as opposed to public behaviour. He was concerned that every activity would get absorbed into the private sphere and that the skills associated with dealing with strangers, and with public discussion of the common good, would atrophy. The privatisation of hotel behaviour might be an instance. So too might it be if the restaurant regime sought to imitate the private dinner party. If customers like Chris were to get their way, and waiting staff came to behave like a hostess, would this reduce the repertoires available for human interaction and signify a process of domestication and privatisation? Alternatively we could suggest that if stiff formality is the mode, mood or tone of interaction in the public sphere, then it is hard to weep over its demise. Part of the more general process of informalisation, the shift of restaurant service towards the more familiar, friendly, entertaining, casual, might be welcomed. But culturally, it may involve the flattening of experience, the reduction of differentiation between different spheres of activity, and the reduction of the manners of public interaction to the familiarities of home.

CONCLUSION

In this chapter we have examined power and resistance around dinner tables outside the home, by comparing food occasions in public venues and private homes and by concentrating our attention on how such occasions are experienced by customers and guests. In summary, our findings suggest that power in commercial venues has shifted away from waiting staff, diners now being more conscious of the establishment regime and of the opportunity for public surveillance in restaurants, both of which demand degrees of self-management and control that depend on the particular character of the commercial operation. One may speculate why such a shift has occurred. One possibility is that it reflects the expansion of the eating out market to include a larger proportion of the population (Mennell, 1984), whose tastes are not necessarily akin to those that prevailed when the activity was more 'exclusive' and exclusionary.

The absence of public surveillance and establishment regime in private homes means that being entertained in this way was seen to offer the opportunity for greater relaxation. This may also be the reason why the private meal was given the appearance of a highly egalitarian and unconstrained social occasion. The only challenge to this came from reflections on the meaning of the work involved in private 'entertaining' and one example where it was felt proper reciprocity had not been possible, both of which generated ambiguous feelings about domestic entertainment. Other evidence (not presented in this chapter) does support the idea that domestic entertaining may indeed be a relatively unconstrained event, where participants are, as David suggested, 'more in charge'. Whilst interviewees had no problem in recording the dinner party in its ideal form, it was clear that they easily improvised on this model. There were several forms of improvisation which involved either less effort for the host(ess) (for instance, by using commercial home delivery services and cook–chill supermarket meals), or a communal effort (for instance, where each person brings a course) or where service became a collective performance between host(ess) and guests. This implies that such occasions are not always bound by set rules and conduct. A thorough analysis of power and resistance around dinner tables at private homes must await more comprehensive sociological examination.

ACKNOWLEDGEMENT

We gratefully acknowledge support for this research from the Economic and Social Research Council, under the auspices of its Programme, 'The Nation's Diet: the social science of food choice'.

NOTES

1. This chapter will thus make little reference to power and resistance around family dinner tables.
2. In this chapter we use the term 'interviewee' to refer to the people involved at the qualitative stage, and the term 'respondent' to apply to those contacted by the survey.

3. By restaurant regime we mean the comparatively clear, rule-governed system for managing the situational and interpersonal aspects of the meal experience.

REFERENCES

Beck, U. (1992) *Risk Society: Towards a New Modernity* (London: Sage).
Charles, N. and Kerr, M. (1988) *Women, Food and Families* (Manchester: Manchester University Press).
DeVault, M. (1991) *Feeding the Family: The Social Organization of Caring as Gendered Work* (Chicago, IL: University of Chicago Press).
Fattorini, J. (1994) 'Food Journalism: A Medium for Conflict?', *British Food Journal,* 96(10): 24–8.
Finkelstein, J. (1989) *Dining Out: A Sociology of Modern Manners* (Cambridge: Polity).
Hochschild, A. (1983) *The Managed Heart: The Commercialization of Human Feeling* (Berkeley, CA: California University Press).
Keat, R., Whiteley, N. and Abercrombie, N. (eds) (1994) *The Authority of the Consumer* (London: Routledge).
Mars, G. and Nicod, M. (1984) *The World of Waiters* (London: Allen & Unwin).
Martens, L. (1997) 'Gender and the Eating Out Experience', *British Food Journal,* 99(1): 20–6.
Mennell, S. (1984) *All Manners of Food: Eating and Taste in England and France from the Middle Ages to the Present* (Oxford: Basil Blackwell).
Murcott, A. (1982) 'On the Social Significance of the "Cooked Dinner" in South Wales', *Social Science Information,* 21: 677–95.
Murcott, A. (1983), '"It's a Pleasure to Cook for Him": Food, Mealtimes and Gender in Some South Wales Households', in Eva Gamarnikow, David H. J. Morgan, Jane Purvis, and Daphne Taylorson (eds), *The Public and the Private* (London: Heinemann), pp. 79–90.
Sennett R. (1978) *The Fall of Public Man* (Cambridge: Cambridge University Press).
Whyte, W. F. (1948) *Human Relations in the Restaurant Industry* (New York: McGraw-Hill).
Wood, R. (1990) 'Sociology, Gender, Food Consumption and the Hospitality Industry', *British Food Journal,* 92(6): 3–5.
Wood, R. (1994) 'Hotel Culture and Social Control', *Annals of Tourism Research,* 21(1): 65–80.
Wouters, C. (1986) 'Formalization and Informalization: Changing Tension Balances in Civilising Processes', *Theory Culture and Society,* 3: 1–18.

6 Marginalisation and Resistance through the Prism of Retirement

MARK THORPE

INTRODUCTION

There is an increasing sensitivity among scholars working in the humanities and social sciences that 'homes', 'households', 'places' and 'spaces' are not immutable environments that act as containers of (passive) lives.[1] Rather, each of these 'categories' is produced through a complex panoply of social relations, tensions, contradictions, fears and, *inter alia*, aspirations. The nature of 'home', for example, owes its production as much to the socialised imaginary as it does to its material constitution. Similarly, places and spaces exist as much in the constellation of images and perceptions produced in the context of social encounters, relations, and struggles, as they do in material cartographies and forms (maps, built environments, etc.). As Henri Lefebvre (1991) has argued, the production and maintenance of places and spaces is inseparable from the networks of meaning and the meaningful networks constituted and lived by people as part of the living of 'everyday life'. As people produce such networks – through contact with others, establishing frames of reference, the routinisation of everyday practice, etc. – so too do they live through these networks. In short, meaningful networks and networks of meaning are both a product of social life and the means through which social life is constituted.

This broad recognition of everyday socio-spatial productions or 'productivities' is an immensely important part of contemporary social inquiry. Widespread recognition of the vitality of human engagement in, and production of, everyday life is a welcome addition to the practical lexicon of the social sciences. However, the distance between such recognition and crude valorisation is often small. This is evident in the movement from the observation of everyday socio-spatial productivities as omnipresent realities to calls for such realities to be seen as inherently radical; the idea being that the production of socio-spatial relations from the 'grassroots' signifies a dissonance with prevailing structural forces and imperatives. Moreover, at times such acts of 'resistance', particularly if sited within 'marginal spaces' (assessed and defined through variables such as 'race', 'ethnicity', 'gender', 'sexuality' etc.), are seen as rich with transformatory potential. The move from observations of the ongoing productivities of everyday life, where people do not just inhabit worlds but actively construct them, to commentaries extolling the latent revolutionary capacity of marginalised lives, is stark. The position adopted in this chapter is that the valorisation of the 'margins' as progressive sites of resistance is often shown to be problematic when tempered with empirical inquiry. The speculative abstractions as to the nature of socio-spatial worlds, particularly those claiming the 'higher ground' for marginalised spatialities, often rest rather awkwardly beside lived-realities. The capacity to produce spaces and relations is not, in and of itself, an indication of politically and socially progressive potential, but is, rather, more often than not a reflection of the 'going on' and 'making do' integral to everyday life.

In this chapter I present a broad critique of the valorisation of the 'margins' and 'resistance' through the prism of ethnographic study undertaken between 1992 and 1995 (Thorpe, 1996). The aim of this work was to develop an understanding of the processes through which everyday lives were constituted by post-retirement-aged people living in, or using, designated institutional spaces. These spaces included multi-occupancy residential housing, day centres and lunch clubs. The research was urban-based and was situated in southern England (and will be referred to as 'Ivington' hereafter).[2] In this chapter, for reasons of scope and the need for clarity, my use of empirical material is restricted to observations and 'structured conversations' originating from research in the day centres and lunch clubs (and not the residential homes).[3] In order to contextualise the illustrations that will appear in this chapter, it is important to point out that the overwhelming majority of my 'respondents' can be broadly defined as 'working-class'. This both reflects the nature of paid employment undertaken by the respondents during their formal working lives (variously skilled manual and blue-collar occupations – from cleaning and catering to labouring and retail shop work) and re-presents a label frequently used by respondents to describe themselves and significant others. In addition, the 'group' was almost exclusively what can be loosely referred to as 'White-English'. Such characteristics obviously make generalisation hazardous. However, my intention in this chapter is not to offer sweeping statements as to the nature of 'old age'. Rather, it is to provide an empirically based dissonance with regard to some of the cruder articulations of the 'margins' and 'resistance'.

It will be argued that, although not unproblematic, the 'language of space' offers the potential for a re-thinking and re-presentation of both theoretical and empirical analysis of social relations. To this extent the work of Henri Lefebvre, primarily his book *The Production of Space*, will be used as illustrative both of how a spatial vocabulary could be constructed and also the ways in which such vocabularies can be applied to the analysis of social relations.[4] The concept of vocabulary is important because it is used to suggest that the use of abstraction should be mediated through a constant dialectical relationship with the concrete relational world. As with any vocabulary, the use of components is dependent upon the task at hand and is limited by the scope for comprehension and the pertinent realms of communication. Vocabularies, then, by their very nature, are both enabling and constraining.

The final task will be to contextualise the discourse of margins and resistance and to question whether my empirical findings suggest ways of thinking or rethinking 'the margins of resistance'. In so doing, it is argued that social life is replete with representational forms and processes which are 'locked-into' relational webs of meanings which themselves interpenetrate, sometimes fuse, separate, repel, and re-form themselves in response to the effervescent energies of everyday experience. Margins and resistance, then, are both 'something' and 'nothing', 'there' but 'nowhere' as one shifts between lived views, imaginative presentations, and localised structures of validity and meaning. The task, then, is to figure the role of specific and localised representational forces and to ask: *why are they there?*; *what do they do?*; and *what is or is not produced?*

EMPOWERING THE MARGINS OF RESISTANCE

There can be few concepts which have a more profound resonance in the social sciences than power and resistance: both have become seemingly ubiquitous in the discourses of social scientists. Whatever the sphere of inquiry it seems as though power is at work, or at least the concept can be invoked to add conceptual and illuminating force to analysis and explication. Undoubtedly, the work of Foucault (in particular, 1967, 1972, 1977, 1980) has had a profound influence in creating a privileged analytical index through which analysts and commentators have attempted to make sense of a seemingly chaotic world. Foucault's power is panoramic. This is meant both in the sense of the concept's prolific reach and in terms of Foucault's influence on the nature of late-twentieth-century social science. It is now difficult to conceive of social relations as anything other than deep-textures which are also power-ridden connections.

As with power, the discursive positioning of resistance has grown as if it were a mirrored form of power's operation. This is not surprising as one of the most striking aspects of the Foucaultian schema is the subtle and sinuous linking of the two 'domains' as if each were the Janus-face hiding in the shadow of its other. The consequence has often been the re-enchanting of the pessimistically (or realistically?) understood social (in which all is power or, at least, all people have power) through turning towards power's twin and energising the discursive presentation of resistance. This has had the effect of making resistance ubiquitous in a similar way to power and, at its most extreme, this culminates in the possibility of any communicative activity being rendered open to representation as resistance.

This coupling of power–resistance has, particularly in more recent years, been supplemented with an accentuation of the 'force' of marginality. These 'margins', ever the stuff of sociological inquiry, are deconstructed, stripped of systemically produced obfuscation, and re-presented as the true vanguard of 'radical' social change. Instead of presenting such margins as the foci of systemic rehabilitation, the new discursive momentum of marginality presides upon a 'positionality' full with transformatory potential. It is as if the class struggle, the once–heralded 'site' of social transformation which has (now) been left to decay in its own historical-material contradictions, has been re-thought, re-configured, and reflexively re-born in 'postmodern' form – disparate, fractured, but omnipresent. There are dangers, however, in uncritically constructing 'the margins' as forceful sites of resistance. David Harvey, for example, reflects that:

> One of the least admirable traits of political argument in recent times has been the romantic turn in radical politics towards 'voices from the margins' as somehow more authentic, less corrupt, and therefore more revolutionary. The idea is that there are those who are so radically 'other', so radically outside of the dominant systems of determination, so marginal in relation to the iron cage of circular and cumulative causation, that they and only they have the capacity

> to see though the fetishisms that fool the rest of us. They and only they have the capacity to generate radical change.
>
> (Harvey, 1996: 100)

For Harvey, the valorisation of the 'voices from the margins' signals a neo-romanticism which weaves together the various 'margins' and presents such marginality as a powerful force with the potential to actualise social transformation. Marginalisation, then, becomes a demystifying dynamic and provides an antidote to the perceived sterility of contemporary social 'order'. As the unrelenting dynamic of capitalism pervades, it is, and can only be (so the implied logic would have it), those who are truly displaced by its maelstrom who are able to recognise the reality of its pathological systemic tendencies.

It is not essential that one shares Harvey's political and theoretical project in order to recognise that, beneath the openly political antagonism of his discourse, there is much to light the fire of doubt *vis-à-vis* the margins as radical sites of resistance. There is, also, a blatant contradiction in his own position, one which stems from his desire to reject essentialist notions of revolutionary dynamics ('the margins') whilst stubbornly holding onto equally essentialist notions ('the class struggle'). If there is anything to be gleaned from the turbulent flows of history it is that there are few certainties. The abstractions of 'the margins' and 'the class struggle' are equally flawed because each relies upon unconcretised abstractions: what and where are the margins (and, for the matter, who is there?) and who, what (where and when also) will represent the 'class struggle'?

Unconcretised theorisations and articulations of 'the margins' work because they could not fail to. 'Power', 'resistance', and 'marginalisation' can be formulated to meet any desire and eventuality when the concept is rendered a floating signifier. Stripped of their contextual humanity 'the margins' are as ubiquitously structural (perhaps more so) than the crudest forms of structuralism so caustically dismissed by 'enlightened' humanism. The danger, then, with both 'the margins' and 'resistance', is to exceed in valorisation and to cast analysis and explication as homilies. Caution is necessary if the excesses of valorisation are not to reduce the 'object' of study to the rank of discursive constituent. If history is regarded as illustrative, then the margins are as likely to produce and contain 'race baiting neo-tribes' (Lash and Urry, 1994: 317–18) as they are agents of progressive social transformation and meaningful resistance; hopes for radical openness stand a significant chance of being met with antithetical closure.

A more adequate understanding of 'the margins' and 'resistance' requires a more cautious approach which resists the temptation to regard marginalisation as imbued with a latent transformatory or revolutionary capacity. If progressive transformations are sought, along with the relational vectors through which to activate and actualise such transformations, then it will be (and is) necessary to render certain fundamental questions visible, not least the question: *what is being resisted?* In so doing the problematic of *scale* is introduced. Does resistance entail a reaction to capitalism and if so where, when, and how? Or is the particular context of resistance one which seeks to negate the threat of local racism? Or, lastly, could resistance, in a specific context, simply be (re-)interpreted as a fight to be left alone, free(r) to pursue such mundane tasks as purchasing cigarettes from an institutional tuck-shop without having to resort to using monopoly tokens rather than (real) money? A further requirement is the formulation of 'processes of concretisation' – the contextualised researching of the everyday life which gives rise to and supports margins – which aim to provide a more situated understanding of relational forces and associational dynamics. This is not to deny the value of abstraction, rather it is to caution against the closure of abstraction which gathers distance from recognisable lived-relational referents.

THE ORDER OF THE SOCIAL WORLD AND THE LIVING OF 'OLD AGE'

Living in these 'postmodern times' one could be forgiven for renouncing all claims to 'order' or 'unity' as hopelessly misguided homilies to a (now) distant fabrication; the reason of order has been dispatched to a retirement home – a 'safe' place in which the moments of the present can wander by without hint of contamination. But yet, as Law remarks, 'something' continues to stir:

> Many of us have learned to want to cleave to an order. This is a modernist dream. In one way or another, we are attached to the idea that if our lives, our organisations, our social theories or our societies, were 'properly ordered' then all would be well. And we take it that such ordering is possible, at least some of the time. So when we encounter complexity we tend to treat it as distraction. Or we think of it as evidence of failure.
>
> (Law, 1994: 4–5)

The desire for order, according to Law, runs against the reality of a 'messy' world in which complexity, perhaps even incomprehension, predominates. Order, then, is but a temporary respite from the 'real' world. Sobering thoughts indeed. Until, that is, one grasps the fact that although the 'out there' of order is problematic (at least to the extent of attaining certainty), localised 'projects' and processes of *ordering* abound. Ethnographic studies (Whyte, 1943; Rosaldo, 1989; Anderson, 1990; Duneier, 1992; Miller, 1994; Back, 1996; Baumann, 1996) are replete with examples of the ordering of 'worlds' according to both particular contingencies and heavily social(ised) 'gospels' of relational association and patterning. Ordering, in this sense, is not only a way of circumventing the deep complexity of everyday life, it is also a fundamental basis for human interaction. Without the constant (and relational) manipulation that takes place by human beings in social and material worlds, meaningful (thus communicative) existence would be impossible. Further, going through the process(es) of ordering can offer the opportunity to re-invent the (temporary) security of the 'modernist dream'.

Many of the pensioners of Ivington with whom I talked, and whom I watched, felt themselves to be isolated fragments in a world that had long since ceased to care about them. The popular image was of a 'crazy' world in which any semblance of order had long been removed via a combination of factors including local government incompetence, the blind greed of 'others', the re-organisation of borough boundaries, and the increasing failure of people to 'do the right thing'. The idea of *doing* the right thing is perhaps most suggestive of what was felt to be missing from contemporary social life. *Doing* suggests process, more specifically process directed towards something: doing has an object and, more often than not, a purpose. Further, doing is also suggestive of knowledge – the appreciation of the practical 'rules' upon which the process of doing depends. Thus, the many references to 'doing the right thing', phrased in a number of ways, indicated a desire to return to a state of social being predicated upon the mutuality of a coherent, and morally just, system of meaning and signification. The call was for a re-ordering of the relational parameters that would facilitate the re-appropriation of order and, thus, meaning also.[5]

Order and the Localisation of Worlds

One day, when talking to a group of pensioners in Wellington Park, a local day centre, an 'event' took place that initialised my thinking on the concept of order and the process of ordering in the lived-relations of these particular elderly people. Five of us were sitting at a table; with the exception of our group the large room was empty, which seemed to allow for the discussion to become quite animated. 'We' were talking about morality in its broadest sense – the way to live the 'good life' and to bring 'social prosperity' back to Britain. A variety of arguments were put forward, but a uniting theme was the view that there had been a moral decline in Britain and that such a decline had much to do with the shared forgetting of the past and, more particularly, the shared forgetting of *ways of doing*. During the 'heat' of the debate Vinny, a man known in the centre for his abrasive manner, entered the room. Vinny listened for a few minutes and then joined the discussion. He talked about 'the thirties' and his involvement in the anti-fascist 'movement' (the term may suggest more structure than there actually was). With a seemingly constant grimace Vinny went on to remark that he no longer believed that he could again feel so intensely about an issue, and he was quick to offer an explanation as to why. 'You see', he argued, 'when once you was someone … now you are like the man from nowhere'. The group nodded and fell silent. Vinny was referring to the changing population of Ivington, both in the sense of the adoption of new sensibilities and in the sense of a demographic shift in which 'new' people moved into the borough (for Vinny, these were primarily ethnic minorities).

Vinny's framing of himself as 'the man from nowhere' said much about *where* he perceived himself to be in contemporary society: he felt isolated and disillusioned by the distance he perceived between himself and the (dominant) world around him. During the 1930s, at which time he would have been in his late teenage years, he felt himself to be very much part of what he considered to be the important social sensibilities of the time. Vinny felt himself to be inseparable from the 'structures of feeling' (Williams, 1977) which pervaded around him and which both supported and determined quotidian processes of doing. In the contemporary, such structures of feeling had been dissolved. As time went on, it was evident that Vinny's brief but poignant narrative was shared and expressed, in a variety of ways, by many of the people with whom I talked. The sense of being *nowhere* infused many discussions.

Thinking back on such discussions, the image that comes most readily to mind is of self-consciously nomadic individuals reflecting upon a moving image (the contemporary social world) in which they repeatedly failed to see themselves. There existed both a restlessness to find a place to 'rest' and a cold 'realism' that such 'places' could no longer exist – the moment, their moment, for the realisation of such ideals had passed. Although such a representation may appear romantic it does, I think, convey both the depth of feeling and the extent of alienation felt by many of the people with whom I talked. However, such a description, although based on what was said to me, also paints a disturbingly one-sided and depressing portrait of the lived-relations of 'old age'. Part of the problem stems from the resonance which alienation has as a one-sided and relatively passive 'experience', one which is both pathological and debilitating. However, as sociological studies have often revealed, human beings are immensely resilient entities and even the most seemingly debilitating experiences can hide, and even produce, creative relational dimensions. In the context of the Ivington people, the narrated experiences of alienation were a dominant feature of everyday conversational life that, no matter how pertinent, powerful, and 'real', often masked the (creative) *processes of doing* in which the pensioners were engaged.

Although often fused with stories of alienation, such narratives were also central in the processes of the production of more creative everyday social relations. This research suggested that narrative was frequently used as a vehicle for the development of a contrapuntal force by which to more clearly define 'one's own' position and to highlight differences between 'the world out there' and 'the world in which *we* live'. Viewed in this way, the 'representational logic' of these narratives functioned to (re-)contextualise the process of doing and, more precisely, the *process of doing the right thing*. In so doing, such 'talk' prepared and offered a 'grid of intelligibility' which served as both an existential guide and a reassuringly constant relational marker.[6] 'Talking (about) the outside' placed morality (as a code of life) within an often simply defined normative–pathological binary. There were four main consequences of this contextual bifurcation. First, the perceived de-rooted and de-routed nature of the contemporary world could be grasped, conceptually contained, and re-presented in a comprehensible form. Second, a process of auto-differentiation could be instigated and energised which facilitated both the thinking and articulation of distinction; the pensioners were able to talk and think themselves as different to the alienating force(s) of the contemporary social world. Third, the seemingly unequivocal normative–pathological binary allowed for the constitution and re-presentation of a scripted morality that was both de-scriptive and pre-scriptive. 'Talk', through the emphasis placed on distinction, was used to consolidate the thinking of the question 'who are we as moral beings' and, once this question had been favourably resolved, the advocation of this 'doing the right thing' as central to the 'rehabilitation' of the contemporary social world. Fourth, such narratives signalled a 'shared internalisation of the world' (Rowles, 1983: 307; see also Rowles, 1978) which served to bind and order the collective experience and the collective attitude.

Returning for a moment to Vinny's proclamation that he had become 'the man from nowhere', the analysis just offered indicates that, contrary to the prevailing disposition of many of the Ivington people, which held that there was indeed 'nowhere to go', the articulated 'recognition' of this disposition worked to create such a desired space. Whilst recognising the immensity of the structural constraints, limitations, and debilitating actualities that appear to be ever-more synonymous with 'old age' (at least for some), many of the Ivington pensioners, more or less successfully, negotiated these obstacles and created cognitive and physical spaces in which they could 'belong'. I refer to this process as *localisation*. The concept of localisation is used to represent the structuring of meaningful 'systems' of validity which are integral to the process of ordering everyday life.[7] By using the concept in this way, no necessary or inevitable link is made with the process of ordering and the fundamental order of the world. Rather, the process of localisation (and thus ordering) is the lived form of the 'modernist dream' to which Law (1994: 4) refers. Indeed, at least in the context of this analysis, it was the perception that the world was fundamentally dis-ordered that made localisation an even greater imperative and social force. Localisation, then, enables the location of meaning and the placing of self (and, as such, converts the *nowhere* into *somewhere*). It also refers to the regulation of doing; more precisely it is the configuration of the conduits through which one is able to engage in the process of doing the right thing. As such, localisation, at least as presented here, is both a practical communicative–relational framework, as well as a moral/ethical 'attitude' towards 'the world'.

Maffesoli (1996a, but see also Maffesoli 1996b) suggests that such binding localised processes are indicative of a growing 'logic' in 'mass society'; the return of the collective (but not collectivism) and the decomposition of individualism signal, for Maffesoli, the increasing emergence of thoroughly social and collective relational secretions and forms:

> one could speak of the rebirth of a *Homo religiosus* who would be just a variant of the *Homo aestheticus*, that is, of the renaissance of a social individual and a society resting not on distinction from the

> other, nor any longer on a rational contract linking to the other, but rather on an empathy that makes me, with the other, a participant in a larger ensemble, contaminated all the way through by collective ideas, shared emotions, and images of all kinds. It is also what I propose calling the 'imaginal' world.
>
> (Maffesoli, 1996a: 91)

Whether such a description is an adequate appraisal of contemporary mass society is debatable, and the sentiments expressed neglect the myriad of antagonisms which evidently prevail in current ('mass') society. But the desire for delimited connection and association were important aspects of the lives of the Ivington pensioners. Further, the enactment of the process of localisation set in motion a 'spatial(ised) imaginative coding' through which the 'world' was placed and a 'where' found that was fit for habitation.

THE ORDER(ING) AND PRODUCTION OF SPACE

The 'spatial(ised) imaginative coding', referred to above, hints at the nature of the explication that is to follow. The phrase suggests *doing*; it is used to emphasise that the living of everyday life on the part of the Ivington people was not a passive experience but an active one, one in which 'new' relational forces and signifiers, coupled with regulated associational dynamics, were 'brought into play' as part of the *process* of living in the world. However, I also want to suggest something else, a point that contradicts the characterisation of retirement as the end of productive life: *the lived-worlds of the pensioners were continually produced and re-produced*. This may seem a fairly obvious comment to make but it does, importantly, serve to problematise the sterile image that so often signifies 'old age' in popular imaginations. Moreover, resisting such an image, which denies the activities and productivities involved in the *making* of social relations and, furthermore, which assumes a causative and resultant constancy, can lead to the genesis of core questions as to *how* and *why* social relations are produced the way they are (and, for that matter, why and how they change).

Prisoners of Space?

In his important analysis of the geographical experiences of 'old age', Graham Rowles summarises what he perceives as the prevailing attitude towards experiences of ageing which, more often than not, are seen as equating to growing spatial imprisonment:

> The elderly gradually become prisoners of space. ... For many older persons physiological decline, economic deprivation, and traumatising effects of rapid societal change, herald physical, social and psychological withdrawal. This withdrawal, it is implied, is accompanied by progressive constriction of the individual's geographical lifespace, and associated intensification of attachment to the proximate environmental context.
>
> (Rowles, 1978: 22)

Whilst the reasons persist for the holding of such a diagnosis of the 'condition' of 'old age', not least of which is the persistent representational–cognitive and material impoverishment of that 'condition' (see Hazan, 1980, 1992, 1994), such a sensibility reflects an inadequate understanding of both the spatiality of everyday life (of which 'old age' is but another dimension) and the vitality of the human condition (which encompasses 'old age'). Further, there often seems to be a reluctance to explore the possibility that 'old age' may not signal an end to the creative energies of human life. The living of 'old age' did not mean that the Ivington people became, necessarily or totally, captives of space but, rather, that they became *captivated* by 'new' spaces, 'new' socio-spatial productivities and, finally, that space became an even more important element in the thinking and placing of the world. Paradoxically, physical, material, physiological, and social constraints were key factors in the energising and development of 'alternative' cognitive 'maps' and social spaces which facilitated the re-routing (and re-rooting) of existential vitality. This is not to suggest that the existence of such constraints was 'good', neither does it seek to valorise the 'benign' consequences of systemic pressures. Rather, the statement is made in recognition of the relational productivities resulting from having to cope with adversity.

From 'External' to 'Internal' Space

For the Ivington pensioners, then, the experience and perception of systemically produced marginalisation and, for some, physiological debilitation, resulted in the making and detailing of particular social and spatial configurations which facilitated a continued presence in, and living of, the 'world'. On a general level, this was undertaken through the ordering of the complexity and change of the 'world out there'; the external world was 'thought through' in the context of the institutional spaces and those spaces were then used as a basis for the social and spatial ordering of the 'internal' world. Important, however, was the maintenance of a seemingly constant tension between these two 'worlds'; the 'internal', lived and structured as authentic and legitimate, required the 'presence' of the 'external' as both a *raison d'être* and a signifier of the calamity produced once the order(ing) of 'lifespaces' was broken. This was most evident at the St Jude's Centre, and it is this centre that will be the focus for the rest of the analysis presented.

The production of internal social space was predicated upon a relational duality in which a necessary 'bleeding' of the internal and external took place. Lefebvre aptly summarises such processes:

> *Social spaces interpenetrate one another and/or superimpose themselves upon one another.* They are not things, which have mutually limiting boundaries and which collide because of their contours or as a result of inertia. Figurative terms such as 'sheet' and 'stratum' have serious drawbacks: being metaphorical rather than conceptual, they assimilate space to things and thus relegate its concept to the realm of abstraction. Visible boundaries, such as walls or enclosures in general, give rise for their part to an appearance of separation between spaces where in fact what exists is an ambiguous continuity. The space of a room, bedroom, house or garden may be cut off in a sense from social space by barriers and walls, by all the signs of private property, yet still remain fundamentally part of that space.
> (Lefebvre, 1991: 86–7)

The social spaces of the St Jude's pensioners were dependent upon the (constantly invoked) *contamination* 'provided' by the conceptual index of the external world. Constructed boundaries failed to prevent such a process of contamination entering the internal spaces of the institutions or the internal lives of the pensioners. However, the dominant search was for existential and relational purity at least, that is, in times when the spectre of (external) crisis was brought to the fore (Sibley, 1995: 36–8).

Narratives of purity, often linked to an ethos of authenticity and legitimacy, were a key aspect of the everyday 'talk' of the pensioners, and were integral to the ordering of relations within the centre. Such narratives were supported by a definitive web of analysis and meaning which both cited and sited the source and constituents of disorder. In the most extreme cases this could lead to self-exploration and anxiety.

Take, for example, the narrative of Flo, who was a key member of a group of pensioners who prided themselves on their 'working-class' heritage and extensive roots in Ivington. One day when talking with Flo she remarked that:

> I can never really be from Farnsbury [a once independent part of the borough] because I've only lived here since after the [Second World] war. Sometimes ... you know ... when they're [the other members of Flo's group] talking ... I just don't say anything ... just stay quiet. I still don't think that I really belong here ... not like they do. I moved here from outside. I don't think until you've lived here all your life that you really belong [here].

These sentiments clashed with the aura hitherto produced and projected by Flo. She had always presented herself, and seemed to be accepted by the others in her group, as a core focus for the 'local spirit' which pervaded much of the discussion that took place in the centre. Indeed, Flo was often the first to voice her dissent over the (perceived) 'corruption' of the local way of doing things. For example, she once greeted my arrival with the following sentiments:

> Look at this. It's a bloody disgrace. All this here [pointing to a local authority publication that was on the table in front of her]. All this and where are we [reference to pensioners generally – but probably those pensioners who 'belonged' in particular]? Just count them a minute. Look. I'll count them with you. There are hundreds. There must be more than a hundred. Look. Lesbians. Gays. Mothers group. All this money. How much does it cost? A bloody fortune. And all the time they say there's no money. There's no money because we don't matter. What's it all for? They can't do anything [for us] but they're doing this. All this. What a waste of money. When things are needed doing, proper things, you get this, lesbians and gays. The moment this lot took over ... took over from Farnsbury is when it started.

The two episodes suggest an ambivalence that was founded upon an entrenched anxiety, one that centred upon a self-reflective questioning of one's own authenticity and the desire to 'fit' within the dominant relational framing existing within the centre. Further, Flo's ambivalence was common to many others in the centre and was often revealed in those quieter moments when others were not around to overhear conversations.

The resistance to the pressures of the external world – filled as it was perceived to be with complexity, disorder, and even chaos – had as its 'dark-side' the possibility or threat of 'externalisation'. Externalisation could be realised in one of three ways, each of which could involve the metaphorical or literal 'casting-out' of individuals. First, the failure, through circumstance rather than choice, of an individual to appropriately place oneself within the localised ways of doing could result in collective censorship of that person. The extent of this process varied, but could range from mild, even playful rebukes, to extended, or even permanent, periods of ostracisation. Second, as already seen with Flo, was the doubt about one's ontological authenticity and, thus, legitimacy within the centre. Again, there was evidence to suggest that such experiences covered a spectrum of intensity, although the research would suggest that such sensations were confined to 'quiet moments' (usually with only the respondent and myself present) in which feelings could be expressed. I have no evidence that would suggest that these feelings were more than fleeting anxieties. Third, there was the knowing rejection of the internalised world and the accentuation of the 'positive' characteristics of the external world. There were several examples of this overt rejection of the relational principles through which the dominant representation of both internal and external worlds was reproduced. The most forthright of the dissenters was Martina, and a brief outline of her 'story' will help to clarify some of the processes and issues involved in the creation and maintenance of internal socio-spatial relations.

The (Production of) Repulsion within: the Mask of Isotopia[8]

Martina's use of the centre was heavily routinised. She would enter the tea room (which was situated on the first floor of the centre) at between 10.20 and 10.30 and would walk to the furthest end of the room, hang her coat over a chair, place a crossword magazine and cigarettes on the table, and then move the ashtray from the centre of the table to the end at which she intended to sit. These activities did not vary and, once they had been completed, Martina would buy a cup of tea (a tea table was located at the centre of the room), return to her seat, light a cigarette and open the crossword book. At intervals she would look up, glancing around the room and occasionally fixing a gaze upon one of the tables where a group would be involved in discussion.

Martina didn't mix with the other centre users; she sat on her own at the table most removed from the activity of the tea room. It was approximately six weeks before I felt able to talk with her because I sensed that she wanted to be alone, and it took this long for me to assess how and when to approach her. Finally, I sat down at her table one morning, after she had bought a cup of tea, and introduced myself. She lit a cigarette as I was piecing together my own (introductory) story and then watched me talking this story through. When I had finished, Martina offered me a cigarette which I took, lit, and began to smoke. Neither she nor I spoke. Her reasons for silence remain with her; mine centred on a frantic searching of a way to 'break the ice' and begin a conversation. After a few minutes I asked a ridiculous question: *do you live in Ivington?* The question was ridiculous because membership of the centre was not only restricted to residents of Ivington but to those living within a mile radius of the institution. She laughed and said 'yes'. We started slowly – talking generally about Ivington and the centre – but as the weeks went on the conversations became more focused and more revealing.

In many ways Martina was a maverick amongst the people at the centre in that she would often express unique views. Her biography offers some clues but not total grounds for explanation. Martina had lived in Ivington 'on and off' for 43 years (she was 65 at the time of the research and junior to most of the users by at least five years).[9] Her early years had been relatively nomadic as her father had repeatedly uprooted the family as he sought work throughout Lancashire. Both parents had died during the Second World War, and Martina still found it extremely difficult to reflect on that experience. She had worked in catering (primarily as a waitress) for most of her adult life because 'it was the one sure way that you knew you would get at least one meal a day'. Her marriage had ended 15 years earlier and she regarded the split as a release. When asked if the separation had been difficult she replied: 'well, you've just got to get on with things, otherwise all you're doing is living in the past, and that doesn't do anyone any good'. This statement, perhaps more than any other, symbolised Martina, at least as I saw her: she saw the past as something to be overcome – a constraining and debilitating series of 'episodes'. Martina felt herself to be an 'outsider' in the centre. She felt pressurised to conform to particular ways of thinking and doing which she sited as having much to do with 'all that rubbish about the good old days'. This common narrative, as Martina perceived it, did not allow people to 'think for themselves'. For Martina, the tea room as a social space, and the centre more generally, was coded through an oppressive narrative of the past that she felt masked her own experiences. My sense was that Martina experienced the dominant narratives as a resuscitation of a past from which she had long since wanted to remove herself. The past, then, was a returning 'pollution'.

Whilst it would be wrong to generalise from Martina's experiences and situation, the 'story' offered does serve to illustrate that dominant ways of seeing and doing in the centre were, necessarily, interspersed with 'conscientious objections'. As this internal world required a projection of the external, so too did it require internal distinctions and 'disruptions'. As Lefebvre observed:

> A homogeneous and utterly simultaneous space would be strictly imperceptible. It would lack the conflictual component (always resolved, but always at least suggested) of the contrast between symmetry and asymmetry.
>
> (Lefebvre, 1991: 200)

As the internal world required projections of the external, so too did it require the 'dwelling' of internal 'contamination'. It is not within the scope of this chapter to explicate fully the variety of circumstances in which similar contamination existed, nor the processes through which such contamination was located, represented, and lived. However, it is important to recognise that the production of space is also the production of repulsion; the represented existence of isotopia masks the fact that space is both isotopic and heterotopic – that is, 'unity' and 'difference' require each other. Further, such a dimensionality of spatial form and process can lead to a more adequate 'thinking through' of both the margins and resistance.

BY WAY OF A CONCLUSION: THE ARCHITECTONICS OF THE MARGINS AND RESISTANCE

In a wonderfully provocative essay entitled 'Choosing the margin as a space of radical openness', bell hooks makes the following proclamation:

> Understanding marginality as position and place of resistance is crucial for oppressed, exploited, colonised people. If we only view the margin as a sign marking the despair, a deep nihilism penetrates in a destructive way the very ground of our being. It is there in that space of collective despair that one's creativity, one's imagination is

> at risk, there that one's mind is fully colonised, there that the freedom one longs for as lost.
>
> (hooks, 1991: 150–1)

hooks uses the 'language of space' in order to articulate a call for a more progressive engagement with the problematics of everyday life. As I read it, her use of a spatial(ised) vocabulary is intended to invoke metaphorical, rather than literal, 'sites' for critical engagements that have as their aim the seeking of cognitive and relational 'positions' through the pervasive taxonomic binaries – of male–female, black–white, rich–poor, etc. – can be 'thought through' and overcome. Thus, the 'margins' become a meta-theoretical and moral project and not literal 'dwelling places'. If this interpretation is correct, then the 'margins' are 'good to think' because 'they' energise a more critical engagement with the 'world'. However, attractive as such an outlook may at first appear, there are problems in regarding the 'margins' as necessarily 'progressive'. As I have tried to show, the 'margins' can indeed be 'good to think' and such thinking (and living) of marginality can produce associational dynamics that create and define new 'lifespaces' which, in turn, re-constitute adversity into a livable realm of quotidian engagement. But, importantly, the *making do* on the margins can also be centripetal in that new centres are produced and performed and new margins created. Further, 'radical closure' can be as likely as 'radical openness'.

The account that has unfolded in this chapter has depicted the Ivington people as engaged in 'resistance' to the perceived force of the external world, a force which was seen to, in a relentless and even systematic manner, annihilate the foundations for traditional *ways of doing (the right thing)*. As part of the process of 'resisting' the perceived 'onslaught' of the external world, the pensioners produced, articulated, and shared a narrative and vision of the 'good life'. In the process of so doing, the margins, their margins, were *made to work*. However, it was made to work through the 'stitching together' of reified forms; in essence, the overriding 'logic' of the existing associational dynamics was the objectification of both external and internal worlds. Here lies the problematic crux of the proposition that the 'margins' and 'resistance' are inherently 'radical'. For what my (theorised) empirical findings would suggest is that the 'margins', whether cognitive or material, are neither a necessary nor inevitable component of fundamental social change. Indeed, this research would suggest that the 'pressure' experienced *vis-à-vis* the perceived processes of marginalisation, resulted in a pervasive reification in which the process of the world was turned 'on its head' so that it became a relationship between fixed objects in space (physical space, cognitive space, relational space). And often, the construction, presentation, and relating (to each other) of these 'objects' would not be seen as 'progressive' by many of those speaking that language. Further, I have serious doubts as to whether it is possible to escape reification and the objectification of human beings and social relations (see Rapport, 1995) and this doubt is premised upon the proposition that reification is central to both the process of cognition and the act of communication.

Adopting such a viewpoint (or arriving at such a conclusion) suggests that the valorisation of 'resistance' and the 'margins', as forces for fundamentally changing the nature of society, says more about an idealism (perhaps a popular one) in academic circles than it does about the 'resistance' or the 'margins'. Perhaps it is an ideal that, deep down, 'we' all share, but this should not prevent 'us' from attempting to see 'resistance' and the 'margins' for what they are in the context of everyday life. Finally, one also has to wonder whether placing the burden of revolutionary change on certain (groups of) people due to the fact that 'they do what they do' and that 'they are what they are' indicates a conceit. The 'margins' and 'resistance', as revolutionary sites, are 'good to think' when one can think them from a distance.

ACKNOWLEDGEMENTS

Thanks are due to a number of people, not least all the Ivington pensioners who allowed me into their lives, in particular to 'Iris', a woman who does not appear in name in this chapter but who is constantly in my thoughts when I think about 'old age'. I hope they all continue to find the time and place to smile. Gratitude also to Jo Foord, Leonie Kellaher, Roger Hallam, Phil Crang, Ian Cook, Elisabeth Wilson, David Sibley, Anne Hartree, Jan Pollock, and Maggie Millman. I also owe thanks to the editors of this volume who offered sympathetic advice on an earlier draft of this chapter. Finally, I would like to dedicate this chapter to the spirit of Vernon Waters who died in September 1996 aged 82. His 'resistance' was a life-long process of making-do in adversity and believing in the fundamental necessity of fair-play, even in times when fairness appeared fairly low on the social agenda. There was much that I learned from Vernon and much more that I was too lazy and ignorant to seek.

NOTES

1. It would be futile to attempt to locate the precise genesis of this sensitivity in a particular text or era. The following are just a few of the influential texts the interested reader may wish to consult: Merleau-Ponty (1962); Bachelard (1969); Relph (1976); Tuan (1977); Buttimer and Seamon (1980); Kern (1983); Lefebvre (1991).
2. All names of places, institutions, individuals, and groups have been changed in order to maintain confidentiality.
3. Structured conversation was the name given to discussions that were loosely structured in order to allow for a more respondent-centred approach. The aim was to allow individuals to develop their own agenda of key concerns. My 'role' was to probe issues raised, to reflect upon, and at times to question, the views and sentiments expressed.
4. For more extended appraisals of Lefebvre's work on space see: Merrifield (1993, 1995); Gregory (1994); Pile (1996).
5. Anthropologists have had a perennial interest in the constitution of local moralities and, in particular, how moralities are used to impose an order on the world. For a contemporary example of this tradition see Howell (1997).
6. I have found the work of Somers (1992) and Somers and Gibson (1994) particularly useful in thinking about the role of narrative in the constitution and framing of social relations.
7. The development of the concept of *localisation* was influenced by the work of Wittgenstein (1953) and, though to a much lesser extent, Lyotard (1984). The paradox of using Lyotard is that his work is often presented as heralding the arrival of the 'postmodern', primarily the devaluation of objectivity. However, my take on Lyotard does not entertain the hopeless fragmentation of some postmodern discourses but, instead, emphasises that meanings are produced within validity systems that can vary in size and influence. Further, I focus upon both the social creation and manifestation of meaning whilst deflecting the now rather tiresome debates as to whether absolute truths exist; on this issue I remain an agnostic whilst recognising that associational dynamics produce a myriad of 'little truths', truths sometimes powerful enough to evoke both contestation and defence when these are challenged.
8. The concept of isotopia is drawn from Lefebvre (1991) and is used to refer to common or analogous social spaces.
9. It is important to bear in mind that 'old age' can mask significant differences in age and that such differentiation can have consequences in terms of 'world views' held and the 'systems' of social organisation adhered to. It

is now common practice to distinguish between the 'young old' (up to 74 years of age) and the 'old old' (those 75 or older). With increasing numbers of people living to their 90s and beyond (in western societies at least) there is likely to be need for further differentiation ('super old'?).

REFERENCE

Anderson, E. (1990) *Streetwise: Race, Class, and Change in an Urban Community* (Chicago, IL: University of Chicago Press).

Bachelard, G. (1969) *The Poetics of Space* (Boston, MA: Beacon Press).

Back, L. (1996) *New Ethnicities and Urban Culture: Racisms and Multiculture in Young Lives* (London: UCL Press).

Baumann, G. (1996) *Contesting Culture: Discourses of Identity in Multi-Ethnic London* (Cambridge: Cambridge University Press).

Buttimer, A. and Seamon, D. (eds) (1980) *The Human Experience of Space and Place* (London: Croom Helm).

Duneier, M. (1992) *Slim's Table: Race, Respectability, and Masculinity* (Chicago, IL: Chicago University Press).

Foucault, M. (1967) *Madness and Civilization: A History of Insanity in the Age of Reason*, trans. Richard Howard (first published in French in 1961) (London: Tavistock Publications).

Foucault, M. (1972) *The Archaeology of Knowledge*, trans. A. M. Sheridan Smith (first published in French in 1969) (London: Tavistock Publications).

Foucault, M. (1977) *Discipline and Punish: The Birth of the Prison*, trans. Alan Sheridan (first published in French in 1975) (London: Allen Lane).

Foucault, M. (1980) *Power/Knowledge*, trans. Colin Gordon, Leo Marshall, John Mepham and Kate Soper, edited by Colin Gordon (London: Harvester Wheatsheaf).

Gregory, D. (1994) *Geographical Imaginations* (Oxford: Blackwell).

Harvey, D. (1996) *Justice, Nature and the Geography of Difference* (Oxford: Blackwell).

Hazan, H. (1980) *The Limbo People: A Study of the Constitution of the Time Universe Among the Aged* (London: Routledge & Kegan Paul).

Hazan, H. (1992) *Managing Change in Old Age* (New York: State University New York Press).

Hazan, H. (1994) *Old Age: Constructions and Deconstructions* (Cambridge: Cambridge University Press).

hooks, b. (1991) 'Choosing the Margins as a Space of Radical Openness', in hooks, b., *Yearning: Race, Gender, and Cultural Politics* (London: Turnaround).

Howell, S. (ed.) (1997) *The Ethnography of Moralities* (London: Routledge).

Kern, S. (1983) *The Culture of Time and Space* (London: Weidenfeld & Nicolson).

Lash, S. and Urry, J. (1994) *Economies of Signs and Space* (London: Sage).

Law, J. (1994) *Organizing Modernity* (Cambridge: Polity).

Lefebvre, H. (1991) *The Production of Space*, trans. Donald Nicholson-Smith (first published in French in 1974) (Oxford: Blackwell).
Lyotard, J.-F. (1984) *The Postmodern Condition: A Report on Knowledge* (Manchester: Manchester University Press).
Maffesoli, M. (1996a) *The Time of the Tribes: The Decline of Individualism in Mass Society*, trans. Don Smith (first published in French in 1988) (London: Sage).
Maffesoli, M. (1996b) *The Contemplation of the World: Figures of Community Style*, trans. Susan Emanuel (first published in French in 1993) (Minneapolis, MN: University of Minnesota Press).
Merleau-Ponty, M. (1962) *The Phenomenology of Perception* (London: Routledge & Kegan Paul).
Merrifield, A. (1993) 'Place and Space: A Lefebvrian Reconciliation', *Transactions of the Institute of British Geographers*, 18(4): 516 – 31.
Merrifield, A. (1995) 'Lefebvre, Anti-Logos and Nietzsche: An Alternative Reading of *The Production of Space*', *Antipode*, 27(3): 294–303.
Miller, D. (1994) *Modernity – An Ethnographic Approach: Dualism and Mass Consumption in Trinidad* (Oxford: Berg).
Pile, S. (1996) *The Body and the City: Psychoanalysis, Space and Subjectivity* (London: Routledge).
Rapport, N. (1995) 'Migrant Selves and Stereotypes: Personal Context in a Postmodern World', in S. Pile and N. Thrift (eds), *Mapping the Subject: Geographies of Cultural Transformation* (London: Routledge).
Relph, E. (1976) *Place and Placelessness* (London: Pion).
Rosaldo, R. (1989) *Culture and Truth: The Remaking of Social Analysis* (London: Routledge).
Rowles, G. D. (1978) *Prisoners of Space? Exploring the Geographical Experience of Older People* (Boulder, CO: Westview Press).
Rowles, G. D. (1983) 'Place and Personal Identity in Old Age: Observations from Appalachia', *Journal of Environmental Psychology*, 3: 299–313.
Sibley, D. (1995) *Geographies of Exclusion: Society and Difference in the West* (London: Routledge).
Somers, M. (1992) 'Narrativity, Narrative Identity, and Social Action: Rethinking English Working-class Formation', *Social Science History*, 16(4): 591–650.
Somers, M. and Gibson, D. (1994) 'Reclaiming the Epistemological "Other": Narrative and the Social Constitution of Identity', in Calhoun, C. (ed.), *Social Theory and the Politics of Identity* (Oxford: Blackwell).
Thorpe, M. (1996) '*Space, Time, and Community: An Enquiry into Localized Social Relations*', unpublished PhD, University of North London.
Tuan, Yi-Fu. (1977) *Space and Place: The Perspective of Experience* (London: Edward Arnold).
Whyte, W. F. (1943) *Street Corner Society: The Social Structure of an Italian Slum* (Chicago, IL: The Chicago University Press).
Williams, R. (1977) *Marxism and Literature* (Oxford: Oxford University Press).
Wittgenstein, L. (1953) *Philosophical Investigations* (Oxford: Basil Blackwell).

7 The 'Local' versus the 'Global'? – 'Individualised Milieux' in a Complex 'Risk Society'

The Case of Organic Food Box Schemes in the South West

JÖRG DÜRRSCHMIDT

> *The discourse of nature that by now invades every aspect of our daily lives both emphasises and conceals the dilemmas of complexity.*
>
> (Melucci, 1996: 126)

INTRODUCTION

The institutionalisation of 'ecology' as a 'masterframe' of contemporary society (Eder, 1996a) has publicly established and re-emphasised a persistent feature of human culture: the mediation of conditions of the social through natural symbols. The extension of the symbolic space provided by the ecological discourse towards the sphere of 'life politics' (Giddens, 1993) exemplifies this link. For the 'greening' of 'life politics' takes place against a profound change in the social condition: the emerging complexity of a 'planetary society' (Melucci, 1996: 2). Accordingly, in this chapter I will argue that 'environmental' concern should be seen as a symbolic expression of people's more general apprehension for the new planetary complexities and consequent uncertainties of living in a 'global risk society' (Beck, 1992).

It is this new complexity of a planetary society[1] which would be concealed by a sociological analysis which takes environmental concern at face value for what it seems to be: concern for nature, care for the environment. Instead, Melucci's argument seems to suggest that we would need to look at a whole new pattern of individual and collective identity formation in which environmental concern is embedded, and which in turn it helps to express.

In this chapter I attempt to indicate some 'issues of complexity' behind that environmental discourse which is possibly closest to individual 'life politics', and most deeply embedded in everyday life: namely the discourse on organic food. My argument is based on field work on organic food box schemes in the Bristol area.[2]

By 'organic box scheme' I shall refer to a network of people who join in a delivery scheme of organic produce, mainly fruits and vegetables, but quite frequently also providing further organic products, ranging from meat to cider. I will argue that organic food box schemes are a prime example of the embeddedness of environmental concern within people's wider social practices, conversely serving the symbolic expression of people's anxieties about living in a global risk society.

Placed in the context of the global versus local debate, organic food box schemes could appear as a form of local resistance against a global economic system, reinforcing the local community. But box schemes reveal more than a form of stubborn local resistance against an overpowering global economy embodied by supermarkets. And they cannot be equated with the resurgence of the local community. Instead I shall argue that, although local in terms of scope, these schemes reflect the generation of globalised individual 'milieux'. The simple decision to eat local organically grown products is the local realisation of globalised 'life politics' which link food into wider planetary issues such as pollution, food miles and poverty in the Third World. Whilst operating in a local context, box schemes are associations between the like-minded, based on personal commitment and shared values, instead of simply reenforcing the ties of a local community.

Box schemes can thus be regarded as an example of 'emancipatory practices' (Hegedus, 1989), or simply as an experiment in the 'enormous laboratory' of everyday life (Melucci, 1996) in which the individual has – paradoxically it seems – to engage in order to live a 'life of one's own' (Beck, 1992: 90; 1995b).

ORGANIC OR LOCAL FOOD?

At first glance *organic* food box schemes seem to indicate people's interest in the equation of a healthy diet and more natural diet, framed by a general questioning of the relationship between the human and the natural world. And yet, as James (1993: 206) argues:

> Although ... organic food now occupies a more central position in contemporary thinking about food, the process of re-presenting 'nature' and the 'natural', which frames its marketing, cannot be [immediately] taken as a sign of the integration of environmentalist principles into contemporary British Culture. It reflects, instead, their absorption and incorporation into a continuum of existing discourses surrounding human beings and what they eat.

This consequently implies, according to James (1993: 207), that 'although the consumption of organic food may symbolise a commitment to environmentalism, quite different meanings may be invoked'. James goes on to identify two sets of recurrent 'binary oppositions' in which organic food is given subtly different meanings: nature/culture and past/future, both overlapping in a third overarching, dichotomy between the city and the countryside (1993: 208).

It is rather surprising to find missing from James' account one framing dichotomy which provides the obvious link of organic food with the complexity of contemporary planetary society: the global–local dichotomy. At least some voices in the discourse on organic food place their thoughts in this context. To illustrate this, I shall refer to a forum which figures quite prominently in the active formation of this legitimising discourse. In a booklet issued by the 'Soil Association' on the occasion of its 1993 conference on 'Linking Farmers and Consumers' (Dale and Booth, 1994) it says in the preface:

> Organic farming has always been about more than producing food.

In particular, it is about local resistance to what is perceived as the destructive forces of globalisation. Norberg-Hodge (1994a,b), for example, argues that globalisation, economic globalisation in particular, is responsible for environmental but also social decline. It not only means 'more transport and pollution, packaging and waste', due to the time–space distanciation between producers and consumers, but brings with it the disruption of local communities with its well-known consequences:

> It [globalisation] means the breakdown of locally-based economies and communities, which in turn leads to increased alienation, crime and violence.
>
> (1994: 4)

In turn, a 'Community Supported Agriculture' which brings consumers and producers closer together again also has, in Norberg-Hodge's argument, apart from its environmental benefits, social applications:

> Perhaps the most significant of these is that we thereby rebuild *real* community. Community is based on close connections between people, and an understanding of their dependence on one another. As we can see when we visit a small shop in a village, people know each other and talk to one another. Nearby farmers that sell to the shop – and know the people who will be buying their produce – are far less likely to put toxic chemicals on their crops. Conversely, people who know the person who grows their food are more apt to help him out in difficult times [my emphasis].
>
> (1994b: 14ff.)

Thus we see the main focus of the previously outlined argument shifting subtly from (local) *organic* food to *local* (organic) food. Organic farming thus serves as a symbolic expression of concern about the complexities of a planetary society, which finds its expression here as the experience of a 'globalisation versus local community' dilemma. Organic 'Community Supported Agriculture' is, on the one hand, being portrayed as means of effectively dealing with environmental problems. On the other hand, the argument has a strong element of belief that *local* organic farming can serve as the nucleus of rebuilding an eroded local community.

What comes to the fore here is a distorted view on globalisation, which conceals the actual 'complexity', in Melucci's sense (1996: 58, 126), behind people's interest in organic food (production) and the new forms of social association, that are presumed to result. Instead I prefer to look at people's interest in organic food as one symbolisation of the much broader attempt to come to terms with the new complexities of a global risk society.

INDIVIDUALISATION AND GLOBALISATION OF MILIEUX

Globalisation, if it is not simply reduced to macro-economic forms and processes, means first and foremost the extension of social relations and the interconnection of social contexts across time and space. This in turn implies forms of 'local transformation', as locale and locality become the site of intersecting distanciated social relations (Giddens, 1994: 64, 108f.). Accordingly, Robertson has suggested the conceptualisation of the dialectical phenomenon of local globalisation and global localisation as 'glocalisation', so that 'the local is *not* best seen, at least as an analytical or interpretative departure point, as a counterpoint to the global'. Instead it should be regarded, 'subject to some qualifications, as *an aspect* of globalisation' (1995: 28ff). Glocalisation finds such a further qualification, for example, in people's 'life politics', understood as 'self-actualisation' in the context of globality (Giddens, 1993: 214).

Seen in this context there is a touch of romanticism and nostalgia about Norberg-Hodge's claim that 'Community Supported Agriculture' could reclaim the 'real' community, that is, a community based on localised social relations and face-to-face interaction. By proposing local organic farming as a form of resistance of the local community against globalisation, she re-emphasises the global versus local dichotomy. Instead, by drawing on the 'individualisation' thesis (Beck, 1995b), I conceptualise these phenomena as forms of people's engagement *within* rather than *against* an emerging global society.

For Beck, globalisation and individualisation are complementary processes. Globalisation continues the detraditionalisation process of modernity: people are released from the relative certainties of industrial society into the complex uncertainties of a 'global risk society'. More precisely, the individual is 'set free' from the collective identities of class, family and nation into a 'life of one's own' (Beck, 1992, 1995b).

> Individualisation in this sense means that each person's biography is removed from given determinations and placed into his or her own hands, open and dependent on decisions.
>
> (1992: 135)

Drawing on the phenomenological approach developed by Scheler (1973), Schütz (1966, 1970) and Goffman (1972), I conceptualise the individual's ongoing attempt to construct a 'life of one's own' as generation of a milieu. By 'milieu' I refer here to a person-related, relatively stable and situated configuration of action and experience, in which the individual actively generates and maintains a distinctive degree of familiarity and practical competence (cf. Grathoff 1989: 344, 434).[3.]

Taking up Beck's argument, I suggest that what Robertson calls 'glocalisation', that is, the blending of the local and global, finds its life-world expression in the *'globalisation of individualised milieux'*. Three complementary processes are involved in this. Firstly, individualisation as the release of the individual's milieu from given localised communities in the context of globalisation processes implies a potential loss of 'ontological security'. It affects people's confidence in the continuity of their self-identity which is based on the security provided by the constancy of *'their'* world (Giddens, 1994: 92). Referring back to Norberg-Hodge's argument, it is not surprising that unease about this development is expressed in terms of locale or locality, insofar as 'ontological security' is primarily 'anchored in the local circumstances of place' (Giddens, 1994: 100ff.).

The 'globalisation of individualised milieux', secondly, poses the task of *'self-actualisation'* in the context of a global risk society beyond the certainties but also constraints of stable local environments and given collective identities. The individual is consequently, according to Beck , 'condemned to freedom' (1995a: 192) in a 'society of multiple options' (Gross 1994). In other words, the construction of a meaningful and practicable milieu turns into a personal and risky enterprise, demanding experiment and invention, as well as the openness to trial and error as appropriate practice (Beck, 1995b: 190ff.).

In this context then we might, thirdly, see the development of a new type of 'social milieux'. These, in distinction from 'communities', emerge wherever individualised milieux overlap to such an extent in their interests and routines that these materialise in shared social practices. In this sense an 'individualised milieu' can be part of many 'social milieux', without being completely absorbed by them.

Considered in this perspective local organic food box schemes are much more a form of self-actualisation in a complex global society, than a form of local resistance against globalisation. At the same time it can be considered as a 'social milieu' in the meaning outlined above. I will now further illustrate these processes.

BOX SCHEMES AND 'SELF-ACTUALISATION' TOWARDS FOOD

In this section I develop these arguments with regard to a particular form of self-actualisation evolving around organic/local food initiatives. I focus on how concern about food indicates the individualisation of milieux inside the complexities of the global risk society with which they are interwoven. The generation of individualised milieux has many aspects. The struggle for 'one's own time', 'one's own space', 'one's own body', 'one's own sexuality' (Beck, 1995: 186) are certainly dimensions of it. Without any doubt this line could be extended towards 'one's own diet'. Joining an organic food box scheme is usually initially about a healthy diet, even though the motivations for a healthy diet are as varied as the people who join. The following statement is a good example of the answers to our question as to why people had joined a food box scheme:

> I simply wanted to have organic fruit and veg, and fresh fruit and veg. ... So, I simply don't like eating certain things, I don't like things that have grown commercially, and I particularly don't like all the stuff on it that's used to preserve it.

In some cases this fairly general dislike of chemically treated fruits and vegetables had simply accumulated over the years, enforced by public opinion, while for others there was a specific event that made them make the link between industrial food and health:

> One thing that raised my awareness of this sort of environmental thing is illness. ... My mother died quite recently of cancer, in fact so many people die of cancer now. ... And obviously you start questioning 'well, what is causing cancer'? Obviously, there is a whole range of things. ... but chemicals in food is certainly one of them. So we started eating more organic fruit and vegetables, they taste nice and you eat something which has less dump in it.

What brings people together in a box scheme is initially a 'commonality of anxiety' (Beck, 1992: 49; James, 1993: 213) about food, expressed as 'fear of impurity' (Eder, 1996b: 155, 159). But why is there this fear about food? One plausible answer could be that food links the individual's milieu with wider society. It becomes one of risk society's 'access point' (Goffman, 1972: 351ff.) to people's milieux.

It is useful to recall at this point our definition of 'milieu' as that zone in everyday life in which the individual generates a distinctive degree of familiarity and practical competence.

In Goffman's terms, it provides the individual's 'Umwelt' for maintaining 'normalcy' and 'self' in everyday life. However, 'the ease he [the individual] attains in his Umwelt presumes that he constantly sustains certain "personal" standards of conduct.' Accordingly, 'normalcy' and 'self' are threatened when the individual loses the practical competence to conduct formerly taken-for-granted routines (Goffman, 1972: 305, 326, 364, 382).

In this sense 'food' has certainly until recently been a 'safe' part of people's 'Umwelten', competently integrated into the individual's 'personal' standards of daily conduct. The revelation of chemicals in food and its potential consequences in general, the salmonella-in-egg crisis, listeria in soft cheese, botulism in hazelnut yoghurt, BST in milk, Alar in apples, and BSE in particular (James, 1993: 214), have certainly undermined the position of food as a taken-for-granted element of people's milieux. Food has turned into a source of potential practical incompetence, into a source of disruption of milieux insofar as it can change familiar features of everyday life overnight.

Consequently, food is one significant element of everyday life that links people's milieux with the interdependencies of the global 'risk society', turning them into 'risk positions' (Beck, 1992). Food as an 'access point' of 'risk society' to people's milieux has lost its status as 'something that can be disattended safely', and become a source of 'alarm' instead, indicating a (potential) loss of 'self', 'normalcy' and 'competence' (Goffman, 1972: 299, 351).

What the individual experiences here with regard to food is a '*double shock*': firstly, the sudden realisation of the risk deriving from formerly familiar and appreciated food items; and secondly, the loss of sovereignty over dealing with the disruption of one's own milieu (Beck 1992: 54). The individual is exposed to a dilemma typical of 'risk society'. Due to the 'scientisation of risks' which devalues the practical 'stock of knowledge', she/he is unable to regain competence *within* the milieu without having to rely on *external* expertise. The sudden revelation of chemicals in certain food stuffs confronts people in their milieu with problems that are neither previously detectable nor permanently solvable within the context of the milieu.

Taking up a previous line of argument, such a disruption of the milieu certainly brings with it a loss of 'ontological security'. Two typical reactions may follow in this situation of lost 'normalcy' and 'competence'. One is given in the tendency to accept or even deny the newly revealed risks, what Beck calls the '*death-reflex of normality*':

> The shattered constructs of normality are upheld, or even elevated, as if they remained intact.
>
> (Beck, 1995a: 48ff.)

In the context of the present case study, this would mean continuing to eat what you like, or what previous generations in your milieu thought was good for you, instead of waiting for the next eating taboo, stimulated by the scientific study of food, to disrupt your eating habits once again.

The other possible adaptive reaction could be described as *empowering engagement*. I see box schemes as an example of this. Engagement in an organic food box scheme hands back to the individual some competence over one of the crucial issues of daily life – 'what to eat'? As Erica, a respondent from Bristol, expressed it, joining the box scheme brought back peace of mind about food issues, at least to a certain extent.

> Yes, in some ways it's easier being in the box scheme, because it's five minutes around the corner, and that's that, and you don't have to do any thinking either, because the food is in there, ... you have to do the thinking later, how to prepare seven meals out of it.

Taking up Goffman's argument, food here again becomes a 'normal' part of the individual's 'Umwelt', something that can be 'disattended safely' for the conduct of the project at hand (cooking a meal). The food box scheme not only provides 'food you can trust' (Delingpole, 1997), in many cases it also facilitates the practical incorporation of organic food into people's milieux by familiarising the yet 'unknown' to a certain extent. Hannah, who is the drop-off point for a box scheme in Bristol, pointed out:

> Martina sometimes puts little leaflets in with the boxes. If she is supplying something that is unusual or different she'll put a little note in it to say what it is and how you can cook it.

This practice could be regarded as a form of providing 'alternative dietetic knowledge' (Eder, 1996b: 155), thus partially rebuilding the previously devaluated 'stock of knowledge' concerning the individual's eating habits. On the basis of partly regained 'ontological security', there is then even scope for limited experimentation, actively broadening the 'horizon' of the individual's milieu. Erica explained this as follows:

> You get stuff you'd never have bought in a shop, I've had stuff like 'spaghetti squash', I would probably never have made the effort to

> buy something like that which I didn't know what to do with, but because it was there we cooked it and found it was really nice. So, you expand your own horizon a little bit.

Thus by returning into people's milieux some of the trust in food, and helping people regain competence over handling daily eating routines 'safely', the food box scheme allows for elements of the 'playing-self' (Melucci, 1996), stressing the creative aspects within an enforced process of 'self-actualisation'.

BOX SCHEMES AND 'SELF-ACTUALISATION' TOWARDS RISK SOCIETY

It is important to stress at this point that box schemes help the individual to regain some of the lost 'ontological security' with regard to food, but do not re-establish the *status quo* before 'risk society'. Instead they rather force the individual to face up to the problems of risk society at large. While polluted food is a more or less sudden and immediate threat to the individual's bodily 'self', it highlights another crucial dimension in which the individual's milieu becomes globalised via the anxiety about food. Conceptualising food as an 'access point' of global risk society to the individual's milieu indicates potential sources of alarm that are for the moment beyond the individual's sphere of immediate reach. In other words, contaminated food raises '*global* alarm' in the individual's *local* 'Umwelt' (cf. Goffman 1972: 351ff.). This links with James's argument, that the threatening pollution of the individual's body by contaminated food is at the same time experienced as a 'symbol of the environmental pollution in which human beings contemporarily dwell' (1993: 214) – a symbol to express a general unease with the way things are in the 'world'. Susan, a freelance consultant from Bristol, mentioned on this:

> Everybody talks about pollution, but I mean what causes pollution ...? And then you walk down the main road to pick up your children, and you see all these people sitting in their cars during rush hour – just frightening! ... I mean the whole thing, the whole world is upside down to me.

Food pollution is possibly the most significant way in which the complex interdependencies of risk society surface in the individual's milieu. The causal processes of food production, and subsequently the risks of food pollution, are so complex that they escape a simple pattern of cause and effect. They are no longer locally bound but temporarily and spatially detached. Realising polluted food as 'access point' of 'global alarm' indicates to the individual that the radius in which 'risk society' can impact on his/her milieu, is open and potentially global (Beck, 1992: 27ff.). People thus experience in their dealings with food what Melucci calls 'the ecological issue as *a systemic problem*':

> That is to say, it reveals behind its surface the phenomenon of planetary interdependence and creates new frontiers of human consciousness and action. We have come to an end of linear causality, of monocausal explanations.
>
> (1996: 58)

Engagement in a food box scheme is in this sense not only a form of practical self-actualisation with regard to the immediate threat coming from contaminated food, but also a realisation of the individual's milieu as a 'risk position' (Beck 1992: 53f., 47) in global 'risk society', and moreover a symbolic self-positioning towards the problems of the global 'natural' environment.

For those who join the box scheme without any wider 'environmental' awareness or concern, the occasional leaflet in the boxes helps to broaden the horizon towards the wider issues linked to a 'healthy diet'. In the introductory leaflet of the farm which delivers to one of the box schemes studied, it says, for example:

> We aim to farm in a sustainable way. ... By developing close links with our consumers, and selling direct, we hope to address the wider environmental problems of excessive transport and packaging.

Thus, while, on the one hand, the *local* box scheme is an attempt to locally refocus the causalities and contingencies of risk involved in food production, on the other hand it facilitates people's attempts to position themselves towards *global* environmental issues via their desire for 'organic' food and their concern for a 'healthy diet'.

Consequently, with the issue of 'local organic food' the contradictory complexity of risk society irrevocably enters the individual's milieu. While the box scheme, by providing 'food you can trust', implies the regaining of 'ontological security' with regard to immediate bodily threat by contaminated food, it simultaneously exposes the individual to the complexities and (moral) uncertainties of global risk society. In other words, it cannot relieve the individual from having to position his/her milieu in the context of wider risk society. That is, instead of concealing the contradicting complexities behind the 'food you can trust', involvement in a box scheme rather triggers people's awareness of the configuration of global and local links into which their milieux are tied. Self-actualisation in terms of 'healthy diet' then intrinsically implies the realisation of the interlinkage between the 'here and now' and global society. What, for instance, about organically grown beans from Kenya? Are they OK to eat in view of 'food milage'? If rejected because of that, what then about the life chances of the people who grow them and hope to earn a living with them?

The individual's 'healthy diet' thus becomes an issue of 'life politics' (Giddens, 1993: 214), linking attempts of self-actualisation directly to global issues. This recognition of food as an issue of people's globalised 'life politics' is, for example, indicated when Hannah explained:

> I don't know whether, I don't really think I think terribly sort of globally, I suppose. I don't particularly ... I mean if you go into a supermarket, you know, the green beans that we are buying now, are likely to come from Kenya. I mean, you know, OK that's supporting a population in another country, but I mean, they could be growing for themselves, you know, rather than for us, or growing a different crop, you know, it just seems crazy if we could be producing it locally over here.

In this sense food box scheme initiatives encourage people 'to view the world through food' (Moore-Lappé, in Eder, 1996b: 156).

THE 'GREENING' OF LIFESTYLES?

Apart form the immediately food-related dilemmas, as expressed by Hannah in the above interview sequence, the consumption of organic food as an attempt of self-actualisation in the context of a global risk society then raises the question as to what extent engagement in a box scheme is linked to wider environmental awareness and a generally 'green(er)' lifestyle? The answer to that seems quite obvious: participating in an organic food box scheme in itself does not make up a 'green' lifestyle. As Hannah, the drop-off point for a Bristol scheme, said quite pragmatically on the embeddedness of the food box scheme: 'It needs to suit your way of life.' In other words, each member of a box scheme has to incorporate and legitimise the engagement with (local) organic food in the motivational and practical context of their respective 'biographical situation' (Schütz, 1970). And yet, the following statement could stand as an example for the 'typical' member of a food box scheme – the temptation, as well as the awareness of the need for a greener lifestyle is there, but the involvement in (a not-yet-greened) everyday life is keeping them away from realising their good intentions. Karen, another box scheme member from Bristol, who also grows some organic vegetables in her allotment, pointed out:

> I would hesitate to say that we have a green life style, if I feel we make too many compromises. ... The box scheme is rather something to do with an intention to move in that direction. ... Yes, there is some concern about the environment, but I feel embarrassed about saying it, because I don't feel that we carry it through, I mean we are not consistent about it, we still buy imported fruit and vegetables which have come all the way around the world, I still haven't kicked the habit of shopping in the supermarket to buy exotic fruits like aubergines. ... Sometimes it feels you haven't done anything, I think the box schemes are exciting, but they feel like a drop in the ocean.

If she wanted to go completely 'organic', Karen feels she would have to take 'time off' from earning a living in 'society', just as she could only start her allotment once she started part-time work:

> I mean I was intending to have an allotment for years, but it wasn't before I stopped full-time work that I got one, I suppose in a sense it had to tie in with the rest of my life. ... And, I mean I simply don't have the time and energy at the moment to grow a full complement of everything organic that we would like to have, I simply don't have the time and the facilities at the moment.

Taking up Karen's point about her engagement in a box scheme feeling like 'a drop in the ocean', it is fair to say that respondents' engagement in local organic food box schemes is a symbol of an alternative lifestyle, rather than an element of an actual alternative lifestyle itself. Box scheme membership seems to imply attempted change 'occurring outside rather than within present social structures' (James,

1993: 212). Consequently, rather than providing evidence for local resistance against globalisation, these statements seem to indicate the tension between 'social structure' and 'personal milieu' referred to by Mills (1959: 321). Moreover, what these statements by box scheme members indicate is people's search for recognition in their attempt to actualise their milieux in the context of a complex risk society. Thus it seems necessary to further explore the link between the individualisation of milieux and new forms of sociation.

INDIVIDUALISATION AND SOCIETALISATION OF MILIEUX

The decision to engage in a box scheme is, as outlined, an act of 'self-actualisation' with regard to eating habits in risk society. It illustrates individualisation processes along risk-issues, insofar as the individual has to take appropriate decisions without being able to fall back on the collectivised taken-for-granted assumptions of a local community, or even family. In a more positive sense, aspiring to create 'one's own diet' can be seen as a symbolic expression of the attempt to live 'one's own life'.

Jasmine, for example, who is the drop-off point for a box scheme in another Bristol area, remembers individualisation tendencies around food issues from her childhood in an Asian family in Tanzania:

> I think part of it is that since I was quite young, I was really into it, so I'm obviously called a 'health freak' in my family. I don't know what it is, I think it's just something, I don't know, because none of my family are into this at all, they think I'm quite crazy really. ... I remember arguing with my mum about using oil every day, and I used to explain to her that the oil was getting rancid, because she used to put it on top of the cooker etc. etc., and she just used to think I was crazy.

Also today in her own family there is by no means total agreement in terms of diet. While she 'always used to be a vegetarian, my [her] son is a complete carnivore'. This is also something mentioned by Hannah about her box scheme, which includes organic meat as well as organic fruit and vegetables. She finds herself catering for 'families where half the family are vegetarians and half the family are meat eaters'. In Hannah's case, there is no actual disagreement with her husband about their diet, but as far as the demanding task of running the drop-off point for an organic food box scheme is concerned, he does not participate at all:

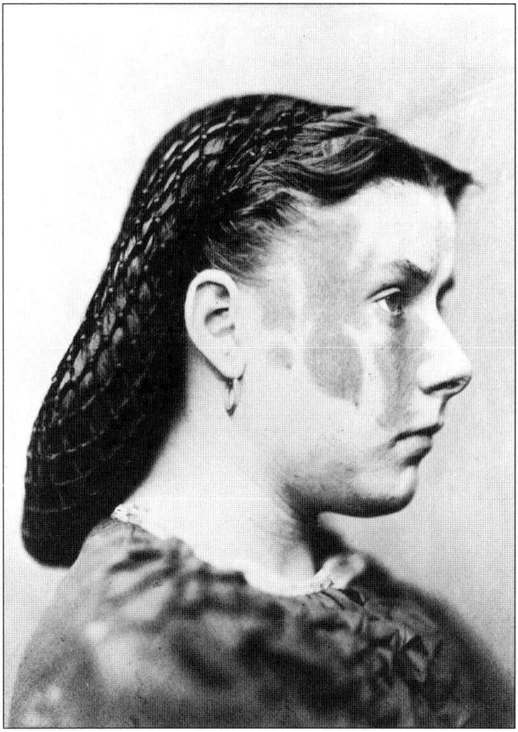

1. Visible pathology: diseases of the skin.

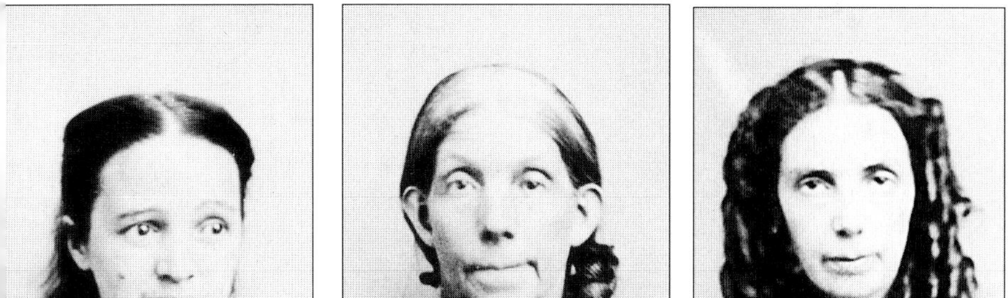

2. Wakefield Lunatic Asylum: portraits of three women patients.

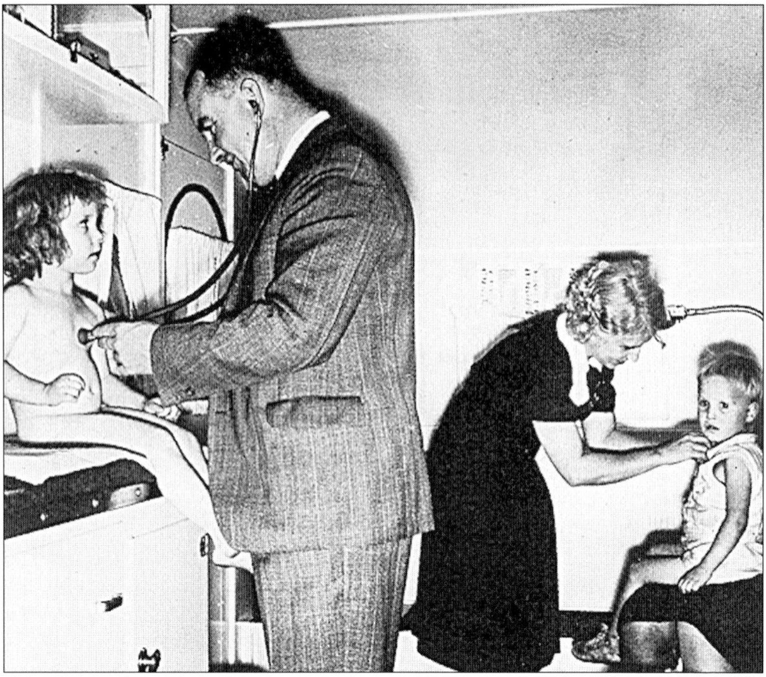

3. An example from the FSA medical files: Dorothea Lange's photograph of a mobile camp for migratory labour, trailer clinic, 1939.

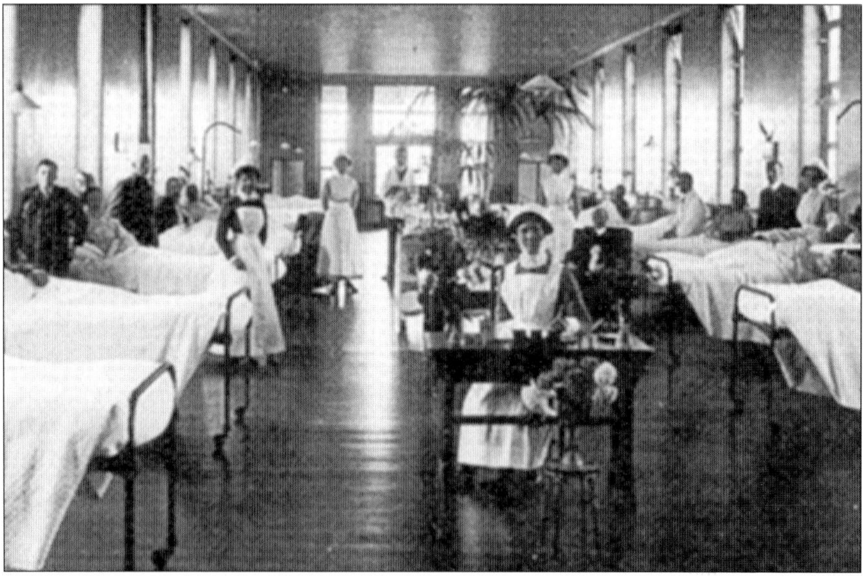

4. Northampton General Hospital, Grafton Ward, 1906.

5. Southland Health Centre Toddlers' Clinic, August 1937.

6 Hither Green Nurses' Home, *c.* 1940s.

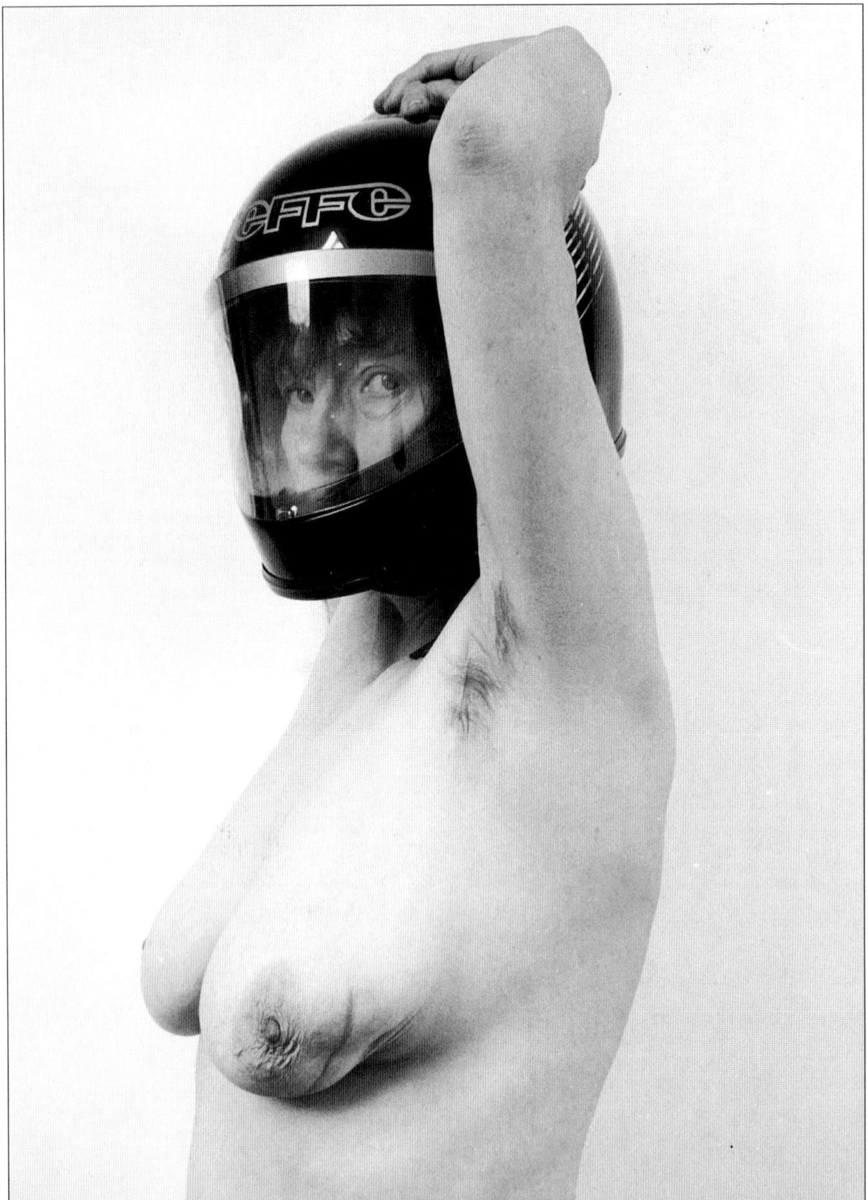

7. Jo Spence/Terry Dennett from the Cancer Project, 1982.

> Martin? [her partner] I don't know whether it was out of choice or something to do with the way he worked, his hours were never … [laughing], no, Martin doesn't, Martin doesn't actually like it [the box scheme], he doesn't like to have any part of it. It's quite strange really, but he'd rather be out on a Thursday night when all this is happening.

These quotes indicate one crucial aspect of the individualisation process outlined by Beck, namely the 'separation of the individual from traditional support networks (for example, family or neighbourhood)' (1992: 93). The daughter going 'organic', or the woman deciding to become the drop-off point for a box scheme, cannot necessarily hope for practical and emotional support from their family or husband.

The box scheme itself can thus be regarded as an '*alternative support network*' between like-minded people, serving the self-actualisation of individual milieux. They are a form of 'collective empowerment' of individual lifestyle decisions, indicating features of a 'self-creative society' where people attempt to manage in an autonomous manner their individual and collective destiny with respect to domestic and transnational issues (Hegedus, 1989: 28ff.).

This research suggests that box schemes in the first instance operate as a technical support service. Whether something more social develops out of them depends on the extent to which the box scheme is or becomes a crucial element of the individual's milieu, and in what kind of social context this milieu is itself embedded. Jasmine, for example, described her box scheme in quite technical terms:

> I'm the collection point for Boxton, so on Thursdays Geoff [the supplier] comes in and drops off the boxes to me, and I have a list of people that want the boxes and I have to ring them once a week. … My number is held at the Soil Association, they have a list of all the collection points around Bristol. So if anybody wants anything, people often ring up and sort of say 'I need to know more about organic veg', so they give the person my name so I get phone calls.

The relationship with her box scheme 'customers' she described as quite anonymous:

> I don't know what sort of people they are, most of them I haven't met, but something has led them to thinking 'I must try this out'.

For most of Jasmine's 'customers' the box scheme is an experiment of integrating organic food into their respectively quite different lifestyles. Accordingly, there is considerable turnover in membership, depending on the success of this small lifestyle experiment:

> It just doesn't suit a lot of people, so people come and try a box scheme and then they never come back, and it's only the dedicated people who do. … Most people, just after a few weeks, get fed up and want something more exotic, or they feel it's too expensive, so then they stop. So it's very exchanging, it changes all the time, like last year I lost a lot of people who aren't carrying on this year.

We can contrast this quite technically organised box scheme with one which is hooked on an existing network of like-minded people. From supplier to 'customer', Hannah's box scheme is based on overlapping networks of acquaintances, and she knows everyone by name. She explained how the box scheme started:

> But in terms of how it all started really, it's because I know Matthew and Janet who own the farm, and when I found out that they were buying a farm, I just casually said 'Oh I'm interested in organic meat, you know, I'll buy it off you, and I'm sure there are several people living around here who would be interested', and they really just took that on board. And straight away, as soon as they got themselves established, they said to me 'will you do this'?

There was no actual 'recruitment' of customers, for example, in terms of leafleting, for again Hannah could rely on the potential like-mindedness of acquaintances in and around her neighbourhood.

> You see, most of the people who collect have known me for quite some time, so I've just mentioned it, I haven't made a big thing of trying to persuade people.

But these links between people have the character of overlapping 'alternative support networks', of which the box scheme is only one example, rather than constituting a closed circle of mutual friends. Participating in one scheme does not necessarily oblige someone to join all other networks, as most of these networks are based on shared specific interests and needs, like having to organise child care. Erica, a member in Hannah's scheme, pointed out:

> Some of us have other links, for example in the baby sitting circle, I know some people in the box scheme from there. So may be people get to know each other through one thing and then they link it to something else. Lots of things really, some people that live around the corner from us share a car, and that's I suppose the same kind of thing … and at least one of those couples is in this box scheme as well, so it's probably *like-minded* people, you know [my emphasis].

These networks of like-minded acquaintances in which the box scheme is embedded, unlike communities in the sense of 'Gemeinschaft', do not absorb the individual milieux completely. They allow for free play of the 'fine distinction' amongst the participating milieux. This is at least what Erica has experienced with regard to her eating habits:

> We got to know Hannah and Martin when our children were small and we joined the baby sitting circle, and then became friends with them. And then this started, and they said to us 'are you interested'? But we are vegetarians, so we are not interested in the meat side at all, and the meat side started first, and the vegetables came a bit later, this was when we joined in.

And yet there are elements of an 'as-if' community life in Hannah's kitchen on a Thursday evening. Unlike in Jasmine's scheme, people stay for a little chat, and might even have a cup of tea. And indeed, respondents stressed the enjoyable character of face-to-face contacts in the context of these Thursday evenings. As Erica pointed out with regard to this Thursday evening chitchat:

> I mean I don't always come, but my partner often comes, because he very much likes all that, chatting to other people and who he sees. … But often I'll meet people who live around, you know if they live in the same street, then you walk back and talk to them on the way.

Does this indicate the resurgence of the lost close-knit local community around the nucleus of a local box scheme? Not at all, for as Lash and Urry aptly remark, the difference between the 'new communities' and 'traditional Gemeinschaften' is 'that people are not born into them. They have to *decide* whether to join or not' (my italics) (1994: 50). Moreover, as Erica's statement reveals, this not only applies for the actual act of joining the box scheme, but also for the different forms of socialising which go with it. Depending on the degree to which each respective individual is inclined to participate, these Thursday evenings are sometimes more, sometimes less sociable, and, as Erica indicated, they are more enjoyable for her partner than for her.

Instead of a resurgence of the local community, what these Thursday evenings rather seem to reveal, is a form of 'socialising without consequences', aptly described by Simmel as 'sociability'. So what we are looking at here is a form of non-committal form of 'sociation'. The aim of this 'play-form of association', as Simmel calls it, 'is nothing but the success of the sociable moment and, at most, a memory of it' (1964: 45). On Thursday evenings in this sense an 'as-if' community is enacted, which has, however, no 'real' consequences for the milieux participating in it.

In fact, these rare occasions of sociability in the 'as-if' community of box scheme members are so enjoyable only because no 'real' community exists. This Thursday evening community is made up of people who otherwise live in their quite individualised milieux, who participate in so different 'sociospheres' (Albrow, 1997), that their daily life paths rarely cross. Hannah stated thoughtfully:

> I think we, I mean everybody leads such a sort of busy lives that you can go for ages without seeing people.

This becomes particularly clear on the few occasions when Hannah really tried to refocus these different biographical paths into a 'bonding exercise', like when the supplying farm invited people out on a 'farm open day'.

> Like this year, ... it was in July, and most people couldn't go, well nobody went from my box scheme at all, because it was just a very busy time, June and July are very busy for people, and there is all sorts of things going on in Bristol. It was actually the Ashton Court [open air festival] weekend.

What this final quotation certainly indicates is the reluctance of individualised milieux towards any form of 'Ver-Gemeinschaftung' (communalisation). Set free in their individual life paths from collectivised frames of reference and habitual orientation into a 'society of multiple options' (Gross, 1994) – 'there are all sorts of things going on in Bristol this weekend, why feeling obliged to join the others and visit a farm?' – the individual is hesitant towards any form of imposed association with 'the other'. It would therefore be somewhat misleading to call new forms of sociation evolving around *emancipatory experiments* like box schemes, 'new communities' (Lash and Urry, 1994: 50) or 'post-traditional communities' (Berking, 1996: 200).

On the other hand, it is also obvious from these personal accounts of box scheme members that the individualisation process going on in contemporary society has not 'successively dried up the social–moral hinterland of our social order'. Instead, some box scheme initiatives could be considered as one of the 'phenomena that signal more an intensification than a diminution of social engagement' (Berking 1996: 192ff.). New forms of 'self'-actualisation require new forms of social engagement. In this sense the box scheme can be regarded as the materialisation of a social milieu, understood as social practice based on like-mindedness in the broadest possible sense. The point here is that these forms of sociation are not based on the more or less imposed expectations and demands of a pregiven 'community', but on what Berking calls 'solidary individualism' (1996: 194ff.), that is, the voluntary extension of solidarity to other like-minded people beyond the confines of family, locality or neighbourhood. A box scheme in this sense then can finally be seen as the materialisation of 'solidary individualism' in an *experimental social milieu*, from which the individual can opt out relatively easily if it no longer contributes to maintaining a 'life of one's own'.

CONCLUSION

Having looked at box schemes from the perspective of the individualisation theses, there is good reason not to immediately see them as a form of local resistance against globalisation, or complementary, as re-enforcement of a local community. People's interest in local organic food can be better seen as an aspect of 'self-actualisation' in the context of a complex risk society.

By participating in a box scheme, people are facilitated in their attempt to:

1. deal with the immediate danger of contaminated food that severely disrupts the 'ontological security' of the individual's milieu;
2. come to terms with the complex reality of a risk society to which their individual milieux is increasingly exposed; and

3. find symbolic reconciliation with nature by incorporating the 'organic' into their milieu.

As one box scheme member put it:

> I've actually made the switch, so I'm really happy to spend much more of my budget every week on organic food, and the box scheme is a way of doing it. ... So I feel really thankful that there is something like that around, I just really like the idea that it has been grown locally and I know that people have grown it, and when I see some caterpillars now I just think, God, this is really good. This means a lot to me, I suppose I care about my food.

This chapter has described the resurgence of the structural tension between society and milieu in the new configuration of global risk society: 'individualised milieux' are exposed to the complexity of global risks, turning them into 'risk positions'. I have examined this in detail with regard to food as an 'access point' of risk society to people's milieux. Box schemes in turn can be seen as an active attempt to solve this tension through 'self'-actualisation. They can thus best be described as forms of collective 'self'-empowerment *within* risk society, rather than a form of parochial resistance *against* the somewhat unspecified threat of globalisation. When milieux become interwoven with risk society, even the daily routines closest to 'home' become the stage for global 'life politics', rather than providing a shelter from globalisation. The 'here and now' thus becomes irrevocably interlinked with global 'risk society' – a 'society of multiple options', in which the maintenance of the individual's milieu becomes an ongoing DIY project.

ACKNOWLEDGEMENTS

This chapter developed in the context of a joint research project on 'Networks of Renewal' at UWE, Bristol. I would like to thank my colleagues Paul Hoggett, Pete Jowers, and Richard O'Doherty for lots of good discussions. I am particularly grateful to our research assistant Derrick Purdue for allowing me to contrast my own interview material against some of his in the second part of this chapter.

NOTES

1. In my argument I will continue both terms, 'planetary society' – when arguing in the context of Melucci's concern with complexity, and 'global society' – when referring to the global implications of Beck's 'risk society'. While the difference between planetary, global and world society would be an interesting topic in itself, it is of no consequence for the argument in this article, and is therefore not addressed. This seems to be in line with Melucci's lenient handling of the difference. While he emphasises the notion of a 'planetary society', he occasionally also uses 'global society' in the same context (1996: 2).
2. The argument in this chapter is based on fieldwork conducted in the Bristol region, using a combination of semi-structured interviews with box scheme members and participant observation in drop-off points. In this text the names of interviewees have been changed. The second part of the argument uses the method of 'maximising differences' (Glaser and Strauss, 1977: 55ff.) by contrasting two rather different box schemes.
3. I am aware of the potential terminological confusion here. Please note that the 'conceptual individualism' of the 'milieu' concept used in my argument is not the same as the 'individualisation' process emphasised by Beck. However, one could argue that the 'conceptual individualism' of the phenomenological notion of milieu anticipated something which becomes only more obvious with the individualisation of milieux in the context of global society, namely the continuous struggle to maintain a unique biography.

REFERENCES

Albrow, M. (1997) 'Travelling Beyond Local Cultures: Socioscapes in a Global City', in J. Eade (ed.), *Living the Global City: Globalisation as Local Process* (London: Routledge).

Beck, U. (1992) *Risk Society: Towards a New Modernity* (London: Sage).

Beck, U. (1995a) *Ecological Politics in an Age of Risk* (Cambridge: Polity).

Beck, U. (1995b) 'Die Individualisierungsdebatte', in B. Schäfers (ed.), *Soziologie in Deutschland: Entwicklung, Institutionalisierung und Berufsfelder, Theoretische Kontroversen* (Opladen: Leske und Budrich).

Berking, H. (1996) 'Solidary Individualism: the Moral Impact of Cultural Modernisation in Late Modernity', in S. Lash, B. Szerszynski and B. Wynne (eds), *Risk, Environment & Modernity: Towards a New Ecology* (London: Sage).

Dale, C. and Booth, E. (eds) (1994) *Food, Farming and Society: Towards a New Model* (Soil Association/International Society for Ecology and Culture).

Delingpole, J. (1997) 'Where the Grass is Greener', *Independent Magazine*, 22 March 1997, pp. 6ff.

Eder, K. (1996a) 'The Institutionalisation of Environmentalism: Ecological Discourse and the Second Transformation of the Public Sphere', in S. Lash, B. Szerszynski and B. Wynne (eds), *Risk, Environment & Modernity: Towards a New Ecology* (London: Sage).

Eder, K. (1996b) *The Social Construction of Nature: A Sociology of Ecological Enlightenment* (London: Sage).

Giddens, A. (1994) *The Consequences of Modernity* (Cambridge: Polity).

Giddens, A. (1993) *Modernity and Self-Identity: Self and Society in the Late Modern Age* (Cambridge: Polity).

Glaser, B. and Strauss, A. (1977) *The Discovery of Grounded Theory* (New York: Aldine).

Goffman, E. (1972) *Relations in Public: Microstudies of the Public Order* (Harmondsworth: Penguin).

Gross, P. (1994) *Die Multioptionsgesellschaft* (Frankfurt/M.: Suhrkamp).

Grathoff, R. (1989) *Milieu und Lebenswelt: Einführung in die phänomänologische Soziologie und sozialphänomänologische Forschung* (Frankfurt/M.: Suhrkamp).

Hegedus, Z. (1989) 'Social Movements and Social Change in Self-Creative Society: New Civil Initiatives in the International Arena', *International Sociology*, 4(1): 19–36.

James, A. (1993) 'Eating Green(s): Discourses on Organic Food', in K. Milton (ed.), *Environmentalism: The View from Anthropology* (London: Routledge).

Lash, S. and Urry, J. (1994) *Economies of Signs and Space* (London: Sage).

Melucci, A. (1996) *The Playing Self: Person and Meaning in the Planetary Society* (Cambridge: Cambridge University Press).

Mills, C. Wright (1959) *The Power Elite* (New York: Oxford University Press).

Moore-Lappé, F. (1978) *Die Öko-Diät. Wie man mit wenig Fleisch gut ißt und die Natur schont* (Frankfurt/M.: Fischer).

Norberg-Hodge, H. (1994a) 'Introduction', in Dale, C. and Booth, E. (eds), *Food, Farming and Society: Towards a New Model* (Soil Association/International Society for Ecology and Culture).

Norberg-Hodge, H. (1994b) 'Globalisation versus Community', in Dale, C. and Booth, E. (eds), *Food, Farming and Society: Towards a New Model* (Soil Association/International Society for Ecology and Culture).

Robertson. R. (1995) 'Glocalisation: Time–Space and Homogeneity and Heterogeneity', in M. Featherstone, S. Lash and R. Robertson (eds), *Global Modernities* (London: Sage).

Scheler, M. (1973) *Formalism in Ethics and Non-Formal Values: A New Attempt toward the Foundation of an Ethical Personalism* (Evanston, IL: Northwestern University Press).

Schütz, A. (1970) *Reflections on the Problem of Relevance*, ed. by R. M. Zaner (New Haven and London: Yale University Press).

Schütz, A. (1966) *Collected Papers*, vol. III: *Studies in Phenomenological Philosophy* (The Hague: Nijhoff).

Simmel, G. (1964) *The Sociology of Georg Simmel*, ed. by K. H. Wolff (London, New York: Collier Macmillan, The Free Press).

Part II

Technologies of Consumption and Waste

8 Photography, Power and Resistance: the Case of Health and Medicine

BARBARA HARRISON and
KAY ARANDA

INTRODUCTION

This chapter considers the role of the photograph and camera technologies within the personal and professional realm of health and medicine. This role will be used as an illustration of how dimensions of consumption and use can be considered within relations of power/resistance. Following a short contextual discussion of photography in general, the case study consists of three main parts. First, it examines the thesis that vision was attributed with an ontological and epistemologically privileged role in the development of science and medicine as forms of knowledge and practice. This examination will commence with a historical analysis of the development of late nineteenth century uses of the photograph, and consider the extent to which the clinical photograph still serves similar purposes in the contemporary context. Outside of the clinical role for photography, the chapter then considers how photographs may in a different way be viewed as documenting and confirming existing hierarchies of power inherent in the social divisions between professionals and between professionals and client/patients, as well as those of class, 'race' and gender. In particular, it will be argued here that the rise of 'publicity' or propaganda photographs during the twentieth century, alongside the production and consumption of popular imagery and personal photographs, can be taken to represent particular ideas of health, illness and medical/health care practice. Finally, the chapter suggests that photography can also be a means of resistance, subverting the discourses of institutional and professional power, providing opportunities for new meanings to be asserted and identities constructed. Such subversion questions the very idea of what photographs may be about

– and as such also confronts and challenges the conventions of photographic practice itself. It is our argument that such dimensions are not exclusive to the topic of health, illness and medicine, but rather it is one case example which clearly indicates the complex relationship between vision, visual products and practice. As a topic of study it further demonstrates the necessity for developing a sociology of photography as integral to understanding the connection between representation, social structure and personal experience.[1]

PHOTOGRAPHY IN SOCIAL CONTEXT

Photographs, like other visual images, take historically specific forms linked to political, economic and social relations, which both determines their mode of production and their ability to constitute the social world itself in particular ways. At any point in time photographs provide us with views of how things are or 'ought' to be. In addition the languages of visual presentation, or in this case the photographic genres employed, draw on wider cultural perceptions, categories and metaphors, so that there seems to be a seamless continuity of the social with the photograph.

The analysis of photographic imagery in the historical and contemporary context will of necessity be as representations. They are forms of text, and analysable as discourses. As with other forms of discourse, photographs are refashioned, and in this process can be separated from their sources or original purposes/producers. This refashioning, as Chaplin (1994: 1) describes it, uses pictorial and textual codes so that the resultant 'pictures' 'can be understood as articulating and contributing to social processes'. Such understandings, therefore, can be distinguished at both the level of production, that is the photographer, and at the level of consumption, that is the many different audiences there may be for any image. There is an important mutuality where representations not only articulate the social but in turn constitute and alter it. In this way, as Fyfe and Law (1988: 1) have argued, visual depiction[2] does social work, such as 'the construction and depiction of social difference'. Importantly, they argue, to understand visualisation is to 'note its principles of exclusion and inclusion, to detect the roles it makes available ... and to decode hierarchies and differences that it naturalises'(*ibid.*). As sociologists we now accept there is a problematic relationship between representation and 'reality' if such a distinction is tenable at all. Interestingly a current advertisement for a camera makes use of the idea that any image is capable of multiple interpretation. It invites producers to 'write their own story'.[3]

As sociologists then, we can have a variety of interests and therefore approaches to the study of photographs as representations. We can be interested in the content of representations – that is what their manifest message purports to be about, or in terms of a purpose such as education, clinical diagnosis or selling products, or with their symbolism – the latent meaning of overt imagery in a similar vein to the art historian's use of iconography, or the semiotician's use of sign (see for example, Williamson, 1980; Pryce, 1996). Whatever our interest in the representational text it will be necessary to consider modes of representation as devices which produce particular types of accounts and/or theories not simply as some kind of 'reflection'. As argued above, the construction of photographs involves the viewer/interpreter as much as it does the photographer who fashioned the original image.

For the sociologist of photography there is a further important factor in considering both representational forms and their productive relations, and that is camera technologies. Technological developments have been a crucial determinant of the kinds of imagery and the amount of it that is available at particular times. Changes in camera technology have been fundamental to debates about the extent to which there can be a clear distinction between professional and amateur images, as well as the relation between the two. As Hearn (1992) suggests, the more sophisticated the technology, the more possible it is for the 'amateur' to aspire to 'professional' image making. The contemporary marketing of cameras has exploited such aspirations. Thus, an important element of photographic production has been the changing consumption of both cameras themselves and of particular representations in particular locations. This applies equally for professional and what might be called 'amateur' or 'everyday' image making. For example, as we shall see, an enormous number of medical and health-care photographs were produced for public audiences. Personally produced images were dependent on the technological developments from the turn of the century which permitted the camera itself to become an item of mass consumption. In addition, there has been a long history of personal consumption of professional images as archives of family portraiture demonstrate.

What a historical and sociological analysis of photography further demonstrates, is that despite a technology seemingly able to be used by everyone, it is evident that there are topics that may or may not be photographed. What is considered appropriate for professional productions for particular purposes, will seldom appear in the personal or family album, and what is included in the personal or private album is a restricted range of topics and images. As Bourdieu (1990) has argued, 'the need to take photographs can be understood as a need for photographs' (p. 25) and stressing that while everything is potentially able to be photographed, amateur pictures draw on a well-defined common range of subjects. We must therefore accept that 'everyday' photography is a socially designated and highly regulated practice.

Outside of the domain of personal and amateur photographs, interest has grown in the coincidence of certain visual technologies alongside particular social and political developments, including that of knowledge itself, and this has opened up new lines of inquiry in the present. This historical perspective following Foucault (1977; also see Green, 1985, Tagg, 1988) has demonstrated the importance of photography in particular, to the capacity for 'scientific observation' and so to the power of scientific knowledge and its place within the developing health and welfare institutions of the nineteenth century. The ability to 'see', whether it be the clinical gaze on or in the body, or the surveillance of working-class working mothers' health, or the thousands of photographs taken of Barnardo children, and the categorisation of human and social types in anthropology and criminology,[4] this surveillance served forms of administration, knowledge and disciplinary power. Even the design – the visual architecture of such institutions, it was argued, allowed for the exercise of power by observers over the observed as part of the regulation of human populations. Bentham's original notion of the panopticon as the 'ideal' form for penal incarceration, was one which theorists, following Foucault's own use of this metaphor, have taken as indicative of a relation between observation, regulation (or 'disciplining'). Here the idea of 'policing' extended beyond the penal to other arenas of social life, and in the medical arena public health officials were referred to in some contexts as 'medical police' (Rosen, 1974).

Disciplinary practice, as Foucault (1977) indicates, was present in a wide range of institutions by the late nineteenth century, the hospital being one. Thus we can see how this articulates with ideas of knowledge, the role of vision and the exercise of power within health and medicine. The panopticon then provided an exemplar for an architecture which facilitated constant observation, identification and the acquisition of information. Architecture, he argues, was no longer built to be seen, but to permit 'an internal articulated and general control, to render visible those who are inside it ... to act on, transform, to know and alter them'. The panopticon provided a 'generalisable model of functioning' (1977: 205), a diagram as it were of how power was exercised. It was the apparatus of the hospital as a whole which produced power, built into medical action and relationships. As with other institutions of disciplinary power, Foucault claims the examination was central and, along with documentary techniques, made individuals into cases. Patients, as individualised bodies, were perpetually examined, and increasingly the hospital became a focus for training and knowledge (see p. 186).

In the development of medicine the clinical gaze was not just to see *voir,* seeing was to have knowledge, *savoir* (Gilman, 1982). In this sense, however, the concept of 'gaze' in Foucault (1977) does not only refer to immediate vision, but includes other forms of perception such as touch and hearing. Doctors, then, needed to be skilled 'observers', a training and competence which it can be argued is, at least in part, a non-codified knowledge acquired at the bedside (see, for example, Jamous and Peloille, 1972). Vision, and visual technologies, are attributed with a capacity to fulfil some aspects of medical work which enable disciplinary power to be exercised. Theorists such as John Tagg (1982, 1988) have, therefore, sought to develop that aspect of Foucault's work which provides a perspective on visual images, especially photographs, as elements of discourses of 'truth' which are bound to systems of power and institutions of regulation. Photography was thus a technique that enabled archives of information to be created, for typologies or classifications to bring bodies, so captured, into constant surveillance, to be known and thence controlled. Moreover, institutionalised visual/camera surveillance provided a further authorisation for positivism as part of this 'regime of truth'. This is important, as Tagg (1988) points out, as photography's privileged status as witnessing actual events is possible only when it functions within particular ideological and institutional frameworks where its evidential quality can be taken as given. As Jenks (1995) has argued also, positivism and the techno-scientific attributions of camera images as literal descriptions, were part of common-sense cultural dispositions towards perception and interpretation, that granted 'objectivity' to pure vision – an empiricist project with a realist aesthetic. Thus by transforming the material world into a representation which appears to be of the objects represented, photography was an important contributor to vision as a vehicle of knowledge and truth, an essential part of modernity's project (Slater, 1995). The confluence of camera technology with positivism's epistemology will be evident in the discussion of medical photographs which follows.

PHOTOGRAPHY IN MEDICINE AND HEALTH CARE: CLINICAL KNOWLEDGE AND PROFESSIONAL PRACTICE

A particular interest in what is broadly called medical photography (mainly on the grounds that early images were a consequence of doctors' interests and initiatives) has been sustained by the theoretical interest outlined above in the relation of seeing to knowing and knowing to power. But there is an added important dimension of the medical–photographic relationship in the nineteenth century where the advocacy of photography by doctors, as individuals and through professional media, contributed to the growth and popularity of photography itself (Fox and Lawrence, 1989). Fox and Lawrence (1989) suggest there were essentially two uses to which this new technology was put, and surviving photographs in the main can be classed in this way. First, there were clinical photographs – those which sought to delineate, understand and record pathology and disease. Camera observations were to be an aid to clinical practice, to aid 'observation' and classification for diagnostic and therapeutic purposes. The second use was to make professional images for public audiences, forms of 'publicity' – photographic documents which served to present and even propagandise the value of medicine and health services, and professionals. In this context also, were those photographs of 'conditions', both urban and rural, which required forms of medical regulation.

Clinical Photographs

In the clinical sphere a significant underpinning for the use of photographic technology by doctors was the belief that the camera produced a mirror image or faithful rendering of what was being recorded. The importance of neutral observation was already a widely held assumption in knowledge production in medicine, as in other areas of science. Jordanova (1987) notes the impulse to 'realistic' and objective representations in medicine preceded the camera, as the use of wax models and anatomical topography in the eighteenth and early nineteenth centuries demonstrates. What all these kinds of representation were required to do was to increase the legibility of the body, to render its features, including those beneath the skin, visible and to delineate difference. That such differences were conspicuously oriented towards gender, it is argued, allowed social roles to be naturalised in bodily difference (Jordanova, 1987: 51), a core component of medical theorising from hereon. Also important in this gendering was the association of nature with the feminine, science requiring access to nature in order to effect control. The 'unveiling' of women's bodies would thus provide knowledge that would allow nature to be 'mastered'. The camera also reinforced gender relations in other respects too, as the 'servant' or 'handmaiden' of science, the passivity and femaleness of the subject as giving themselves up to the camera was a necessary correlate of its 'objectivity'. As such it also masked the operation of power (McGrath, 1984).

Visible difference was important to medical knowledge in other respects also. Early clinical photographs are dominated by images of extraordinary illnesses, diseases or disabilities, what McGrath (1984) refers to as a kind of 'freak voyeurism'. But this was also to develop into a more widely used genre where the aim was to demarcate the abnormal from the normal, that is the difference or pathology was 'seeable' (see Plate 1). It was common in the latter part of the nineteenth century to use pairs in one image or paired images, one representing the normal, the other the visible departure from it. There were similar uses of photographic practice in other disciplines, such as anthropology, where formal portraiture of individuals and groups served to demarcate the other – and indeed provide the data for more precise measurement of 'racial' physiognomy (Green, 1984). As Gilman (1982) points out, an important dimension of categories in human culture is their polarity, and the reliance on visual features that distinguish one from the other. Both this idea of visible difference and its necessary corollary that the outward appearance of the body could be read as revealing an inner nature, was clearly articulated in the context of psychiatric photography. For the sane that 'otherness' relied on an appearance of difference – typically facial or cranial features, expression, body build and gestures. Even now the idea that people 'look crazy' is deeply ingrained. As with medicine generally, ideas of visualising madness had been around before cameras. Images were integral to picturing madness as the object of knowledge and psychiatric practice (Gilman, 1982; Rose, 1990).

Some of the most prominent theorisers and practitioners of medical photography in the last half of the nineteenth century were based in asylums. Hugh Diamond (Superintendent of the Women's Department in the Surrey Asylum) presented the case for his photographic work not only by reference to its accuracy but also the permanency of it as a record, as he noted it 'makes them not only observable now but forever ... a perfect and faithful record, free from horrific painful caricaturing' (cited in Gilman, 1982: 164). As with other psychiatrists who embraced the camera as a diagnostic aid at this time, Diamond affirmed the ontological relationship between inner states and outward appearance – a necessary precondition for the epistemological weight given to camera images as a means to knowledge. It records, he stated:

> with unerring accuracy the external phenomenon of each passion as the really certain indication of internal derangement, and it exhibits to the eye the well known sympathy that exists between the diseased brain the organs and features of the body.
>
> (*Ibid*., p. 164)

As Gilman (1982) documents, there was little divergence among other practitioners, such as Crichton Browne, the Medical Director at Wakefield Asylum, from the view that photographs provided an 'objective portrayal of signs and symptoms of specific classes of illness', and Connolly at Hanwell also saw them as presenting clinical description (see Plate 2). There were also some practitioners who considered photographs might serve to destigmatise the insane – to show that their essentially 'normal' appearance could permit a return to a world outside the asylum. Visual records of 'reform' were made by using before-and-after photographs. There was certainly a rationale that they had therapeutic value for patients (who could see for themselves their visible improvement). This may of course have been a justification for the intrusion into patient privacy.

It is important to stress that the ideas which underpinned the use of photography were central to nineteenth-century neurological and psychiatric theory itself – so that existing theorisation provided at one and the same time the rationale for photographic use. Seeing and photographing the insane became an almost inseparable relationship, further reflected in the work of Darwin in developing his 'scientific theory' of emotional expression. There were issues which proponents themselves raised, however, about the interpretation of photographic images and increasingly about the value of the posed photograph. Darwin, for example, commented that:

> although photographs are incomparably better for exhibiting expression than any drawing, yet I believe it is quite necessary to study the previous appearance of the countenance.
>
> (Cited in Gilman, 1982: 181)

There were technical limitations in moving away from the static image in the earlier years of psychiatric photography, so that some practitioners advocated the use of unposed images, sequences of images and then moving film. The in-house photographer at Saltpêtrière increasingly adopted sequencing in relation to epilepsy and hysteria, and it is perhaps interesting that students of the latter returned to etchings in order to map and sub-classify the appearance of the hysterical crisis (see Gilman, 1982: 198–9). So here, as elsewhere, drawing and other forms of representation continued to be important because of technical limitations rather than any epistemological shift, but it was not to last. The impact of Freud's ideas was to lead to just such a epistemological shift in psychiatry – a theory and practice which rejected visual observation and gave primacy to listening to patients themselves. Words were now to be the means of making the inner worlds of patients visible.

Psychiatric photography provides an example of how 'clinical' imagery ostensibly used as an aid to diagnostic practice contained other discourses. That many of these images were of women patients was not just an accident of location, but fundamental to ideas of managing women and madness. Personal appearance was an indicator of natural feminine qualities, those that become disordered (including a diagnosis of extreme vanity) and those which indicated the 'success' of management strategies. This helps to explain the use of portrait genres with appropriate 'props', since these conformed to wider conventions about proper decorum, and a domestication of the patient, while also defining women's necessary subservience to the doctor and the male gaze. As Showalter (1987: 97) concludes:

> that we should have so many remarkable pictures of Victorian madwomen and so few of their words, reminds us how strongly the power of definition rested with the male observer. In the photographs ... we are made to see the moral management of female insanity, as well as its reduction ... to visual conventions. All sit at the doctor's bidding, they surrender to his lens; they are at his service.

To return to the clinical photograph in physical medicine, there were, alongside the enthusiasm for the photograph, some doubts about its technical limitations. There were doctors who tried to apply photography in the study of morbid anatomical specimens in the same way as drawing and engraving had been used. There was a good deal of debate about the ability of the photograph to show the appropriate detail which the use of colour and texture had previously, but photographic practice developed in other directions in physical medicine as an aid to clinical decisions and therapy. Observation and tools of observation remained central to knowledge production. The challenge was to see 'inside' the body and not be reliant on its external features. The early years of X-ray technologies, as Pasveer (1989) observed, have had surprisingly little scrutiny given this continuing aspect of medical science. Like photographs, X-rays were also presumed to provide images that 'truly' reflected health and disease. The problem, however, as he points out, was the nature of the world it was presumed to reflect. That world still required making before the images could give up their knowledge. Seeing by means of X-rays had to be learned, and their content interpreted. It was on the basis that this was more than an everyday competence that allowed for the formation of specialist professionals in the production and interpretation of images for clinical purposes, and for such skills to be contested.

X-ray techniques have remained a dominant form of visualisation throughout the twentieth century, and while rendering visible aspects of the body's interior, there have been continuing problems of differentiation, its restriction to single-angle shots, and its ability to move from structure to function. New forms of 'looking at the body' that have developed more recently, that access new interior surfaces, hold out the possibility of diagnostic accuracy, but do they 'structure a new way of knowing the body?' (Kember, 1995: 104). Tomography, a form of advanced X-ray, produces colour-enhanced, three-dimensional reconstructions using digitalised computer translations of the images. The detail provided now exceeds the capacity of the human eye, so the challenge to medical authority lies in the ability to understand and use imagery that requires a unique visual literacy (see Kember, 1995).

Magnetic resonance, as in ultra-sound technologies, also raises other issues about the 'uses' of the clinical photograph. This is especially so in respect of the routine use of this technology in pregnancy. As Kember (1995) remarks, there have been proponents who have suggested a liberatory or at least egalitarian quality to such non-invasive forms of visualisation but, she argues, these remain images which 'unveil' the female body, a process which obliterates or writes out the role of the mother, giving the doctor direct access to the foetus. Ultra-sound surveillance provides an example of how a highly technological and professional form of imagery has become an item of popular consumption. Not only are mothers and/or parents given access to the imagery during examination, but they are given personal copies. The ultra-sound image of the foetus has begun to assume a 'pride of place' in family albums as the baby's first picture. It might be argued that it will be difficult to change client expectations about routine use of ultra-sound when it and its visual products have become forms of consumption. Ultra-sound images thus present a paradox. The images have become personal, occupying 'first' place in the chronicles of childhood, a form of bonding between mother and child, and such electronic forms of imaging are still instruments of surveillance and the exercise of disciplinary power. Pregnant women are required by these means to submit to the authority of the doctor, an authority that rests in part on what ultra-sound reveals. This example serves to emphasise that technologies of visualisation are not autonomous from culture or institutional practices. And, as Petchesky (1987) has demonstrated, the consumption of ultra-sound images is not restricted to parents, but they have been harnessed as a tool in the political struggles of anti-abortion activists.

Public and Professional Imagery – Official Perspectives

To turn to the second major type of medical photograph, professional or public imagery, where the context, purpose and audience for the images is much more variable, especially over time and place. These factors are important in evaluating photographs. In particular there are issues for the historian who might be inclined to consider these provide additional sources of documentary data, since these are highly contrived, even when using candid or 'realist' genres. Let us take the example of the use of photographs, including the medical ones, by the Farm Security Administration (FSA) in the USA in the 1930s, as an integral part of New Deal social policy making. The images in the medical files of the everyday delivery of primary health care, in the often-desperate context of economic depression, need to be analysed as part of a co-ordinated programme of propaganda to make visible to a wider public that interventions, including the new pre-paid health plan, were working to improve life (Stoeckle and White, 1985; see also Plate 3). Thus the vernacular tradition adopted here, of the ordinary and everyday nature of images of, and understood by, 'ordinary' people, is itself a restricted and interpreted account of the photographers who operated within a particular institutional and political context, one which was evidently highly manipulated (Tagg, 1982). Over and above this, the FSA photographs conformed to a new visual language that had wider currency – that of photojournalism. We may question the extent such photographs can be read as 'documenting' the ordinary when, as Sontag (1978) reminds us, 'realism' is itself a contrived aesthetic. From this time onwards, however, the photo-story had established itself and it was not unusual to find that the photo-story included topics in health and illness, and they were accompanied by major changes in representation. Patients, for example, were now to be seen as recipients of health-care work.

At various times then photographic images were used to construct a distinct image of medical or health care, those personnel who delivered it and their qualities, and the social relations between them and patients or clients. What is photographed will also depend on the institutional concerns and practices of those who commissioned the photograph at particular times. Just as the FSA photographs reflected particular policy developments, the same is also true of UK collections. For example, the London County Council-generated collection has a large number of images of welfare clinics for mothers and babies, and the work of health visitors and school nurses. It was these aspects of health-care delivery which dominated local authority responsibilities in the first half of the twentieth century, continuing into the post-NHS 1950s. Similarly it is evident that the public health section was a major instigator of photographic records.

Fox and Lawrence (1989) have noted a number of substantial changes in the way the social roles of doctor, nurse and patient were represented over time. In early institutionally based photographs doctors were frequently absent, instead appearing in individual or group photographs posed outside of work, which they suggest was to reinforce their middle-class dignity and respectability when doubts existed about expertise. Nurses, on the other hand, are clearly visible with patients in hospital settings, but they are not at work either. These images also conform to visual conventions of formality, domesticity and sometimes family portraiture – although the patient, often sitting in bed staring at the camera, reminds us this was not merely a domestic scene (*ibid.*, p. 42). What the images of wards convey is neatness and cleanliness; hospitals as ordered and disciplined but also 'homely' places to be (for example, the presence of plants and other objects recognisable as part of Victorian domestic environments; see Plate 4). The ward with nurses at the centre thus served to emphasise the caring component of hospitals rather than medical intervention. American photographs, on the other hand, departed significantly in this respect; hospitals were shown as places of work.

Shifts in British imagery still tended not to show medical work being done in hospitals, with the exception of increasing numbers of surgery or clinic photographs. The rituals and separate space occupied by surgery in these images constituted it as a distinct arena of medical practice. Nurses were increasingly seen in other settings outside hospitals, in homes and clinics, but despite showing them at work in all cases there was still an absence, as Fox and Lawrence (1989: 45) comment, on 'blood, sweat and tears'. From the 1930s photographs begin to identify spaces or particular surroundings, where encounters between health-care workers and patients – especially mothers and children – took place. Work was done: babies were weighed, mothers were instructed, and patients themselves were to assume a more active role in the imagery. Thus even the frequent images of the 'patient' patients in the waiting room emphasised that the public good was being realised, and that health care was now to be thought of as not only dealing with disease, but with individual biographies and 'communities' (see Plate 5). From the inter-war period, general practitioners who were absent from earlier photographs were now included, and health centres celebrated. Wartime images also broke with the more formal posed images of previous hospital photographs. At the same time there is still a distance between the inner rooms where 'clinic' work is conducted, and those who wait their turn; and between the 'expert' and the client.

It is evident from photographic collections that nurses were a popular source of imagery, including picture postcards (O'Neill, 1989, 1991). The uniform was a defining quality of their 'professionalism', a visible display of discipline and order, and of their femininity. Where they were photographed with doctors their place in the hierarchy was also confirmed. Increasingly, the uniform as 'proper dress' (Apple, 1988) became a perpetual indication of nursing as vocation. In photographs in classroom settings and nurses' homes, whether off or on duty, the uniform remained (see Plate 6). Recruitment campaigns made extensive use of these kinds of images.

The overwhelming impression of these images of health-care workers, including nurses, is of 'idealised' and normatively constructed pictures. Like most forms of 'publicity' they draw on conventions for public consumption in which the photographic subject remains subservient to the needs of the commissioner and their agent – the photographer. It might be argued, therefore, that if nurses had generated their own images of themselves and their work they would be significantly different, as Short (1995), using one example, suggests. We would argue this might be less than supposed, even in the case of images produced for essentially private purposes. We do not have much of this kind of material to work with, but isolated examples suggest that both kinds of production draw on similar conventions – both cultural and photographic, and Short's own example of the Australian nurse, Mabel Bamber, do not we suggest differ markedly from the 'stereotyped images' of photographs of nurses through the eyes of hospital administrators, doctors or a nursing leadership. Despite different purposes and audiences, they draw on similar discourses and genres just as family or holiday photographs might do (see, for example, Williamson, 1984; Bourdieu, 1990). Even for those who choose to challenge or change stereotypical representation many still employ particular commonly used discursive themes to do so.

THE USE OF PHOTOGRAPHY AS A FORM OF RESISTANCE

To move to the final section of this chapter, we want to suggest that there is also the possibility for such photographic imagery to be subverted – to have alternative definitions, meanings and political purposes. This may be true for professional or personal forms of camera imagery. Furthermore, if photography is viewed as a means by which people themselves interpret, give meaning to and make sense of their experiences, then the possibility of photography as a form of resistance, a challenge to existing structures and the definitions of self and experience by others, must be acknowledged. These might be 'ordinary' everyday experiences or events which disrupt and require new and different responses from both self and others, including the construction of new social identities. Illness and other changes to the body provide one particular form of disruption that has provided opportunities for using photographic approaches. Some focus on particular illnesses or disabilities while others examine aspects of people's experiences as carers for children and others. Personal narrative approaches have tended to dominate within this tradition, through the use of visual journals, essays and diaries, often within a written text. The suggestion is that disruptions, such as those caused by illness or death, require some personal journey of 'making sense'. Some authors, such as Barthes (1981), would also argue that this does not require images to be self-generated, since the symbolic form of photographs (or indeed other imagery) invites the 'speaking about' the experience of others, and by this means perhaps also oneself.

As with drawing and painting, photographic projects can have the explicit or implicit aim to use self-generated imagery to symbolise and make visible aspects of the self in social and physical environments. Such work has been used in research also, with the expressed aim of giving back to research participants some control over the articulation of their experience from their point of view. Ziller (1990), a pioneer of this approach in psychology, describes this kind of work as photobiography. Participants are encouraged to use the camera in order to address fundamental questions of identity – who am I? There is a similar argument underlying the compilation of various kinds of photographic journals. Such journals may reveal 'unfamiliar and unknown aspects of human health experience'. In one example (Hagedorn, 1994) eight families were asked to take photographs of their experience of caring for a child with chronic illness, which were then a source for 'spontaneous story telling'. There are examples such as this, where the photographer as amateur has produced images for research purposes, and there needs to be critical attention paid by researchers to the extent that such techniques, in research settings, can be empowering of research participants. It is possible that what commences as the participants' representation of their experience is undermined by research-led agendas.

There are certainly some researchers who would argue that, with careful attention to 'ownership' and 'control' over participants' image production and the images themselves, in some contexts photographs provide a means for greater political participation by community members, and a means by which social policies can be directed at their own needs. This technique of 'photovoice' has emerged in the context of some health and development projects, For example, Wang *et al.* (1996), who have used cameras within a women's health and reproduction project in Yunnan, China, argue that this involves more than making oppressed groups more visible, 'it is a tool for participation, for grassroots planning and implementation, and for reaching policymakers' (p. 47). While they are cautious about a potential to overromanticise this technique as giving 'voice to the voiceless', they equally suggest it does increase participation and people's access to power. The assumption is that people themselves have insights and expertise that professionals and outsiders lack. While this project is about a specific political process of evaluation, it is useful to remember that visual imagery has long played a role for groups in political struggle (see, for example, Loftus (1988) on Northern Ireland).

Phil Cohen (1989) suggests there is a model that provides for a explicit political reading of photography involving critical analysis and space for alternative representation, and projects with young people in which he has been involved demonstrate the potential for productive relations or knowledge to be re-defined, and space provided for young people to generate an analysis of 'race', gender and class. The examples discussed above suggest also that 'everyday' photographic images may provide some opportunities to put representation and interpretation back into the hands of the non-professional producers. In addition to the personal orientations which they may reveal, there is within the genre examples of how such productions may be used to challenge stereotypical or conventional imagery – both in content and acceptable aesthetic criteria. There are individuals who have also embarked on such work in order to 'make sense' of their experience, and as such it can be viewed as serving therapeutic purposes. In the context of health and illness there are clear examples of such work coming from individuals 'living with' their own experiences of acute or chronic illness, and/or who use their 'art' to find alternative meanings and subjectivity.

In the UK a number of photographic projects have sought to redefine and challenge the conceptions of others about health, illness and disability. Camerawork's two projects on Disability (1988) and Women's Health (1990) combined both text and image to challenge medical and media images, as have a number of other photographic projects around disability (see Hevey, 1992). The person who has done most to take this approach forward and to develop not just a political model (both feminist and socialist) for photographic projects, but the therapeutic, is Jo Spence. Her work had always been autobiographical, but became increasingly so when she was diagnosed as having breast cancer. The diagnosis of, and treatment for, her breast cancer became a major impetus for the use of her photographs as a way of having a dialogue with and for herself, or 'revisioning illness and asking new questions' (1991: 79). It was also to become more than a document of 'what was happening to me' where the exhibition and publication of 'A Picture of Health' became a vehicle that would allow others, particularly women, to share in a critique and reappropriation of their bodies from the medical establishment (see Plate 7). It is argued that a critical component of such a reappropriation is that, in being an active subject of one's own investigation, one is no longer simply an object of medical discourse. With Rosy Martin she then continued to work through the possibilities of photo-therapy. Here, it is argued, 'The body is a site of struggle – the sign is a site of struggle. I am trying to make available visually what is usually unknown, unseen or feared by most people' (Spence and Martin, 1988). In their latter work Spence and Martin used photographic work as forms of psychic healing: a way of revisiting childhood, of understanding and exploring relationships, and arriving at new understandings of self. Women's bodies have always been the subject of representation, so it is not surprising to find photographers among those many feminist artists creating new forms of imagery that aim to celebrate and redefine the body, sexualities and female identity. Equally, however, it is important to interrogate ideas of empowerment that such photographic strategies imply. Spence (1991) herself is cautious about what the process involves:

> I'm not saying that because you have other knowledge you rid yourself of the disease. I am saying that armed with new knowledge you are able to make choices to act rather than be acted upon.
>
> (p. 188)

Rosenblaum (1991) noted that the ability of the camera to access subjectivity is limited. It is a universalising instrument that results in seeing things as human, rather than individuals, and there is a danger that images 'devolve into cultural clichés' (p. 243). Inevitably, she argues, photographic accounts may be impoverished in charting someone's personal journey with, as in her case, dying.

Photographic discourse can thus be both political and therapeutic in the context of people's experience of health and illness. It is suggested here that a component of this is using such visual images or techniques as a means by which persons or communities may present the subjective experience of illness. An additional form of power is confronted in the process whereby 'barriers' to taboo areas – to bodies which are sick and dying in particular, are challenged (Bertoia, 1993). It has been in the model of collaborative projects with people, whether in research, development or therapeutic settings, in which relational aspects of power have been the main emphasis. The power relations challenged in this way are largely conceived of to be those between professional (research or health care) and lay people or patients; those of gender where male-dominated medicine is viewed as at odds with women's experiences; and able-bodied presumptions of how we should 'see' those whom we have 'disabled', including through our use of imagery.

The forms of photographic re-presentation that we have considered above as forms of resistance, will achieve this in part through public consumption of these images. While many projects initially begin as a personal or collective project of redefinition, or of making sense of experiences, they often reach far wider audiences. In other cases the aim at the outset is to 'shock', to challenge, to create new forms of visibility for public consumption. Examples such as the Camerawork projects and Jo Spence's work were public exhibitions. In a recent exhibition Marilyn Manchot showed 40 nude photographs of her mother. The series confronts, the photographer argues, 'a real taboo around ageing – particularly about showing older women's bodies' (Lacey, 1997) and the wider invisibility of older women, which underpins the work, again suggests a merging of personal production with wider political agendas for public consumption.

There is one further power relation that has been addressed in the context of imagery production as a means of resistance – that of professional dominance of doctors over nurses. To date the focus for this redefinition of the relation of nursing to medicine (and of women to men) has been to revisit ideas of 'art' versus 'science'. In nursing, the value placed on the visual is as 'art', and an explicit contrast is thus drawn between ideas of science and its related concept of cure (the medical model) and 'art' as related to the caring component of nursing work. In reclaiming an aesthetic component of nursing as an art, some nurses have suggested the caring component of nursing can be likened to that of the artist producer (see Hess's (1995) discussion of her work as a stained-glass maker and nurse).[5] However, it remains to be seen whether returning to a dualism of art versus science, and cure versus care will be a successful political strategy for nurses in their struggle over occupational boundaries, expert knowledge and skills and the claim to professional power, although it may open up new understandings of suffering which those for whom they care experience.

CONCLUSION

In this chapter, the role of vision, and photography as one form of visual technology, has been considered in relation to Foucauldian arguments about the growth of institutions permitting the exercise of disciplinary power. Knowledge and power, it is argued, are inextricably bound up with observation and documentation. Photographic records provided both of these within health and welfare institutions of the late nineteenth century, and it can be argued such forms of surveillance continue through new techniques into the present century. Through an examination of medical photography these themes were explored, commencing from the presumption that photographs used to aid the daily work of medical practitioners indeed might even be regarded as essential to it, and those which are integrated into institutional publicity practices that are designed to sell models of professionalism, and the successes of health-care work, serve to maintain existing power relations between doctors and nurses, between health-care professionals and patients or clients. Equally, such representations maintain the power/knowledge relationship, most evidently seen in contemporary uses of camera images which may only be 'read' by those with highly specialised knowledge and skills.

Finally, the chapter suggests that photography may be used to increase the political participation of people, and provide them with personal perspectives on their health and on health-care services. Examples here suggest that this may be a way of making sense of one's situation for oneself, or it may act as a challenge to other definitions and stereotypes, thus providing a resistance to existing power relations. There is a necessary caution to the political possibilities of imagery, especially as it can be difficult to find new visual codes that can break out of conventional genres of representation.

In this chapter we have aimed to demonstrate that the possibilities of the exercise of power and forms of resistance through the use of photographic technologies and imagery involve ideas and social relations of consumption. Indeed, the traditional divisions of photographic production between amateur or 'everyday' or personal imagery, and professional, official or public imagery are not clear-cut. Productions by one can be consumed by others, the public by the private and the private in public forms. There are two commodities, the camera and the photograph, and producers and consumers become part of a complex set of social relations that are often obscured when seeing and seenness seem to be one process. Furthermore, the very content and compositional structures of photographic images suggest that social convention and social symbolism are utilised by amateur and professional image makers alike, as holiday photographs exemplify. To do the 'work' of communicating particular messages to audiences or viewers, similar conventions will be employed. This is the case with the exhibitions of types of 'resistance' imagery as it is with advertising. Williams (1980) argues that mass camera consumption has necessitated a control over image production, citing 'the very folders our snaps are returned in' as an example. Equally, however, the development of photographic conventions may not be a one-way traffic. Drawing on everyday and personal imagery may ensure the social function of other types of photographic imagery.

An understanding of the social role of the photograph also requires attention to its historical location, as this case study has demonstrated. It can be argued that in modernity photography was not only important to knowledge but also to the communication of identity. In a fascinating study of the history of photographic practices in Mali by Elder (1997) the heterogeneity and changing nature of the practice and imagery served to confirm identities in place and space and in relation to the world of goods. In this way photography inscribes people with identities as consumers, as configuring social position. In Mali, Elder argues, it was 'a "tool" to assemble and organise not only the world of meaning but also the practical exigencies of the modern world' (p. 245) as in the practice of ID photography. Historical and contemporary analyses suggest that there are many different types of photographs, taken in different settings for different reasons and for multiple audiences. The consumption of images in terms of their interpretation and meaning can also be local despite an increasing tendency to their consumption as part of global forms of communication. These complex relations and social practices involved in camera use and productions over time offer considerable scope for further scrutiny by sociologists, who must eschew the modernist project of privileging camera observations as visual documents of 'truth'. Rather we need to locate photography as a set of visual practices within a historical and social or cultural context, including the possibilities for power/resistance.

NOTES

1. For this reason and to assist the further development of what remains a relatively underdeveloped area of sociology, an extended bibliography is included.
2. Fyfe and Law use the term visual depiction to refer to both the process of production and the product, whereas we would prefer to use the word depiction solely as a descriptor for photographic images as representations.
3. This advertisement for Canon cameras shows an image of a woman in a smock-like uniform being confronted by two policemen, with the caption 'actress? inmate? recruit?'

4. These historical uses of the photograph, and the relation between science and art, were addressed in a recent exhibition 'In Visible Light' at the Museum of Modern Art, Oxford, March–July 1997.
5. This dualism of the lost art of nursing in a paradigm dominated by science has been used to defend the use of artistic works in pedagogical practice in order to give nurses access to private worlds of suffering (Darbyshire, 1994)

REFERENCES

Apple, R. (1988) 'Image or Reality? Photographs in the History of Nursing', in Jones, A. H. (ed.), *Images of Nurses: Perspectives from History, Art and Literature* (Philadelphia, PA: University of Pennsylvania Press).

Armstrong, D. (1983) *The Political Anatomy of the Body* (Cambridge: Cambridge University Press).

Barry, A. (1995) 'Reporting and Visualising', in Jenks, C. (ed.), *Visual Culture* (London: Routledge).

Barthes, R. (1981) *Camera Lucida* (New York: Noonday Press).

Bertoia, J. (1993) *Drawings from a Dying Child: Insights into Death from a Jungian Perspective* (London: Routledge).

Betterton, R. (ed) (1987) *Looking On: Images of Femininity in the Visual Arts and Media* (London: Routledge).

Bourdieu, P. (1990) *Photography: A Middle-brow Art* (Cambridge: Polity).

Camerawork, (1988) *A Sense of Self* (London: Camerawork).

Camerawork (1990) *Silent Health: Women, Health and Representation* (London: Camerawork).

Chaplin, E. (1994) *Sociology and Visual Representation* (London: Routledge).

Cohen, P. (1989) *Really Useful Knowledge: Photography and Cultural Studies in the Transition from School* (London: Trentham Books).

Darbyshire, P. (1994) 'Understanding a Life of Illness Through the Art of Frida Kahlo', *Advances in Nursing Science,* 17(1): 51–5

Edholm, F. (1992) 'Beyond the Mirror: Women's Self Portraits', in Bonner, F., Goodman, L. *et al.* (eds), *Imagining Women: Cultural Representations and Gender* (Cambridge: Polity, in association with the Open University).

Elder, T. (1997) *Capturing Change: The Practice of Malian Photography* (Linkoping: Linkoping University, Sweden).

Foucault, M. (1977) *Discipline and Punish* (London: Allen Lane).

Foucault, M. (1980) 'The Eye of Power', in Gordon, C. (ed.), *Power/Knowledge: Selected Interviews and Writings, 1972–77* (New York: Pantheon).

Fox, D. and Lawrence, C. (1989) *Photographing Medicine: Images and Power in Britain and America since 1840,* Contributions in Medical Studies, No. 10 (New York: Greenwood Press).

Fyfe, G. and Law, J. (1988) (eds) *Picturing Power: Visual Depiction and Social Relations,* Sociological Review Monograph 35 (London: Routledge).

Gilman, S. (1982) *Seeing the Insane* (New York: John Wiley and Sons).

Green, D. (1984) 'Classified Subjects', *TEN-8*: *Quarterly Photographic Journal*, 14: 30–7.
Green, D. (1985) 'On Foucault: Disciplinary Power and Photography', *Camerawork*, 32 (Summer) 6–9.
Hagedorn, M. (1994) 'Hermeneutic Photography: An Innovative Aesthetic Technique for Generating Data in Nursing Research', *Advances in Nursing Science*, 17(1): 44–50.
Hamilton, P. (1997) 'Representing the Social: France, Frenchness in Post-War Humanist Photography', in Hall, S. (ed.), *Representation: Cultural Representations and Signifying Practices* (London: Sage).
Harper, D. (1994) 'On the Authority of the Image', in Denzin, N. and Guba, E. (eds), *The Handbook of Qualitative Research* (Beverley Hills: Sage).
Hearn, J. (1992) *Men in the Public Eye* (London: Routledge).
Hess, J. (1995) 'The Art of Stained Glass: A Metaphor for the Art of Nursing', *Nursing Inquiry*, 2: 221–223
Hevey, D. (1992) *Creatures that Time Forgot: Photography and Disability Imagery* (London: Routledge).
Hudson Jones, A. (ed.) (1988) *Images of Nurses: Perspectives from History, Art and Literature* (Philadelphia, PA: University of Pennsylvania Press).
Jamous, H. and Peloille, B. (1970) 'Changes in the French University Hospital System', in Jackson, J. (ed.), *Professions and Professionalisation* (Cambridge: Cambridge University Press).
Jenks, C. (ed.) (1995) *Visual Culture* (London: Routledge).
Jordanova, L. (1987) *Sexual Visions: Images of Gender in Science and Medicine Between the Eighteenth and Nineteenth Centuries* (Brighton, Harvester-Wheatsheaf).
Karpf, A. (1988) *Doctoring the Media: The Reporting of Health and Medicine* (London: Routledge).
Kember, S. (1995) 'Medicine's New Vision?', in Lister, M. (ed.), *The Photographic Image in Digital Culture* (London: Routledge).
Lacey, H. (1997) 'Flesh and Blood: A Voyage Round My Mother', *The Independent on Sunday*, 21 September 1997, p. 5.
Loftus, B. (1988) 'Northern Ireland 1968–1988: Enter an Art Historian in Search of the Theory', in Fyfe, G. and Law, J. (eds), *Picturing Power: Visual Depiction and Social Relations*, Sociological Review Monograph, 35 (London: Routledge).
McGrath, R. (1984) 'Medical Police', *TEN-8: Quarterly Photographic Journal*, 14: 13–18
Mayes, S. and Stein, L. (eds) (1993) *Positive Lives: Responses to HIV – A Photodocumentary* (London: Cassell).
Mulvey, L. and Wollen, P. (1987) 'The Discourse on the Body', in Betterton, R. (ed.), *Looking On: Images of Femininity in the Visual Arts and Media* (London: Pandora).
O'Neill, C. (1989) *A Picture of Health: Hospitals and Nursing in Old Picture Postcards* (Meadow Books).
O'Neill, C. (1991) *More Pictures of Health: Hospitals and Nursing in Old Picture Postcards* (Meadow Books).
O'Neill, J. (1995) 'Foucault's Optics: The (in)vision of Mortality and Modernity', in Jenks, C. (ed.), *Visual Culture* (London: Routledge).

Pasveer, B. (1989) 'Knowledge of the Shadows: the Introduction of X–ray Images into Medicine', *Sociology of Health and Illness*, 11(4): 360–81.
Petchesky, R. (1987) 'Foetal Images: the Power of Visual Culture in the Politics of Reproduction', in Stanworth, M. (ed.), *Reproductive Technologies: Gender, Motherhood and Medicine* (Cambridge: Polity).
Pryce, A. (1996) 'Visual Imagery and the Iconography of the Social World: some Considerations of History, Art and Problems for Sociological Research', in Lyon, E. S. and Busfield, J. (eds), *Methodological Imaginations* (London: Macmillan).
Rose, N. (1990) 'The Visible Invisible: Picturing Madness', *Free Associations*, 20: 75–84.
Rosen, G. (1974) *From Medical Police to Social Medicine* (New York: Science History Publications).
Rosenblaum, B. (1991) 'I Have Begun the Process of Dying', in Holland, P. and Spence, J. (eds), *Family Snapshots* (London: Camden Press).
Short, P. (1995) 'Our Pictures of Us', *Nursing Inquiry* 2: 224–6
Showalter, E. (1987) *The Female Malady: Women, Madness and English Culture, 1830–1980* (London: Virago).
Slater, D. (1995) 'Photography and Modern Vision: the Spectacle of "Natural Magic"', in Jenks, C. (ed.), *Visual Culture* (London: Routledge).
Sontag, S. (1978) *On Photography* (London: Penguin).
Spence, J. (1986) *Putting Myself in the Picture: A Personal, Political and Photographic Autobiography* (London: Camden Press).
Spence, J. (1991) 'My Consultant Wouldn't Like It', in Camerawork, *Silent Health* (London: Camerawork Press).
Spence, J. (1995) *Cultural Sniping* (London: Routledge).
Spence, J. and Martin, R. (1987) 'The Use of the Camera in Therapy', in Betterton, R. (ed.), *Looking On: Images of Femininity in the Visual Arts and Media* (London: Pandora).
Spence, J. and Martin, R. (1988) 'Photo-therapy: Psychic Realism as a Healing Art', *TEN-8: Quarterly Photographic Journal,* 30: 2–17.
Stoeckle, J. D. and White, C. A. (1985) *Plain Pictures of Plain Doctoring: Vernacular Expression and New Deal Medicine* (Cambridge, MA: MIT Press).
Tagg, J. (1982) 'The Currency of the Photograph', in Burgin, V. (ed.), *Thinking Photographically* (London, Macmillan).
Tagg, J. (1988) *The Burden of Representation* (London: Macmillan).
Wang, C. and Burris, M. (1994) 'Empowerment through Photo Novella: Portraits of Participation', *Health Education Quarterly*, 21: 171–86.
Wang, C., Ling, Y.Y. and Ling, F. M. (1996) 'Photovoice as a Tool for Participatory Evaluation: the Community's View of Process and Impact', *Journal of Contemporary Health* 4: 47–9.
Williamson, J. (1980) *Decoding Advertisements* (London: Marion Boyars).
Williamson, J. (1984) 'Family, Education and Photography', *TEN-8: Quarterly Photographic Journal*, 14: 20–3.
Ziller, R. (1990) *Photographing the Self: Methods for Observing Personal Orientations* (Newbury Park: Sage).

9 'It was the way we were watching it': Young Men Negotiate Pornography

RACHEL THOMSON

It was the way we were watching it, it was more than to get sexual enjoyment out of it, it was a laugh, it was.

(Young man, esw[1], working class, aged 19)

INTRODUCTION

Heterosexual pornography is an increasingly visible presence in contemporary Western culture, a presence that demands both acknowledgement and negotiation. Yet, there is surprisingly little empirical work concerning the place of pornography within everyday life, or what Ross has called 'the social practice of pornography' (Ross, 1989: 175).[2] These everyday negotiations have been largely ignored by an academic and political debate that became absorbed by questions of cause, effect and definition (Itzin and Sweet, 1993; Segal 1993). In this chapter I hope to move beyond these questions and positions in order to account for the processes through which young men 'make sense' of pornography and through which pornography 'makes sense of them'. By reflecting on the way a group of young men describe accessing, witnessing and consuming pornography, I explore how the cultures and the technologies of pornographic consumption are implicated in the everyday processes through which boys become men.[3]

The widespread presence of heterosexual male pornography within a culture is, however complicated, an expression of and a resource for the social and cultural power of its intended audience. Studies of masculinity have identified pornography as playing a part in the development of homosocial (Hearn, 1985) and hegemonic (Connell, 1989) masculinity, through bringing men into identification with other men through the exclusion and objectification of women.[4] Feminist responses to pornography continue to be polarised, and characterised on one hand by a commitment to confront pornography as an expression of male power (for example, see Itzin, 1993) and on the other by a curiosity about the operations of the pornographic narrative and gaze and the potential to disrupt them through transgressions of performance and identification (for example, see Church Gibson and Gibson, 1993). The complexity of the pornographic narrative has been pursued by a number of commentators who have observed that, while heterosexual pornography may be an expression of the social power of men, pornography may also reflect and deflect a neediness that lies at the heart of heterosexual masculinity (Dyer, 1985; Moye, 1985; Segal, 1990).

The social practices of heterosexual pornography can be seen as providing an interface between the masculinities of individual men and heterosexual masculinity as a collective project. In this respect pornography can be seen as a collective form of exemplary masculinity, which Connell (1995) describes as 'the use of culture for disciplinary purposes: setting standards, claiming assent and discrediting those who fall short' (Connell, 1995: 214). Pornography brings young men into identification with a form of homosocial masculinity, a masculinity that defines itself oppositionally. The rewards of this form of homosocial masculinity are collective rewards: identification with other men, the assertion of gender difference and the creation of male spaces. Yet, I will suggest, the disciplines of pornography also operate at a more intimate level and in ways that can jeopardise the masculinity of individual men. By entering into the pornographic narrative and by accepting the fantasy of 'male transcendence and female passivity' (Segal, 1993: 12) men risk undermining a sense of masculinity that is based on 'real' sex with 'real' women in the 'real' world. While the social disciplines of heterosexual pornography can signal and affirm the power of heterosexual men, the intimate disciplines may reveal the dependency that lies at the heart of the forms of masculinity through which this power is claimed.

I begin by looking at the circumstances within which young men report *encountering* pornography, and suggest that this encounter is one of the ways in which young men are implicated in a collective masculinity. Looked at in this way the display and circulation of pornography becomes a 'conversation between men' through which young men are brought into an identification with other men across generation and social divides. This is an identification with a homosocial masculinity, that signals the masculinity of physical, social and imaginative spaces through the exclusion of women. I then consider young men's accounts of how they *engage* with pornography, paying particular attention to how they position themselves in relation to, if not within, a disciplinary pornographic narrative. I suggest that, although pornography appears to offer young men power, it also presents a threat to the masculinity of individuals. I present a number of young men's accounts of how they read, watch or witness this material, which are, I suggest, primarily accounts concerned with resistance to these disciplines. Commonly asserted distinctions between 'ways of watching' pornography (including denials of arousal, assertions of humour and the questioning of the relationship between reality and representation) reflect considerable ambivalence towards being the subject of the sexual narrative of pornography.

DRAWING THE LINES OF A MAN'S WORLD

The young men's accounts discussed here show clearly that the environment and relationships within which pornography is encountered play an important part in shaping the meanings that are made of it. Traditional boundaries of gender and space, including gendered notions of 'public' and 'private', have been disrupted by changing patterns of employment as well as the consequences of advances in media technology. Pornography can be seen as one vehicle through which these spaces are renegotiated and contested. One of the most intriguing examples of this is the way in which the presence of pornography can signal masculinity within the domestic space. The growth of home video, satellite and cable television has brought pornography from marginal spaces of the public into the front room and into the heart of the domestic (Ross, 1989).

All except one of the young men in this study, who were asked about pornography, reported having seen either or both pornographic magazines or films. This level of familiarity is reflected in the findings of surveys which suggest that over 90 per cent of young men have seen pornography by the time they are 16 (Kelly *et al.,* 1991). While the reactions of these young men to this material varied, it was widely understood to be a ubiquitous presence in the culture.

> **Q:** Would you say that a lot of young men look at porn?
> **A:** ... I think everybody; 99 per cent of the population would have looked at them, looked at videos.
>
> (Young man, esw, working class, aged 20).

Yet while pornography is understood as a fact of a wider, public culture, it was encountered within the private or domestic space and in the context of relationships with other men. All of the young men who reported encountering pornography in this study, did so through other men. In some cases this was male peers and in others older male relatives.

> They had got them off their Dads and all that. All the friends had brothers and that's where they get them from.
>
> (Young man, working class, ac, aged 17).

> I slept round my cousin's and his friends were in there and the video was on. And I came down and they said 'what are you doing? Get out'. I said 'what do you mean?' ... I remember him saying 'You're not ready for it yet man'.
>
> (Young man, working class, ac, aged 16)

These young men cannot be said to 'choose' pornography, but rather they encounter it as a fact of life. The process through which they learn to accommodate the images that they see in pornography and the associated meanings, with what they come to know of real men, women and sexuality is beset with contradiction and tension. Positioning themselves in relation to pornography is one part of the process of negotiating what kind of man to be, and while there is nothing inevitable about how they will manage this process, they are likely to confront an identification of pornography with masculinity and the sexuality of adult men. For a number of young men, the image of adult male sexuality that they read from pornography was disturbing and unattractive.

> I used to stay at my sister's flat, her boyfriend used to have them, I use to call him pervert, sexual pervert.
>
> (Young man, working class, esw, aged 16)

> I don't really like them ... Just the insensitiveness of them and the hardness ... older people, it turns them on because they're used to everything else, in a way, and you're always looking for new things if you're older.
>
> (Young man, middle class, mixed, aged 21)

> First time I saw it I thought ugh, is that what it looks like ugh! ... I went to see the film and then ugh! Ugh! Like making all these noises and I think why doesn't she kick him off her if it's hurting her

> so. I just couldn't understand why they just accepted it, but that's how it is.
>
> (young man, working class, ac, aged 16)

Implicit in the identification of pornography with the sexuality of adult men comes an assertion of gender difference – the recognition that pornography excludes or is at the expense of women. While women can and do participate in and even disrupt the gaze of heterosexual pornography (Kotz 1993; Williams, 1993), more commonly women respond to such imagery with discomfort (Kelly *et al.*, 1991; Itzin and Sweet, 1993).[5] Such discomfort or opposition was widely cited by the young men in this study, although a number of them questioned how genuine these responses were. Although some young men reported sometimes watching pornography in mixed friendship groups, it was nevertheless understood to be an activity that excluded women, including girlfriends:

> Not with the girlfriends around. You know what I mean? ... They make out that they're not into that, but really they are. They're just embarrassed because they are trying to say its disgusting and they're going like this. They feel they have to say 'Oh God horrible, switch it off.' I have watched a few in front of a few girls but they always complain so we switch it off.
>
> (Young man, working class, mixed, aged 19)

female friends:

> Some of them don't like it, some of them don't mind it and don't give a shit what happens. But I think the majority of girls don't like you watching it ... they just think you are perverted.
>
> (Young man, working class, esw, aged 16)

and mothers:

> At first it taught me a lot, so in a way I think it's a good thing ... it's not a good thing if it gets into the wrong hands, like little boys or your mum. People who don't like it because they think it's revolting.
>
> (young man, working class, ac, aged 16)

The young men's frequent use of the words such as 'disgusting', 'revolting' and 'perverted' to describe the response of women to pornography, as well as some of their own response to the material, suggests that pornography transgresses the boundaries of both femininity and of respectability. Part of the association of pornography with masculinity and with homosocial culture appears to be this exclusion of the 'obscene' from the 'on scene' or mainstream (Williams, 1993) or, as Ross suggests in his account of the popularity of pornography, the large stake that pornography has in celebrating delinquency (Ross, 1989). As the following young man suggests, pornography is not supposed to be socially acceptable:

> It was, I don't know, it was a bit, it's not social acceptance, it's still not socially acceptable to watch porn films, that's why you have to make copies and get them off your mates, if it was socially acceptable you would have it on television and so the situation you was in was a bit of a laugh, look at the size of them and all the rest of it, it was a big joke.
>
> (Young man, working class, esw, aged 19)

However, as several young men noted, the increasing availability of pornography through home-based popular media, such as cable and satellite, as well as the increasing visibility of the sexual in mainstream media, suggests that the lines between the obscene and the mainstream may be less clearly drawn than in the past:

> There's Sky now ... and sometimes when you're flicking through you'll see things that are quite, well not shock you, but I mean, you'll think maybe it shouldn't be on television and it's very close to quite graphic porn.
>
> (Young man, middle class, esw, aged 17)

> It's in every other book, you see it in newspapers, see it on the tele, it's just a way of life.
>
> (Young man, working class, esw, aged 16)

And changes in the imagery of some heterosexual pornography, including the push towards a female market and the rise of the 'couple's film', also disrupts the traditional associations and uses of pornography:

> Some of the videos are just women but in other ones there are blokes in it as well, so I think everyone these days would just laugh.
>
> (Young man, working class, esw, aged 20)

While these shifts in the pornographic market may have disrupted the gender identifications of heterosexual pornography, the social practices of pornography reported by the young men in this study suggest that pornography continues to play a part in the assertions of gender difference. For example, while sexual imagery may have proliferated in mainstream media, watching pornography in the home, and more specifically in the house of your mother, can still be a deliberate and meaningful act. At least one young man explained that it would be impossible for him to watch 'sex films' at home (the house of his aunt) for this reason, and that he would need a place of his own or he would have to watch it in a cinema or at a friend's house. The following young man's account of watching a hard-core video before sitting down to dinner with his parents is particularly revealing. The only person not in the joke is the mother and without the mother, the joke would not be funny

> [There was] quite a famous film around school that somebody had, I borrowed it off him, went back to my house with a couple of friends to watch it and my Dad came in. And he was like watching it as well, looking at us, going 'disgusting people', and then we had dinner and it was pork chop and all of a sudden (this guy had been bonking a pig) and I've never eaten pork since, it's disgusting.
>
> (Young man, middle class, esw, aged 20).

The family politics surrounding the consumption of pornography within the home are intriguing and would bear further investigation. While few young men reported receiving any explicit sex education from their fathers, the expression of vicarious pleasure at their son's sexual activity, as well as the sharing of pornography, provided the sole forms of communication about sex with their fathers for a number of the young men in the study. The following extracts suggest that pornography can facilitate identification between men over generations. In taking up the position of viewer, men are implicated in a community of interpretation which Moye (1985: 53) describes as being characterised by a shared 'gaze and itch in the groin'.

> **Q:** Your father was quite happy to let you watch it?
> **A:** Yes, when he went to bed at night, all you heard from downstairs was the video winding forward then stopping and watching then going forward again, he was watching it as well.
>
> (Young man, middle class, esw, aged 20)

Dad's got some, when I'm down in his room and look at them and things.

Q: Does he know that you look at them?

A: He knows that I look at them.

Q: Does he mind?

A: No, he don't mind, it's part of growing up.

Q: What about your Mum, does she know?

A: She knows I've got a video, but she doesn't actually ask if you know what I mean, so I just keep it away from her.

(Young man, working class, esw, aged 17)

This assertion of a masculinity defined in opposition to femininity and women can also facilitate identification between men across other social divides,[6] such as the case of the following young man who reported being discovered by his boss reading a pornographic magazine:

> I had this burning feeling in my shoulder I looked round and it was my boss and I went Ahhhhh. This bloody centre fold opens and this woman and I just turned the page. And he said 'Gordon Bennett! My wife looks nothing like that'. He was alright about it ... so he said 'I know what it's like'.
>
> (Young man, working class, esw, aged 20)

This suggests that one of the ways in which men use heterosexual pornography is to signal and assert the difference of masculinity and to create masculine space. In almost all cases the young men in this study reported using pornography with other men, thereby, I would suggest, creating homosocial spaces. For younger respondents this generally meant the territory occupied by male friendship groups ranging from 'huddled around a classroom desk' to 'some abandoned place', 'down by the canal' and 'over at my mates'. For older respondents this could include public spaces such as snooker halls and for a few, the workplace.

> One morning you will come in and there will be a porn mag on there, everyone comes in and has a look through it, she's nice, I wouldn't mind going to bed with that and all the rest of it. There is always a film floating around at work.
>
> (Young man, working class, esw, aged 19)

or the space occupied by workmates

> We basically watch them at work, so its basically around Christmas time, we can go out, you get your porno, you watch it, you go out for a meal and then you go out to a club or something.
>
> (Young man, working class, esw, aged 20)

The effects of the public display of pornography are to simultaneously assert the masculinity of a space and to challenge the presence of women or to affirm their absence. Studies of the workplace suggest that the circulation of pornography provides a means through which men can communicate with each other, with women acting as the currency rather than the subject of communication (Hearn, 1985; Ross, 1989; Collinson and Hearn, 1996). It is a conversation between men that requires female silence or complicity and which is vulnerable to subversion through female ridicule (see Blackman, 1995).

The circumstances and relationships through which young men encounter pornography shape its meaning. In one respect young men encounter pornography as an expression of broader relations of power. The fact that porn exists and is accessible is an expression of the power of men within the culture. Yet young men also encounter pornography within relationships with other men through which they are implicated in a collective and exclusive form of masculinity. While young men may resist or refuse this identification, and while they may not actively choose or seek out pornography, they nevertheless have a relationship with it.

> I said I'd never bought one, never felt the need to buy one. Never hired a porn film out. Dad tends to have them out more than I have, but then again that doesn't happen very often, say two or three times in the last couple of years or something. It's just, you know, seeing as it is there I'll have a look at that.
>
> (Young man, working class, esw, aged 20)

It is this tension between the individual and their investment in (or complicity with) broader social relations of power that provides the focus of the next section, through an exploration of young men's accounts of the ways in which they watch pornography.

THE WAY WE WATCH THEM: HUMOUR AND THE NEGOTIATION OF AGENCY

The most common circumstance for the consumption of pornography reported by young men in the study was the gathering of a group of male friends within the home to watch a video.[7]

> I used to pick my video up, trundle off over to his house and we would have a group of us sitting there having a few cans of beer and watching sort of porn films.
>
> (Young man, working class, esw, aged 19)

> Most of my mates have got pornos of some sort, videos or magazines. ... When I go out and when I've got friends round we sit and watch it.
>
> (Young man, working class, esw, aged 16)

While most young men spoke positively of this pastime, the words of the following young man show how participation in such group activities may be difficult to avoid:

> You have to sit and watch these, it's disgusting. I feel like putting 10p in the slot or whatever.
> **Q:** What, so you don't watch them?
> **A:** Well, I watch them but I don't like them, I just sit and watch it.
> **Q:** Maybe they are all doing that.
> **A:** Half of them want to watch them, I think. When the new thing comes on that they would never know, then they say 'I'll remember that'. Half the time I go and raid their cupboards, open up their fridge and have a pint of milk and biscuits and crisps and bars of chocolate.
>
> (Young man, working class, esw, aged 16)

Although readers and researchers may contemplate the homoerotic charge of such situations in which young men collectively negotiate the meanings of pornography, such an interpretation was dismissed by the young men.

> **Q:** When you used to watch it with groups of friends, I mean how did that feel, sitting around with them.

A: That didn't bother me funny enough. It was because the way we were watching it, it was more than to get sexual enjoyment out of it, it was a laugh.

(Young man, working class, esw, aged 19)

The acknowledgement of homoerotic potential in such circumstances was more common among middle-class young men, some of whom took pains to explain that they watched these films in mixed company.

Q: Was it an all male group or was it a mixed group of friends?
A: No, I think every time I have its been mixed. ... Yeah, every time I've watched them, only once or twice anyway, its been with mixed ... we've just put it on for a laugh. Never actually watched one seriously, you know, sex in front of one or watched one to get turned on.

(Young man, middle class, mixed, 21)

A more oblique defence against a homoerotic reading of such cultures of consumption, which transcended differences of class and culture, was the widespread distinction that young men made between consuming pornography 'seriously' and watching or reading it for 'a laugh'. While 'watching seriously' was associated with either being alone and masturbation or with watching with a sexual partner, 'watching for a laugh' *required* the participation of a group. For most of these young men, it appears that the participation of a group insures against the meanings, if not the feelings associated with the erotic.

It's more humorous than a sexual kind of thing.

(Young man, working class, esw, aged 20)

I don't read them on my own, just with friends, for a laugh, not as a stimulant for sex.

(Young man, middle class, esw, aged 16)

It is notoriously difficult to interpret humour or to find a single interpretation to fit in any one situation. I would suggest that the assertion by these young men that such situations were funny is a sign that there is an instability or ambiguity of meaning. The assertion of humour suggests that these young men are, at some level, seeking to subvert what they take to be the intended meanings of the pornography.

There are a range of ways in which we could interpret this expression of humour and denial of arousal. At one level humour can express the shared meanings of a group providing an effective check on membership. Joking and laughing unite people; 'this integrating and boundary-setting function is, of course, of special importance when the group is somehow endangered or threatened' (Zijderveld, 1983: 47). To not get the joke, to not think 'its a laugh' is both to question and to be excluded from the spoils of masculinity. Humour has been identified as characterising the homosocial activities of heterosexual men and boys. Jokes that ritually objectify women may in some way serve to protect against homoeroticism (Collinson and Hearn, 1996). Laughter can then be a response to, or even a practice of, objectification, necessary for the protection of a heterosexual masculinity that is premised on an identification with other men.

There is a further explanation of the assertion of humour that is concerned with the dispersal of agency and the avoidance of the disciplines of the pornographic narrative (Moye, 1985; Dyer, 1985). From the young men's accounts it is possible to identify a boundary between pornography as part of the banter and humour that characterises the collective world of men, and pornography as revealing the desires and vulnerabilities of the individual. While many young men were comfortable with the former, few were comfortable with the latter, which was most commonly invoked through the figure of the 'pervert'. By policing a boundary between 'respectable' and 'dangerous' masculinities within a dichotomised discourse of male sexuality, the figure of the pervert safely carries the ambivalent feelings about adult male sexuality experienced by these young men, while also serving to displace any fears of dependency that might be suggested by pornography.[8]

Q: Why do you say that people who look at porn are perverts?
A: If somebody goes out of their way every 5 minutes to look at porn things and mags I suppose they are perverted in a way.
(Young man, working class, esw, aged 20)

The 'pervert' is someone who 'needs' pornography, someone who buys pornography, someone who watches or looks at pornography on their own and who is aroused by it. Although several young men did report being aroused by pornography, and using it for masturbation, they were careful to distinguish the source of their arousal.

Q: What was the attraction around it then?
A: The fact that it was forbidden I suppose.
Q: It wasn't sexually exciting?
A: Yes, very arousing. I think, yes it was, but whether it was the actual acts going on, or the actual act of watching and thinking 'the dirty idiot', I don't know. Yes it was arousing, that was the normal sex in it.

(Young man, middle class, esw, aged 20)

For most (and particularly for middle-class young men), the means by which pornography was accessed, the degree of agency involved in accessing it, and extent of ownership implied by a relationship of consumption became centrally important in their accounts.

> I don't go out of my way to watch it but if it happens, I'll like spend a few minutes watching.
>
> (Young man, middle class, esw, aged 17)

> I've never had my own, maybe looked at other people's, but I've never actually bought magazines. I mean I've seen porn videos round at friends houses but I've never actually had my own.
>
> (Young man, middle class, mixed, aged 20)

> I would never use pornography as a stimulant for masturbation or anything like that so whenever I watch it was for a laugh, a thing to do like, with blokes and girls just sitting around laughing at it, because it's sort of a funny thing.
>
> (Young man, middle class, esw, aged 16)

If we accept that this ethical ambivalence is more than the absence of a vocabulary to describe pleasure (Ross, 1989) or a reticence to identify themselves in an interview situation with something that they consider to be socially unacceptable, it appears that at some level these young men are avoiding an individual relationship with pornography. The avoidance of agency that can be heard in these young men's accounts is strongly reminiscent of that which infuses young women's descriptions of sexual encounters (Holland *et al.,* 1996). Sex 'happens', it is not done. Our analysis sought to explain this absence of agency as a consequence of a discourse of heterosexuality within which subject and object positions are gendered male and female respectively. Would an extension of this reading to the young men's accounts of pornography indicate that they are rendered the objects of a pornographic discourse? I suggest that within these young men's accounts lies the sense that there is something potentially disempowering, or emasculating about the visual language of pornography which 'to work must establish a universe in which all men are sexually desirable because they are desired ... it works by denying the reality which men know and often believe to be true' (Moye, 1985: 55). This was something that was implicit in most accounts, but recognised explicitly by the following young man who points out, at the heart of heterosexual pornography there is a seductive lie, that the model is looking at and desiring you.[9] The way in which her gaze is met has significance for individual agency and masculinity.

> Everybody always thinks that the girl is actually looking at you, and they are not. That's why I would rather look at the letters and stuff like that. Because all the girl is doing is looking at the camera smiling, or having a look of lust on her face and getting paid for it. You look at a girl and you think 'I wouldn't mind knocking her off' and stuff like that. But most of the time it's just lust.
>
> (Young man, working class, esw, aged 20)

Although laughing at pornography with a group of others can be a powerful expression of masculinity, becoming subject to the disciplines of this pornographic narrative through 'watching it seriously' or believing what it shows, presents dangers. As Moye points out, 'masturbation, not sex with a woman, is the natural counterpart to pornography' (Moye, 1985: 53) and the pornographic narrative can lead 'real men' away from the 'real world' and 'real women' (see also Hite, 1981). If the dangers of pornography for heterosexual men lie in complicity with the gaze of the centrefold, then resistance appears to lie in the demystification of the pornographic fantasy.

The same young man who observed the dangers of the model's gaze, explains how the disjunction between the world of pornographic representation and fantasy and his and his friends' experience becomes a source of humour.[10]

> Everybody just sits back and laughs at it, because like all these sounds that you hear them making, they hardly ever really happen. You know, 'give it to me, give it to me'. When you're actually sleeping with someone you don't say that. ... The things that they say to

> each other ... 'suck harder', we just crack up laughing, because can you imagine a girl saying that? More like 'shut up – go away'.
>
> (Young man, working class, esw, aged 20)

While some young men were clear that the representations of pornography presented a fantasy world of female submission, this distinction was not always clear or stable. While I do not suggest the operation of simple causal relationships between representation, fantasy and reality, the accounts of this group of young men do suggest that the domains of the pornographic representation and their own intimate relations exist in an state of 'unresolvable tension' (Kotz, 1993: 108). This tension can be illustrated in many ways. For example one young man reported asking his first girlfriend to strip naked so that he could check if the images that he had seen in pornography were 'true' or, in his words 'like some kind of cartoons' (working class, ac, aged 16). Another responded to the shock of seeing his first porn movie by checking the box of the video for an explanation of the status of the images. Were they consensual? If they were staged, does this make them real?[11]

> The first time I see it I thought Ugh is that what it looks like ugh! Look at that ugh! And like seeing a girl putting high heels up her fanny and all that, I said ugh no, it must hurt her. I said check the back, is she supposed to be getting hurt, is that what she wants sort of thing? Why would they do that. What do they hurt themselves for. I just looked on it as torture to their body ... I just couldn't understand why they accepted it, but that is how it is.
>
> (Young man, working class, ac, aged 16)

Others suggested that girlfriends might resent or become jealous of their 'relationships' with the girls in the magazines and movies. The ontological status of pornographic performance and narrative are both 'notoriously complex' (Butler, 1990a, quoted in Kotz, 1993: 107) and subject to controversy and contestation.[12] This complexity can be found in the accounts of these young men: their concern with the ethics of production (was she really enjoying it?), and the ethics of consumption (does she really want me?) are bridged by dilemmas of personal agency (do I want or need her to want me?). What is particularly interesting and revealing about these young men's accounts is the way that a rejection of the fantasies of pornography (and by association masturbation) in favour of the realities of 'real sex' can become implicated in the assertion of masculine agency and identity.

For example, a number of young men talked about only 'needing' pornography when they were without a sexual partner, or only having used it before they became sexually active.[13]

The rejection of pornography on the grounds that 'a real man does it with a woman' offered by the following young man, is worth quoting at length. At first sight his denial of any qualitative difference between the world of pornographic representation and the world of flesh-and-blood women appears to be a powerful expression of the transcendence of a male gaze across the divisions of representation and reality. However, his account confounds both the expectations of the interviewer and any simplistic interpretation of the meanings and effects of pornography.

> I don't see how people can get off on watching other people having sex. I'm alright, I can go home and have sex. It's not doing you any good just sitting there watching it, it's better when you're doing it ... I don't see why I should look at this woman with her fanny showing, when I can go home and see my woman with her fanny showing. What's the difference apart from like that's unavailable and that's available. It's both the same thing, they both mean the same thing, they both look the same, there's no difference.

Q: Right, so you've got no problem with the fact that porn exists?
A: No.
Q: What do you think women think of porn?
A: Nothing, some must like it and some mustn't.
Q: What do you think women think of men that use porn?
A: They must think they are unloyal.
Q: Unloyal?
A: Unloyal. Why are they watching that when they can come home and get it here, trying to make me jealous aren't you, kind of thing, you are pissing me off.
Q: So, what do you think of the idea that porn exploits women?
A: It's about the male thinking he's superior.
Q: So what's your view on that?
A: Total bollocks there.
Q: What, total bollocks that porn exploits women?
A: No, that the man thinks he can exploit the woman.
Q: Does he though?
A: Yes, of course he does. That's only because the man hasn't come to terms yet with the woman being as equal as him.

(Young man, working class, esw, aged 19)

By refusing the independence or separateness of meaning in the fantasy world of pornography and in his intimate relationships, this young man resists the operations of the pornographic narrative which serves to maintain the splits and dissociations integral to homosocial masculinity. In doing so he relinquishes the power that appears to be on offer in the world of pornography in favour of engaging as an equal in the 'real' world of 'real' women. Ironically, he does this through an assertion of his individual heterosexuality, masculinity and potency.

CONCLUSIONS

In these young men's accounts we find a simultaneous expression of complicity and resistance. The young men identify with and through the pornography that is part of their environment, but they also find a need to 'look back' and 'talk back' at the pornographic gaze (Gordon and Kay, 1993). An examination of the way young men tell us they encounter, negotiate and engage with pornography reveals a complex interplay of meaning and practice which seems to be grounded in the inconsistencies of masculinity and the contingencies of these young men's lives. While young men inhabit different masculinities shaped by class, culture and style, and while these differences have significance for the kind of cultures within which pornography is consumed, the negotiation of pornography implicates them in a community of interpretation that connects men across and through their differences. Although this identification is achieved by the exclusion of women, paradoxically, it is a process that is also dependent on women. While young men's accounts reflect differing investments in homosocial male culture, they are nevertheless implicated in it through their investments in masculine heterosexuality.

Butler has suggested that heterosexual gender is a 'construction that regularly conceals its genesis' (Butler 1990b: 140). The contradictions that attend the consumption of pornography are an example of the enduring paradox that lies at the heart of heterosexual masculinity, dependent on both the exclusion and the inclusion of women – and which can be found in other practices of heterosexuality which, under scrutiny, reveal both asymmetry and dependency (Holland *et al.*, 1998).[14] While the homosocial masculinity that is signalled by pornography appears to provide access to individual and collective power, this collective project of identification between men brings with it dangers. These dangers are evident in the ambivalence expressed by many of these young men about using pornography. While pornography both misrepresents and objectifies women, in Lynne Segal's words, 'it is rather less obvious just who is being controlled and exploited in the penis-worship of pornography' (Segal, 1990: 218).

We can learn something by looking at pornography within the social context of its consumption. We can see it used as a means of communication between men that both confirms and gives rise to resistance to adult male sexuality, the values and power of women and the disciplines of the pornographic narrative and gaze. We can also see the challenge that pornography poses to young men's understanding of the sexual politics of gender: their surprise at their girlfriends' responses; their confusion as to the status of the images; the struggle to learn to enjoy what they see. Pornography provides a commercial arena of representation within which sexual politics are mediated. As consumers these young men enter into this arena, seeking to make sense of the product and of themselves. Ultimately this 'sense' is as contradictory, unstable and yet as powerful as the gender relations to which it contributes.

NOTES

1. We have identified the ethnicity of respondents as follows: esw (English, Scottish, Welsh), ac (African Caribbean), a (African), Asian (South Asian), mixed (parents from two different ethnic groups).
2. Discussions of pornography arise only in passing in ethnographic and other accounts of young people's sexual cultures (Mac an Ghaill, 1994; Blackman 1995) and are better accounted for in studies of the worlds of adult men, including at work (Hearn, 1985; Collinson and Hearn, 1996) and in all male environments such as prisons (Thurston, 1996).
3. The data presented in this paper arise from interviews undertaken with young men as part of the Men, Risk and AIDS Project, a qualitative investigation of young men's sexual experiences, attitudes and beliefs undertaken between 1991 and 1992, funded by the Leverhulme Trust. The study of young men followed a larger study undertaken with young women funded by the ESRC. In addition to the author the team for the MRAP project included Tim Rhodes, Janet Holland, Sue Sharpe and Caroline Ramazanoglu. Discussions of pornography were incidental to these interviews for which the primary interest was in sexual communication, negotiation and the dynamics of sexual risk taking. Only half of the sample (24) were asked about pornography, 23 out of 24 of those asked reported some familiarity with it and the resulting discussions

varied in terms of focus and duration. The interviews were undertaken by one man and two women, not including the author. In all but one instance the discussion of pornography was prompted by the interviewer, and most usually in the context of the process of learning about sex.

4. While I do not have the space or the data to explore this area, others have examined the relationship between heterosexual and homosexual pornography (Stoltenberg 1993) and explored the operation of a homoerotic gaze in the construction of contemporary consumer masculinities (Nixon, 1996).
5. Women's distaste for pornography appears to be associated in part with the environment within which they see it. Most women report accessing pornography through male partners or friends, and report that watching pornography in these circumstances is 'embarrassing' or 'degrading' (Itzin and Sweet, 1993). However, evidence from our own study of young women suggests that, where young women are in control of the material themselves, they can enjoy and learn from sexually explicit material (Thomson and Scott, 1991).
6. In a study of relations within prisons, Thurston (1996) argues that, by giving prisoners access to pornography as a Christmas treat, prison officers sought to achieve a shared identification of masculinity at the expense of 'others'.
7. See also Kelly *et al.* (1991), Itzin and Sweet (1993).
8. Collier has argued for the interdependency of respectable and unrespectable masculinities which he suggests 'are in fact, two sides of the same coin' (Collier, 1995: 229). Dyer goes further in suggesting that the notion of perversion is integral to the 'whiteness' of heterosexual masculinity: 'dark desires are part of the story of whiteness ... the whiteness of white men resides in the tragic quality of their giving way to darkness and the heroism of their channelling or resisting it' (Dyer, 1997: 28).
9. The irony that the core figure of pornography is the sexually insatiable woman has been noted by many commentators – who variously suggest that this figure could be understood as a mockery of feminist demands of a female-centred sexuality (Segal, 1990), as a catalyst of male impotence (Baker, 1993; Moye, 1985) or a postmodern joke (Williams, 1993).
10. Dyer (1985) has pointed out that the source of much sexual humour is the gap that exists between the fantasy of the phallus and the reality of the penis, 'while the apparent butt of sexual comedy is often the woman ... as so often with images of women, the joke is really on the man' (p. 34).
11. For a recent discussion of the ethical dimensions of 'seeing photographically' see Lury (1997).
12. This controversy can be seen in discussions of the meaning of 'performance' in relation to artists such as Annie Sprinkle (see Kotz, 1993), debates about the real effects of pornographic cultural productions (see Kappeler, 1993), and 'realist' interpretations of the relationship between pornography and sexual violence (Itzin, 1993).
13. Dyer (1997: 30) describes pornography (alongside romance, adultery and rape) as one of 'the great narrative dilemmas' of white masculinity,

which must simultaneously reproduce and transcend the body. It is interesting to locate the alienation of masturbation that characterises these young men's discussions of pornography within Dyer's discussion of the homosociality and a corresponding fear of sterility that haunt white (heterosexual) masculinity.

14. For example, for a man the achievement of a positive sexual reputation, while dependent on access to women's bodies, can only be affirmed by other men. See Holland *et al.* (1998).

REFERENCES

Baker, P. (1993) 'Maintaining Male Power: Why Heterosexual Men use Pornography', in Itzin, C. (ed.), *Pornography: Women, Violence and Civil Liberties – a Radical View* (Oxford: Oxford University Press).

Blackman, S. (1995) *Youth: Positions and Oppositions* (Aldershot: Avebury).

Butler, J. (1990a) 'The Force of Fantasy: Feminism, Mapplethorpe and Discussion', *Differences*, 2(2): 105–25.

Butler, J. (1990b) *Gender Trouble* (London: Routledge).

Church Gibson, P. and Gibson, R. (eds) (1993) *Dirty Looks: Women, Pornography, Power* (London: BFI).

Collinson, D. and Hearn, J. (1996) '"Men at Work": Multiple Masculinities/ Multiple Workplaces' in Mac an Ghaill, M. (ed.), *Understanding Masculinities* (Milton Keynes: Open University Press).

Collier, R. (1995) *Masculinity, Law and the Family* (London: Routledge).

Connell, R. W. (1989) *Gender and Power* (Cambridge: Polity Press).

Connell, R. W. (1995) *Masculinities* (Cambridge: Polity).

Dyer, R. (1985) 'Male Sexuality and the Media', in Metcalf, A. and Humphries, M. (eds), *The Sexuality of Men* (London: Pluto Press).

Dyer, R. (1997) *White* (London: Routledge).

Gordon, B. and Kay, K. (1993) 'Look Back/Talk Back', in Church Gibson, P. and Gibson, R. (eds), *Dirty Looks: Women, Pornography, Power* (London: BFI).

Hearn, J. (1985) 'Men's Sexuality at Work', in Metcalf, A. and Humphries, M. (eds), *The Sexuality of Men* (London: Pluto Press).

Holland, J., Ramazanoglu, C., Sharpe, S. and Thomson, R. (1998) *The Male in the Head: Young People, Heterosexuality and Power* (London: Tufnell Press).

Hite, S. (1981) *The Hite Report on Male Sexuality* (New York: Knopf).

Holland, J., Ramazanoglu, C. and Thomson, R. (1996) 'In the Same Boat? The Gendered (In)experience of First Heterosex', in Richardson, D. (ed.), *Theorising Heterosexuality: Telling It Straight* (Milton Keynes: Open University Press).

Itzin, C. (ed.), (1993) *Pornography: Women, Violence and Civil Liberties – A Radical View* (Oxford: Oxford University Press).

Itzin, C. and Sweet, C. (1993) 'Women's Experience of Pornography: UK Magazine Survey Evidence', in Itzin, C. (ed.), *Pornography: Women,*

Violence and Civil Liberties – A Radical View (Oxford: Oxford University Press).

Kappeler, S. (1993) 'Pornography: The Representation of Power', in Itzin, C. (ed.), *Pornography: Women, Violence and Civil Liberties – A Radical View* (Oxford: Oxford University Press).

Kelly, L., Regan, L. and Burton, S. (1991) *An Exploratory Study of the Prevalence of Sexual Abuse in a Sample of 16–21 Year Olds*, final report to the ESRC, Child Abuse Studies Unit, University of North London.

Kotz, L. (1993) 'Complicity: Women Artists Investigating Masculinity', in Church Gibson, P. and Gibson, R. (eds), *Dirty Looks: Women, Pornography, Power* (London: BFI).

Lury, C. (1997) *Prosthetic Culture: Photography, Memory and Identity* (London: Routledge).

Mac an Ghaill, M. (1994) *The Making of Men* (Milton Keynes: Open University Press).

Moye, A. (1985) 'Pornography', in Metcalf, A. and Humphries, M. (eds), *The Sexuality of Men* (London: Pluto Press).

Nixon, S. (1996) *Hard Looks: Masculinities, Spectatorship and Contemporary Consumption* (London: UCL Press).

Ross, A. (1989) *No Respect: Intellectuals and Popular Culture* (London: Routledge).

Segal, L. (1990) *Slow Motion: Changing Men, Changing Masculinity* (London: Virago).

Segal, L. (1993) 'Does Pornography Cause Violence: the Search for Evidence', in Church Gibson, P. and Gibson, R. (eds), *Dirty Looks: Women, Pornography, Power* (London: BFI).

Stoltenberg, J. (1993) 'Pornography, Homophobia and Male Supremacy', in Itzin, C. (ed.), *Pornography: Women, Violence and Civil Liberties – A Radical View* (Oxford: Oxford University Press).

Thomson, R. and Scott, S. (1991) *Learning about Sex: Young Women and the Social Construction of Sexual Identity* (London: Tufnell Press).

Thurston, R. (1996) 'Are You Sitting Comfortably? Men's Storytelling, Masculinities, Prison Culture and Violence', in Mac an Ghaill, M. (ed.), *Understanding Masculinities* (Milton Keynes: Open University Press).

Williams, L. (1993) 'A Provoking Agent: The Pornography and Performance Art of Annie Sprinkle', in Church Gibson, P. and Gibson, R. (eds), *Dirty Looks: Women, Pornography, Power* (London: BFI).

Zijderveld, A. C. (1983) 'The Sociology of Humour and Laughter', *Current Sociology*, 31(3).

10 The Dialectics of Walking: Walkman Use and the Reconstruction of the Site of Experience

MICHAEL BULL

> *Personal space is gone, in town anyway. I think it's inverted. I think your personal space is inside. In the music.*
>
> (Walkman user)

> *Inhabited space transcends geometrical space.*
>
> (Bachelard, 1988: 47)

> *To each his own bubble, that is the law today.*
>
> (Baudrillard, 1993: 39)

This chapter investigates the manner in which Walkman users lay claim to the urban spaces that they transitorily inhabit. Are Walkman users empowered through the re-creation of their own space or are they merely the colonised recipients of industrially produced sounds, which creates the illusion of autonomy and control? I argue both of these alternatives fail to provide an adequate understanding of everyday Walkman use. To understanding the relationship between the site of experience, technology and the street, I draw upon the work of Critical Theory, Gaston Bachelard and Henri Lefebvre. Much of the early work of Critical Theory concerned itself with just such an analysis which has been largely ignored in both contemporary accounts of urban experience and subsequent commentaries on Critical Theory itself. This oversight is unfortunate as the dialectical tension in their analysis of technology and experience focuses very usefully upon the ambiguous relationship that technology has in relation to the 'colonisation' of experience and to strategies of defence in everyday life.

Walkmans provide us with a useful artifact with which to discuss the problems of autonomy and control. They have been phenomenally successful since their introduction in 1979, with sales registered in the hundreds of millions. Their success has not been particularly dependent upon massive advertising campaigns and neither are they a fad of the period, like the 'Rubik cube', for example. The sale of personal stereos continues to grow and includes an increasingly wide user group, beyond teenagers and commuters, who use them regularly as part of their daily routine. Given this immense success, Walkmans have been strangely invisible within sociological literature. What accounts have been given are either anecdotal,[1] situated in the realm of 'representation',[2] or are theoretical meditations upon 'imaginary' Walkman use.[3] Actual Walkman practice remains strangely invisible in these accounts and we find no attempt to investigate how Walkmans are actually used or what significance might be attached to types of use. Existing accounts are united in a common evaluation of Walkman practices as representing a positive 'moment' in the relationship of technology to experience and stress the liberatory aspect of Walkman use.[4] This chapter does not contest this evaluation, but provides what I refer to as the 'negative' moment in the evaluation of technology and experience with relation to Walkman use. The aim is to move towards an evaluation of experience that can incorporate both approaches. This material is presented in terms of a phenomenological description, and as such Walkman use is discussed in terms of modes of use rather than types of user.[5] The resulting analysis attempts to move away from the reification of user types to a methodology of use akin to a Bergsonian concept of experiential time in which experience is not parcelled up in ways that distort the experience of subjects. This draws on recent empirical study of the social meaning of Walkman use in London.[6]

Walkmans have several distinct structural features that are relevant to the task in hand. Their use transforms the 'site' of everyday experience aurally. Music is pumped into the ears directly, thereby replacing the sounds of the street with the user's own soundworld. Walkmans can be used almost anywhere, with users generally not restricted by geographical limitations.[7] They permit a reorganisation of public and private realms of experience where what is traditionally conceived of as 'private' experience is brought out into public realms in the act of individualised listening. It is important to recognise, however, that Walkman use questions the very constitution and meaning of 'private' realms of experience in a manner that is not confined to geographical, social or historical divisions. Walkman use also allows the users to prioritise their experience in relation to their geographical, social and interpersonal environment, and as such enables them to attempt to exist within their own private soundworld. The site of experience is therefore reconstituted through the medium of the Walkman.

In this chapter I investigate the possible meanings that might be attributed to this transformation of the site of social experience through Walkman use, by concentrating upon Adorno's notion of 'we-ness' or 'false acquaintance' which represents the re-creation of direct experience by and through technologically mediated forms of experience.[8] The significance of Adorno's understanding of 'we-ness' in relation to Walkman use is then developed in the final section in relation to the work of Bachelard and Lefebvre, where their analysis of 'habitation' and 'representational space' is examined through the work of Critical Theory.[9]

CRITICAL THEORY: THE 'SITE' OF EXPERIENCE AND THE NATURE OF THE 'HORIZON' OF SOCIAL EXPERIENCE

Critical Theorists in their work on new communication technologies did not merely analyse forms of reception but also considered the space within which reception is received as crucially significant to an understanding of those experiences. With Walkman use 'private' space becomes mobile, reconfiguring the relationship between the user and representational space. The awareness of this ambiguous relationship between control and invasion is brought to our attention in the following observation of early radio users:

> Who could resist the invitation of those dainty headphones? They gleam in living rooms and entwine themselves around heads all by themselves; and instead of fostering cultivated conversation (which certainly can become a bore), one becomes a playground for Eiffel noises that, regardless of their own potentially objective boredom, do not even grant one's modest right to personal boredom. Silent and lifeless, people sit side by side as if their souls were wandering about far away. But these souls are not wandering according to their own preferences; they are badgered by the news hounds, and soon no one can tell anymore who is the hunter and who is the hunted.
>
> (Kracauer, 1995: 333)

Kracauer, an early collaborator of Adorno's, notes that it is primarily the headphones that create the private space for the user whilst the radio messages are deemed to vaporise and de-spatialise space. The relation of the 'far away' to the physical domain of the listener is rendered problematic. It is through the technological medium of radio signals and the headphones that the listeners 'intentionally' put themselves 'elsewhere'. The distinction between the receiving and the creating of experience is already blurred in Kracauer's description. This ambiguity concerning the location and meaning of experience is an early example of the spatial and conceptual re-organisation of experience typical of Walkman use. Adorno points to the significance of the role of technology in enacting this type of transformation through the example of the following poem:

> Just arrived in this region.
> Much more than very rich
> In his hand a telescope
> Came a mister by the name of Pief
> 'Why shouldn't I look.'
> Said he, 'onto the distance as I walk?
> It's also beautiful somewhere else
> And here I am at any rate.'
>
> (Busch, quoted in Bloch, 1988: 2)

In the poem the experiencing of distance is transformed by the telescope. Adorno appropriates and transforms the original impulse of the poem and recasts it in a contemporary mode. He also demonstrates his awareness of the role of technology in delivering magical or utopian aspirations to subjects; in this instance through the technology of the telescope which transforms the ability of the user to traverse distance. The utopian element in Adorno's account is thrown back upon itself because it realises itself merely aesthetically. The everyday world of the subject remains stubbornly resistant in its materiality. The attempt to magically transform experience falls short and becomes normalised. Adorno concludes that the results of this are by no means innocent:

> Numerous so-called utopian dreams – for example, television, the possibility of travelling to other planets, moving faster than sound – have been fulfilled. However, insofar as these dreams have been realised, they operate as though the best thing about them has been

> forgotten – one is not happy about them. As they have been realised, the dreams themselves have assumed a peculiar character of sobriety, of boredom.
>
> (Adorno, quoted in Bloch, 1988: 2)

Technology thus becomes a tool for failed utopian aspirations. Adorno significantly recognises the colonising or appropriating nature of the above experience. The telescope user does not merely look, he also appropriates. This appropriation:

> assumes a horrifying meaning today in the realisation of technological utopias, that 'here I am at any rate' also takes possession of the 'somewhere else'.
>
> (*Ibid*., 3)

It is precisely in terms of the 'here I am at any rate' and the 'somewhere else' that the significance of the transformation of representational space can be understood. The role and significance of technology in transforming the experiential nature of space will become apparent in the following analysis of Walkman use. Adorno points out that the somewhere else is consumed and appropriated by the here and now. In the act of consumption, space becomes subjectivised and immediate experience fetishised. This potentially results in the negation or aestheticisation of urban experience. Notions of 'difference' become one victim of this process and, to paraphrase Baudrillard: if subjects exist in their own bubbles then how can they recognise the 'other'? Paradoxically for Adorno this flattening out of experience contains a latent utopian element. It is precisely to this utopian desire for a fulfilled life that the products of the culture industry orientate themselves whilst colonising the life world of the subject. The world and experience become directly mediated by the manufactured content of messages received. Adorno describes this as 'false acquaintance' and it becomes central to Critical Theory's account of urban experience. Adorno elsewhere refers to it as states of 'we-ness' which are built into our reception of polyphonic music together with other forms of representation and reception from opera, soaps, radio chat shows to news programmes.[10] Everyday life thus undergoes a process of 'de-privatisation' which is dialectically related to the notion of 'we-ness'. De-privatisation signifies the industrially produced construction of an illusory private realm which confounds traditional notions of private and public.[11] It is in reference to the contradictory nature of the creation of a perfectly private personal sphere by Walkman users that Adorno's following observations appear most relevant:

> By circling them, by enveloping them as inherent in the musical phenomenon – and turning them as listeners into participants, it contributes ideologically to the integration which modern society never tires of achieving in reality. It leaves no room for conceptual reflection between itself and the subject, and so it creates an illusion of immediacy in a totally mediated world, of proximity between strangers, the warmth of those who come to feel a chill of unmitigated struggle of all against all. Most important among the functions of consumer music – which keeps evoking memories of a language of immediacy – may be that men's suffering under the universal mediations, as if one were still living face to face despite it all.
>
> (Adorno, 1972: 46)

Without necessarily endorsing the implied totalitarian nature of technology in the above quote, Adorno does point to the powerful aural quality of music and the social construction of states of 'we-ness' within it. This is then located within a simultaneous analysis of technology in relation to a transformed notion of the 'social'. The site of experience in Adorno's work collapses within the historical transformation of 'bourgeois interiority' which is replicated phenomenologically in the behaviour of individuals in their everyday experience. However, as Wolin (1994) has observed, it is a mistake to relate Adorno's work in this area to a 'one-dimensional' model of collapse and colonisation. There is an inherent tension in Critical Theory's discussion of these issues where a dialectic is at play between technology as invasion and technology as resistance, between the principle of domination in the social system and the notion of resistance to that system. To argue for colonisation would be to argue for an identity between subject and object in the form of an identity theory which is alien to Adorno's work and to Critical Theory in general. It is precisely the notion of non-identity, for example, which attracts the anti-foundationalist interest of postmodernists to Adorno's work on an epistemological level, if not in terms of cultural analysis. I now move on to consider the transformation of representational space and the 'site' of experience as described by Walkman users in their accounts of everyday Walkman use.

WALKMAN USE AND THE RECONSTRUCTION OF THE SITE OF EXPERIENCE

In this first empirical section I concentrate on Walkman users' descriptions of their Walkman practices in terms of their sense of being 'connected' with the source or content of what is being listened to through the Walkman. This ambiguity of place and experience is highlighted by the following user:

> I don't necessarily feel that I'm there. Especially if I'm listening to the radio (on the Walkman) I feel I'm there, where the radio is, because of the way, that is, he's talking to me and only me and no-one else around me is listening to that. So I feel like, I know I'm really on the train, but I'm not really ... I like the fact that there's someone still there.

This woman of 21 uses her Walkman to travel across London each day. She, however, listens to music habitually, waking up to it and going to sleep accompanied by it. The Walkman initially appears to constitute a form of company for her whilst she is alone in public, and as such it provides her with a sense of immediacy and intimacy. Public space becomes habitable for her and any sense of isolation is transformed into a state of 'being with'. Just as television changes the structure of experience in the home,[12] so the Walkman changes the structuring of experience in public. In this sense Walkman use can be described as providing the user with a 'mobile home', a 'canopy' or a 'bubble' with which they experience public spaces. Walkman use provides an opportunity for the user to extend states of 'being-with' engendered by other forms of communication technologies used in the home and elsewhere. The following user also remarked on her 'need' for sound to alleviate feelings of isolation:

> I can't go to sleep at night without my radio on. I'm one of those people. I find it very difficult. I don't like silence. I'm not that sort of person. I like hearing things around me. It's like hearing that there's a world going on sort of thing. I'm not a very alone person. I will always have something on. I don't mind being by myself as long as I have something on. ... Because I haven't got the external sort of noises around me I feel I'm in a bit of a world of my own because I can't really hear so much of what is going on around me.

Two processes are operative in this description. The Walkman is used to create the experience of being 'cocooned', either through a separation of the user's subjective realm from the outside world or, alternatively, the subjective realm of the user 'moves outwards' and colonises that space. At present it is sufficient to state that a dualism exists in the categories operationalised by many Walkman users. Within this dualistic experience the Walkman works as a form of 'boundary marker' (Goffman, 1971). Within this reconfiguring of space and experience Walkman use is invariably described as 'filling' the space of experience:

> The space whilst you're walking. ... It also changes the atmosphere as well. If you listen to music like and you're feeling depressed it can change the atmosphere around you.

The aural nature of listening can be all-engulfing. The atmosphere within which Walkman experience is sited is transformed from the inside out. As such it can be described as colonising the space within Walkman use:

> When you have the Walkman it's like having company. You don't feel lonely. It's your own environment. It's like you're doing something pleasurable you can do by yourself and enjoy it. I think it creates a sense of kind of aura sort of like. Even though it's directly in your ears you feel like it's all around your head. You're really aware it's just you. Only you can hear it. It makes you feel individual.

Listening constitutes company:

> If there's the radio there's always somebody talking. There's always something happening.

This is contrasted to the observation that 'nothing happens' if there is no musical accompaniment to experience. The aura collapses. When the Walkman is switched off the 'we-ness' falls away and the user is left in what is often described as an experiential void. Users refer to experiencing feelings of anxiety when there is nothing there to distract them or when they are left alone with only their thoughts for company. Walkman users often describe feelings of empowerment whilst using their Walkmans. The following 30-year-old user describes using her Walkman whilst cycling. For her the state of 'being with' is very specific. She uses one tape in her Walkman for several months. At the time of the interview it was *Scott Walker Sings Jacques Brel*, which she described as a 'special' tape evoking romantic associations. She describes feeling more confident and secure whilst listening to the tape, experiencing that time as a form of 'being with':

> Yeh. It's me and Scott [Walker] on the bike.

This observation is common amongst Walkman users who feel protected whilst accompanied by their personalised music. Their own space becomes a protected zone, as the following statement makes clear:

> If I'm in a difficult situation or in new surroundings then I think nothing can affect you, you know. It's your space.

Listening to the Walkman whilst alone constitutes company and familiarity. To paraphrase Adorno, instead of company the music installs itself. Walkman use works to enhance and transform the user's experience of space and time. As such it becomes 'taken-for-granted' and 'everyday' in relation to the user's experience. Experience without the Walkman is seen as either void or inferior to experience with it. The spacing of experience thus becomes transformed, as described by the following users:

> It fills the space whilst you're walking.

> It also changes the atmosphere as well. If you listen to music you really like and you're feeling depressed, it can change the atmosphere around you. It livens everything up. Everything's on a higher level all the time. It makes you a bit busier. You get excited. Everything's happening.

The invigoration and heightening of the space of experience enacted through Walkman use collapses the distinction between private mood or orientation and the user's surroundings. The world becomes one with the experience of the Walkman user as against the threatened disjunction between the two. Walkmans colonise space for these users and can also transform their mood, orientation and the reach of their experience. This often takes the form of voyeuristic or aesthetic heightening, as the following quote from a 32-year-old Walkman user indicates:

> But when I'm out I'm looking for things that I see – in the world, human interaction – beautiful things that I think can touch my soul – you know. That certain sound at a certain time and it will just move me to tears – and it is filmic. But it's very real. I'm not seeing anything that isn't there. That woman in the street. She's really there. She doesn't have anywhere to sleep but it's because I'm listening to music that's really tender, it moves me even more.

The quality of such experiences is invariably dependent upon the continued use of the Walkman. This is graphically demonstrated by the following respondents who are 17 years old. In a group interview they were asked to describe how the atmosphere changes with the switching off of their Walkmans:

> An empty feeling.
>
> Got nothing to do.
>
> Just sitting there and get bored.
>
> It's like when you're in a pub and they stop the music. It's an anticlimax. Everyone just stops. You don't know what to say.

Switching off becomes tantamount to killing off their private world and returning them to the diminished space and duration of the outside world.

WALKMAN USE: TAKING YOUR 'HOME' WITH YOU

Using a Walkman in public is described by some users in terms of never leaving home. Urban space is transformed and re-created into a personalised experiential realm and becomes domesticated in the process. In effect Walkman users can take their home out with them. Using a Walkman can allow the users to maintain feelings of security which they associate more commonly with feelings of 'home'. This is one reason why many Walkman users regularly play music which has personal associations or connotations. The following response from a hairdresser typifies this point:

> I like to have a piece of my own world. Familiar and secure. It's a familiarity. Something you're taking with you from your home. You're not actually leaving home. You're taking it with you. You're in your own little bubble. You're in your own little world and you have a certain amount of control and you don't have so much interruption. ... What it evokes for me is that I didn't really have to worry about it at all because there's someone there who'll take care of me. In a sense like when you're little and you have your mum and dad. So that's what it would evoke for me, a feeling of security that it will be all right. ... I don't like it [the urban] to totally take over. I have to have a piece of my own world.

The tapes are associated with her own world of memories. She, however, does not visualise this sense of home in terms of concrete memories but rather relates to it as a sense of well-being and security. Certain tunes or songs remind her of her childhood and family. Many other users describe travelling back into their own narratives, visualising situations or re-creating pleasurable feelings whilst listening to their Walkmans. Their imaginary journey into their own narrative takes precedence over their actual physical journey and their actual 'present' is overridden by their 'imaginary' present. These experiences are not to be confused simply with daydreaming. Walkman users describe having great difficulty conjuring up these feelings and images of home and narrative without the use and prompting of their Walkman. As such daydreaming becomes mediated, constructed and constituted through the technological medium of Walkmans.

Walkmans can also help users to reconceptualise their experience of the body as the 'site' of action heightened its sense of presence. This is the case not only for those who use the Walkman for sporting activities, such as working out in gyms or jogging, but also for those engaged in more mundane use such as walking down the street. Users sometimes describe these situations as an 'empty out' of thoughts from the body through Walkman use, which I describe later as the 'clearing' of a space. Walkman users can also, however, become more aware of the body as the site of action:

> I'd enjoy the feeling of my body working hard. It made me more concentrated on that. I enjoyed the feeling. It was channelling you in on that feeling. I'm used to riding a bike as well. Riding the push bike for the same reason. Focussing inside. Getting in a rhythm. Certain tracks, get into a rhythm, follow the bass line. It's always

> dance music. It's got energy. It's like clubbing or dancing. I get the same energy working or cycling. You become part of the bicycle.

The above experience can be described as a form of 'de-consciousnessing', by which I mean the giving over of oneself to the body as 'action'. The body in the above example is experienced as merging with the activity of cycling. As such the body tends to lose its weight and resistance and becomes consumed in the present; in the physical action of the user. Whilst the above accounts are related to Walkman use whilst cycling or doing heavy manual labour a similar description or awareness of the body as site comes from the following 27-year-old artist who describes walking down a crowded and noisy London street. This is not an example of de-conciounessing so much as an awareness of the ambiguous nature of the body as 'boundary marker':

> I suppose you could say it's part of my body. I've got a special pocket for it. It's got its home. It's been a therapy putting it on outside. Because I'm rushing out, doing something. It's an important part of relaxation. Because what I've been doing is something visual. Sound is something else. You feel it's slower, slower than light. You hear things not just through your eardrums but through your whole body. Your whole body is vibrating. I suppose it cancels out the vibrations of the traffic around you. If energy is going in through your ear it vibrates all of your bones, every single bone in your body. You're moving. You've got energy inside you. It's in you. You're not just hearing it.

The success of the experience in creating a zone of protection for the body – an empty out of thoughts from the body or becoming one with the body – is often related to the intensity of sound emanating from the Walkman.

WALKMAN USE AND CLEARING A SPACE

Walkman use can enable the user to exert control over both the external environment, albeit aesthetically, and the internal cognitive processes. Using a Walkman can be described in terms of clearing a 'space' for thoughts, and can also act as a stimulant for the workings of the imagination. The random nature of the sounds of the street does not produce the correct configuration or force to successfully produce or create the focusing of thoughts in the desired direction for many Walkman users. For those who are habitually accompanied by music there arises a need for accompaniment as a constituent part of their everyday experience. This is related to the habitualness of Walkman use, as well as the type of environment within which the experience takes place. For example Walkman users are just as likely to wear their Walkmans down deserted streets as on congested trains or crowded streets. The following descriptions are not unusual:

> It kind of helped me think in perspective. It helped me think things through. It takes the situation out of the immediate surroundings. You're just somewhere else so you can think about things.

> I'm locking myself in a bit more. It locks the rest of the world out. There's nothing to distract you. There's just the journey and the music. you're in to yourself. You don't feel anxiety. I feel less stress.

Using the Walkman is thus described as excluding the 'outside' in order to re-organise the 'inside'. A 'free' and 'mobile' space is described as being created through Walkman use – free in terms of freeing the user from unwanted thoughts enabling them to focus more successfully on their body, their physical activity or alternative thoughts. The above user is describing using a Walkman whilst cycling, whereas the following example is a description of a manual worker using a Walkman whilst working on a motorway:

> There's a lot of empty spaces in your head. Too much time to dwell on your everyday problems [at work]. ... It [Walkman use] distracted you from what you were doing but it helped you with what you were doing.

When the confusion of the world intrudes upon them Walkman users often describe turning to their Walkman, as described graphically by the following 18-year-old user:

> I argue a lot with my parents. When I go out of the house it calms me down. It starts the day off better. It helps me to keep me in the clouds. I know all the words. I know something, I can concentrate on that. My thoughts are more structured when I have the Walkman. It's more positive.

This not untypical description demonstrates the process of blocking out the external world in order to clarify and fill the 'private' realm. Her experience is being constituted through the music with which she is familiar. Similarly other users play rhythmic music loudly in order to produce a similar response, but one that prioritises the movement of their bodies. Walkman use can also allow the user to escape from unwanted thoughts and feelings.

> I associate it with a time when I wasn't getting on well with my parents, and doing these walks, listening to these tapes. It used to take me away from it until I got to where my friends were.

In this instance using a Walkman fills time and space between contact with others, transporting her out of place and time into a form of weightlessness of the present. This she describes as an experience of colonisation or engulfment:

> The music is not like a background. It's all around you. It takes over your senses. It can be quite isolating.

This sense of isolation or of being transported away from the world is apparent in the following quote from a 23-year-old secretary who is an intermittent Walkman user. She is not escaping from unpleasant thoughts but is rather absenting herself from her situation on the tube whilst returning from work. She does not want to think but merely to relax into her state of tiredness:

> It's background. It's something to drown out the noise of the train. If you want to switch off and be in a room of your own you put that on and you close your eyes and shut your ears and it's a way of not being bothered.

The use of the Walkman drowns out the world and places her into 'a room of her own' by 'closing her ears and shutting her eyes'. Users like this describe Walkman 'states' as enclosing; a shutting-off of the senses from the physical environment allowing them to drift off within a hermetically sealed world of their choosing. The environment is thus re-appropriated and experienced as part of the Walkman user's desire. Through listening to, normally, music the listener gets more out of the environment not by interacting with it but precisely by not interacting. Walkman users often focus on themselves as personally receiving the environment via their Walkmans. Music listened to through the Walkman creates the world and places them in it. The use of a Walkman allows for the re-creation of space to accord with the wishes of the user. This is achieved by the user re-possessing space as part of or constitutive of their subjective desire.

THEORETICAL REFLECTIONS: REPRESENTATIONAL SPACE AND THE SITE OF EXPERIENCE

The analysis so far confirms that the site of experience and the nature of representational space is transformed by Walkman use. In developing this analysis further I draw on the work of Bachelard and Lefebvre. Bachelard (1988) provides an account of the 'site' of experience as a form of 'being in the world' via an analysis of metaphors of 'enclosure' found in nineteenth- and twentieth-century poetry. He points to the phenomenological status and significance of the site of experience conceptualised in terms of metaphors of 'home'. Whilst his analysis points to a dialectics of home articulated in terms of safety and danger he fails to provide any historical contextualisation of the experiencing of 'home'. I am interested in what relationship might exist between Bachelard's phenomenology of 'home' and contemporary Walkman users' description of 'home'. In essence I want to extract Bachelard's analysis of the significance of 'home' found within poetic metaphors and re-appropriate it within the mediated technological universe of the Walkman user for whom the metaphor of 'home' seems to resonate as a form of phenomenological intentionality. Bachelard comments that a phenomenology:

> Should therefore have to say how we inhabit our vital space, in accord with all dialectics of life, how we take root, day after day, in a 'corner of the world'. ... All really inhabited space bears the essence of the notion of home. The imagination functions in this direction whenever the human being has found the slightest shelter: we shall see the imagination build 'walls' of impalpable shadows, comfort itself with the illusion of protection.
>
> (Bachelard, 1988: 4)

Bachelard analyses metaphors that indicate the creation of subjective enclosures in an effort to explain their relationship to the site (inner experience) and context of experience (outer experience). His analysis, as such, creates a dichotomy between the two. The progressive moment of Bachelard's analysis is represented by the descriptive richness of his analysis of the subjectivity of enclosure. For Bachelard 'a poem possesses us entirely' and through it we are able to 'experience resonances, sentimental repercussions, reminders of our own past'. Walkman experience equally may engulf and absorb the Walkman user, whose experience can be directed into the imaginary reconstruction of a narrative past. Yet instead of re-creating this sense of 'home' in the meditative or imaginary realm constructed out of a poetic 'text' the Walkman user does this in a conceptual mobile home created by the Walkman where he can continually re-create this experience of home. Inhabited space therefore transcends geometrical space through technological mediation. Bachelard claims that in his description the subject is free in his 'imaginary' state and in doing so his analysis points in the direction of a phenomenology of utopian intentionality.

> But phenomenology of the imagination ... demands that images be lived directly, that they be taken as sudden events in life. When the image is new, the world is new. And in reading applied to life, all passivity disappears if we try to become aware of the creative acts of the poet expressing the world, a world that becomes accessible to our daydreaming.
>
> (Bachelard, 1988: 47)

In this act of freedom through the workings of the imagination space is reconstituted and 'flees the object nearby and right away it is far off, elsewhere, in the space of elsewhere' (Bachelard, 1988: 184). Bachelard provides us with a description of the re-inscription of space through the imaginary creation of the site of experience as that of a self-enclosed 'shell' that freely takes the subject into a freer realm of 'inhabited space'. Yet his description bears greater resemblance to the dreaming that Rousseau recounts on his solitary walks than to today's technologically mediated imaginary space of the Walkman user. For Bachelard, dreamers dream in silence. This picture of isolation, as we have seen, is precisely what Walkman users invariably fear. Walkman users tend to feel isolated with no sound. Their home has to have sound even if the sound within 'geometrical' space is extinguished. Their own technologically mediated sound constitutes their 'inhabited space' which correspondingly transcends the sounds of 'geographical space.'

Whilst Adorno would agree with Bachelard's description of the progressive or utopian moment of subjectivity his own analysis dwells more frequently on the historical process of the 'colonisation' of the 'site' of experience by the social network. Adorno's subjects live in an urban world saturated with technologically reproduced sound.

> We might conceive a series leading from the man who cannot work without the blare of the radio to the one that kills time and paralyses loneliness by filling his ears with the illusion of 'being with' no matter what.
>
> (Adorno, 1976: 15)

Adorno points to the problematic nature of the 'site' of experience as well as to the problematic nature of the phenomenological construction of subjective intentionality. He perceives this dressing up of the site of experience as an 'illusory realm' filled out by society. The subjective impulse to create this 'illusory realm' is where Adorno's analysis coincides with Bachelard's. In order to discuss this problematic relation of the site of experience to that which is 'experienced' it is useful to draw upon Lefebvre's concept of 'representational space' and discuss it in relation to Adorno's notion of 'we-ness'.

Adorno argues for a very specific spatial redistribution of experience through technology that contributes to the manufacture of states of 'we-ness' in contemporary culture. This process, he argues, is built into the very mechanics of the communicative process. What we might ask signifies or constitutes a successful experiential manoeuvring of the 'subject' into a state of security, and what is the status of this security? Critical Theorists discuss this question dialectically through the idea that technology is both invasive and defensive. In their analysis whilst an orientation towards the constitution of subjectivity plays an important role they do not place that subjectivity as a 'given' within culture but rather perceive it as being structurally constituted. It is precisely in this dimension of their analysis that Critical Theorists such as Adorno are more able to situate subjective experience of space and time through technology than many subsequent theorists. The work of Lefebvre in this respect is theoretically close to Critical Theory. It is Lefebvre's notion of representational space that interests me most in relation to Walkman use. The 'site' of experience takes place within representational space and can be described phenomenologically in terms of direction, situation and relation. In this respect Lefebvre goes beyond Bachelard precisely by understanding that representational space is both conceptual and geographical. The 'subject' 'overlays' experienced space in a variety of ways described above by Lefebvre. His analysis would seem to lead to a qualitative and multilayered evaluation of experience in relation to its surroundings. However, Lefebvre also appears to fall into an either/or dichotomy of experience that sits uneasily with his otherwise dynamic analysis of experience within representational space. He argues below that lived space is passively experienced, by which he means 'given', and that it is only through the imaginary or symbolic activity of the individual that 'passion' or intentionality is 'lived' out. Urban space as a contemporary example of representational space seems to be colonised already, as is apparent from the following quote:

> Living bodies, the bodies of 'users' – are caught up not only in the toils of parcelised space, but also in the web of what philosophers call 'analgons'; images, signs, symbols. These bodies are transported out of themselves and emptied out, as it were, via the eyes; every kind of appeal, incitement and seduction is mobilised to tempt them with doubles of themselves in prettified, smiling and happy poses; this campaign to void them succeeds exactly to the degree that the images proposed correspond to the 'needs' that those same images have helped fashion. So it is that a massive influx of information, of messages, runs head into an inverse flow constituted by the evacuation from the innermost body of all life and desire. Even cars may fulfil the function of analgons, for they are at once extensions of the body and mobile homes, so to speak, fully equipped to receive these wandering bodies.
>
> (Lefebvre, 1991: 99)

For Lefebvre representational space, in which he prioritises vision, is saturated. The eyes consume the 'analgons' which 'void' the subject of the occupancy of their own experience and, as such, even the 'overlaying' of physical space by the imagination merely appears to constitute an additional form of superimposed or structurally determined meaning. As in Adorno the structural takes precedent and even constitutes the 'imaginary'. This later account mirrors Kracauer's analysis of some 30 years earlier in the description of the colonisation of space by signs and the mimetic impulse and consequence of this for the experiencing subject:

> In the evening one saunters through the streets, replete with an unfulfillment from which fullness can sprout. Illuminated words glide by on the rooftops, and already one is banished from one's own emptiness into the alien advertisement. One's body takes root in the asphalt, and, together with the enlightening revelations of the

illuminations, one's spirit – which is no longer one's own – roams ceaselessly into the night.

(Kracauer, 1995: 332)

With Walkman use sound can be conceived of as an additional and powerful 'analgon' which prioritises itself and importantly reconfigures the relationship between the aural and visual analgons of culture. However, the dialectic of invasion/resistance seems to be lost here. Resistance is perceived here merely as another, albeit sophisticated, form of 'colonisation'. When looked at structurally Lefebvre's analysis, as does Adorno's at times, seems to imply that there can be no way out, and that even in the aesthetic re-appropriation of urban experience freedom becomes socially prescribed and controlled.

CONCLUSION

The chapter has discussed ways in which it is possible to theorise the transformation of the site of experience within an approach that is loosely connected to the parameters of Critical Theory. The tension in the dichotomy between colonisation and resistance that has been highlighted in the chapter has stressed a fundamental ambiguity in the relationship that cannot be cleared away merely through linguistic terminology (for example, replacing 'management' for control and invasion). The negative moment of these transformations has been stressed not as an ontological position but as a strategic one. The qualitative nature of sites of experience and the nature of spaces within which those sites are placed are questions that the above theorists addressed. They in turn provide, so I argue, a corrective to more recent work which provides for a more positive evaluation of these questions yet which begs the questions as to the nature of the site of experience or the constitution of representational space. However, it is my contention that the work of Critical Theorists, and Lefebvre in particular, can also be used to discuss and develop more positive evaluations of these positions. There are openings in the work of both Adorno, whose work on urban experience has been largely neglected, and Lefebvre, that point to experiential moments of utopian desire that might be articulated through a phenomenology of everyday experience. If these openings are to be fruitfully explored in relation to the workings of new communication technologies and everyday experience then more empirical work needs to carried out that critically interrogates both the constitution of the site of experience and its problematic relationship to notions of representational space. Merely falling back on unreflective notions of free or liberatory urban experience, or on blanket notions of colonised experience, merely perpetuates a theoretical dichotomy that itself might need to be overcome, whether by theoretical deconstruction or political challenge.

NOTES

1. William Gibson does, however, recognise the transformative nature of Walkman use in relationship to the user's experience of space, saying that: 'The Sony Walkman has done more to change human perception than any Virtual reality gadget. I can't remember any technological experience since that was quite so wonderful as being able to take music and move it through landscapes and architecture' (Gibson, 1993: 49).
2. This is the case with the recent publication by the Open University team (du Gay and Hall, 1997) in which representation is confounded with use. Throughout the publication no empirical evidence of Walkman use is presented to substantiate any of the claims being made.
3. Typical of this is a little piece written by Ian Chambers (1990) which is invariably invoked as evidence of Walkman use. Alternatively there is the work of Hosokawa (1984) which perceives Walkman use through the work of de Certeau (1984), but again with no reference to empirical material.
4. This perspective stresses the visual prioritising of much urban experience. Walkman use becomes a form of 'flanerie', and as such constitutes a form of urban aesthetics. This position draws upon Walter Benjamin's (1973) views concerning the relationship of technology to the visual coupled with a negative prognosis of urban experience (Sennett, 1990; Bauman, 1993; Buck-Morss, 1991).
5. This is typical of psychological approaches towards technology and experience as in the work of Moebius and Michel-Annen (1994), in which Walkman users are constructed in terms of psychological types. Individual Walkman users in fact drift into many different types of use.
6. The study was carried out primarily in London over a two-year period from 1994 to 1996 and consisted of in-depth qualitative interviews with over 100 Walkman users. Interviews were conducted both with individual Walkman users and in groups. Supplementary material was gained through the use of diaries. Subjects represented a cross-section of Walkman users in terms of age, gender, ethnicity and occupation.
7. The chapter restricts itself to Walkman use in the street. However, Walkmans can be used virtually anywhere. For example, employees sometimes wear them at work or in their breaks. A cleaner might find their daily working routine becomes more pleasurable using a

Walkman. Issues of authority and control also come into play here, as they do in the fairly widespread activity of teenage use in school. Equally, Walkmans are sometimes worn in the home. All of these situations may bring into play issues of the relationship of gender, technology and authority. There is also an interpersonal dimension to Walkman use which relates to how subjects manage a variety of social situations whilst wearing Walkmans.

8. In Adorno's analysis the urban subject is not so much protecting the site of experience from others as creating, albeit ambiguously, a utopian space of habitation. The fragility of this space is rendered more secure as the space becomes 'occupied' by signifiers of an imaginary and reassuring presence. This is what Adorno means by the term 'being with'. It represents the re-creation of direct experience by technologically mediated forms of experience. Adorno's understanding of modern urban experience prioritises music reception, thus enabling us to understand central aspects of contemporary Walkman use more adequately.
9. Lefebvre describes 'representational space' in the following way as space: 'directly lived through its associated images and symbols, and hence the space of "inhabitants" and "users". ... This is the dominated – and hence passively experienced – space which the imagination seeks to change and appropriate. It overlays physical space, making symbolic use of its object. ... Representational space is alive: it speaks. It has an affective kernel or centre: Ego, bed, bedroom, dwelling house; or: square, church, graveyard. It embraces the loci of passion, of action and of lived situations, and thus immediately implies time. Consequently it may be qualified in various ways: it may be directional, situational or relational, because it is essentially qualitative, fluid and dynamic' (Lefebvre, 1991: 39–42).
10. As such it does not really matter whether we listen to the Spice Girls or Brahms. Adorno is not referring to hierarchies of taste. Neither does he argue that we are always involved in the same activity when we listen to music. Neither is he claiming that historical reception remains invariant (Adorno, 1976, 1991).
11. This concern is also taken up in the later work of Habermas (1989) in his distinction between lifeworlds and systems world.
12. In this way such an analysis does not necessarily conflict with elements of studies that deal directly with response-orientated features of use (Morley, 1992).

REFERENCES

Adorno, T. (1972) *Minima Moralia* (London: New Left Books).

Adorno, T. (1976) *Introduction to the Sociology of Music* (New York: Continuum Press).

Adorno, T. (1991) *The Culture Industry: Selected Essays on Mass Culture* (London: Routledge).

Bachelard, G. (1988) *The Poetics of Space* (Boston, MA: Beacon Press).
Baudrillard, J. (1993) *Symbolic Exchange and Death* (London: Sage).
Bauman, Z. (1993) *Postmodern Ethics* (Oxford: Blackwell).
Benjamin, W. (1973) *Illuminations* (London: Penguin).
Bloch, E. (1988) *The Utopian Function of Art as Literature* (Cambridge, MA: MIT Press).
Buck-Morss, S. (1991) *The Dialectics of Seeing: Walter Benjamin and the Arcades Project* (Cambridge, MA: MIT Press).
Chambers, I. (1990) 'A Miniature History of the Walkman', *New Formations: A Journal of Culture/Theory/Politics*, No. 11, pp. 1–4.
De Certeau, M. (1984) *The Practice of Everyday Life* (London: University of California Press).
Denzin, N. K. (1995) *The Cinematic Society* (London: Sage).
Du Gay, P. and Hall, S. (1997) *Doing Cultural Studies: The Story of the Walkman* (London: Sage).
Gibson, W. (1993) *Time Out*, 6 October, p. 49.
Goffman, E. (1971) *Relations in Public: Microstudies of Public Order* (London: Penguin).
Habermas, J. (1987) *The Philosophical Discourse of Modernity* (Cambridge: Polity).
Habermas, J. (1989) *The Structural Transformation of the Public Sphere* (Cambridge: Polity).
Honneth, A. (1993) *The Critique of Power* (Cambridge, MA: MIT Press).
Hosokawa, S. (1984) 'The Walkman Effect', *Popular Music*, vol. 4, 165–80.
Kracauer, S. (1995) *The Mass Ornament: Weimar Essays* (Cambridge, MA: Harvard University Press).
Lefebvre, H. (1991) *The Production of Space* (Oxford: Blackwell).
Moebius, H. and Michel-Annen, B. (1994) 'Colouring the Grey Everyday: The Psychology of the Walkman', *Free Associations*, 4(4): 570–7.
Morley, D. (1992) *Television, Audiences and Cultural Studies* (London: Routledge).
Sennet, R. (1990) *The Conscience of the Eye: The Design and Social Life of Cities* (London: Faber and Faber).
Wolin, R. (1994) *Walter Benjamin: An Aesthetic of Redemption* (Berkeley, CA: University of California Press).

11 The Mediated 'Interaction Order'

SHAUN MOORES

I

The purpose of this chapter is to delimit a field of study, to define its distinctive objects of inquiry, and to give that field a name. I will call it a sociology of the mediated 'interaction order'.[1] Of course, in the general sense of the term, all social interaction – including that which takes place between co-present participants – is 'mediated' by the signs of language or gesture. However, my specific concern here is with various forms of *electronically mediated communication* between absent others, or else with those situated interactions in which the media play a crucial part. This covers relations between performers and audiences in broadcasting, communications via telephone or computer networks, and routine negotiations over the use of electronic media in everyday life.

While there is much existing work which could be considered to lie within the boundaries of this field – my chapter reviews selected examples of that literature – it is still unusual, even in a media studies context, for these technologies and forms of communication to be grouped together as objects in a single domain of investigation. Traditional divisions between 'mass' and 'interpersonal' communication have tended to obstruct the formation of such a field.[2] By assembling ideas and findings from a range of writings, I am making a case for the convergence of this theory and research around a shared interest in the dynamics and consequences of mediated interaction in modern society. The chapter concludes by proposing some ways in which new work on the cultural significance of the media might now be developed.

As a prelude to the discussion that follows, I want to begin by highlighting three central themes which run through this chapter.[3] The first of these is the position of different media in *social arrangements of space and time*. Television, radio, telephones and computers are communication technologies that have contributed to a significant shift in the spatial and temporal organisation of social life. Alongside other technological systems and institutional mechanisms in the modern world, they have served to 'lift' social relations out of face-to-face contexts and 'stretch' them across potentially vast distances, dislocating space from place. For instance, it has become possible for us to witness far-away events 'live' as they unfold in time, or to engage in dialogue with a distant interlocutor. In turn, the character of place is transformed as everyday settings are increasingly touched by remote forces.

My second theme in the following discussion is *cultural experiences of modernity*. Here, the question is 'how it feels' to live day-to-day life in contemporary conditions – and, more particularly, what difference communications technology has made to the nature of routine social experience. In modern society, for example, patterns of familiarity and estrangement have shifted quite dramatically. Although we may enjoy a relationship of 'intimacy at a distance' with a TV personality or fellow Internet user, many of our daily contacts in urban settings can be with people who are completely unknown to us, the impersonal sea of faces through which we pass on a city street. Presence and absence are themselves experienced in new ways as our opportunities for instantaneous access to distant or virtual locations are increased.

A third key theme is the role of electronically mediated communication in *constructions of self-identity and community*. With the spatial and temporal changes outlined above, that lifting and stretching of human relationships, comes a rapid expansion in the stock of symbolic resources which are available to social subjects as they actively shape their individual and collective identities. If the self is best understood as the product of an ongoing autobiographical 'narrative', then we need to ask where the raw material for our personal stories is obtained. To what extent are those resources extracted from the flow of mediated interactions? Similarly, it is important for us to recognise that modern communities are imaginative constructs, 'fictions' manufactured at the point where private lives and public discourses intersect. Senses of community are less place-bound than they once were before the arrival of electronic media.

II

Let us consider the case of broadcasting and examine that type of communication which John Thompson (1995) calls 'mediated quasi-interaction'. He employs a prefix to signal the fact that, although performers and audiences in television or radio are 'linked together in a process of … symbolic exchange', relations between them will not be characterised by 'the degree of reciprocity and interpersonal specificity of other forms of interaction' (Thompson, 1995: 84). In other words, because of a separation between the place of cultural production and multiple contexts of consumption, broadcast communications are typically 'monological' rather than 'dialogical' – there is a one-way centralised transmission of messages to geographically dispersed groups of viewers and listeners. Nevertheless, partly as a result of their distance from the message producers, those consumers may be able to exercise a degree of choice and interpretative agency in their engagements with TV and radio.[4]

In addition, because the moments of transmission and reception in broadcasting are virtually simultaneous, viewers or listeners can experience a sense of liveness – capturing some of the feelings of 'immediacy' which have traditionally accompanied face-to-face encounters. This phenomenon was originally observed by Donald Horton and Richard Wohl (1956) – who coined the phrase 'para-social interaction' to describe that routine, taken-for-granted yet quite remarkable relationship which the various 'personalities' of television or radio construct with their unknown, absent addressees. Speaking from the institutional site of the studio and orienting their utterances to the circumstances of everyday reception, presenters and show hosts will often employ relaxed and informal styles of talk which are designed to simulate certain aspects of co-present conversation amongst friends or acquaintances. As Horton and Wohl (1956: 215) noted, a public figure of this sort 'uses the mode of direct address' and 'talks as if … conversing personally or privately', even though he or she is actually communicating with a scattered audience of strangers. Across space and over time, regular viewers or listeners may form a 'bond of intimacy' with a personality they feel they have come to know.

We need not see such emotional attachments as pathological. Indeed, while they are quite remarkable, it could also be argued that they are a perfectly normal outcome of para-social interaction in broadcasting. The use of familiar or conversational speech, the electronic illusion of immediacy – and the organising principles of seriality and regularity in TV and radio output – all combine to create the conditions in which mediated 'friendships' might reasonably be expected to develop. It is true that this kind of intimacy is non-reciprocal. Television or radio personalities cannot possibly know all their audience members personally, but their performances will frequently be constructed so as to appear sociable and sincere (Scannell, 1996). Most of these figures have achieved celebrity status not through being extraordinary or special, but precisely by constituting themselves as homely and down-to-earth. John Langer (1981: 355) put it well when he said that broadcasting's personalities display a 'will to ordinariness'.

Nowhere is this will to ordinariness more evident than in the presentation of a TV magazine programme like *This Morning* (Moores, 1997: 223). The husband and wife who host the show each weekday morning are known to viewers by their first names, Richard and Judy, and they inhabit a studio set which is furnished in the manner of a family living room. To enhance that simulation of domesticity, guests are thanked for 'dropping in' or invited to 'visit again'. At particular points in the programme it is crucial for the presenters to reproduce their para-social relationship with the audience by speaking directly to camera in a casual fashion. For example, those greetings and farewells which are routinely uttered by Richard and Judy – 'morning to you', 'hiya', 'bye' and 'see you tomorrow' – get drawn from the sociable discourse of situated interaction in ordinary daily life.

Of course, as Karen Lury (1996) reminds us with her typology of performance styles on television, there are varying degrees of formality or informality displayed by personalities in different programmes and genres, from the serious and authoritative tone of a newsreader on the BBC's *Nine O'Clock News* through to the more playful or comedic presentation of a show such as Channel 4's *The Big Breakfast*.[5] Taking into account its position in the schedule, its content and projected audience, the producers of a TV programme must arrive at what they consider to be an appropriate mode of address for consumers. However, given what Norman Fairclough (1995: 10) calls a 'relaxation of the boundary between public affairs and entertainment' in broadcasting, there is now a tendency for even an established genre like news 'to become increasingly conversationalised'. There, in order that they might appear both believable and personable, presenters have long sought to combine the qualities of authority and familiarity – yet the balance between these two elements is shifting as news gets gradually less formal in style. Changes of this kind are especially evident at the level of regional or transnational broadcasting. I have witnessed them on the ITV bulletin *Scotland Today*, and on the *Sky News* channel.

As it offers access to mediated entertainment and information, inviting identifications with its personality system, broadcasting also provides viewers and listeners with a constant stream of symbolic materials from which to fashion their senses of self. Alongside those resources that are 'to hand' in situated cultures, this flow of images and sounds is selectively and creatively appropriated by social subjects as they try to 'put together' personal identities and lifestyles. Television and radio programmes, their narrative structures or substantive contents, can feed into that ongoing process of identity-formation in two main ways. Firstly, they may be contributing to what Richard Ochberg (1994: 113) terms the 'storied nature' of contemporary selfhood. Secondly, to borrow an important idea from Anthony Giddens (1991), they supply knowledge which is then incorporated into everyday actions and strategies of living – helping to facilitate the 'institutional reflexivity' of modernity.

It is clearly the case that, in the course of our day-to-day lives, one of the means by which we seek to sustain a coherent sense of 'who we are' is through our inner speech or narratives (Johnson, 1986) – stories we routinely tell ourselves in an effort to impose some sort of order on the fragments of modern cultural experience. These stories are concerned, for instance, with structuring personal histories or planning possible futures. They are private accounts that are told inside the head, and yet they often rely on external public representations to give them shape and meaning. Certain genres of broadcast fiction such as the continuous serial or the family drama, along with human-interest documentaries or interview programmes, provide suitable plots and formats for this type of internal account. Which TV soap opera viewer has not at some point compared an aspect of their own life situation with that of a fictional character? Similarly, which Radio 4 listener has never thought about compiling their individual list of *Desert Island Discs* or imagined themselves 'on air' recounting key biographical episodes from the past?

In turn, this revisable 'narrative of the self' is part of a more general reflexivity that is essential for the functioning of modern society. Giddens (1991: 20) is careful here to distinguish between 'the reflexive monitoring of action intrinsic to all human activity' and what he prefers to call an institutional reflexivity, 'the regularised use of knowledge about the circumstances of social life as a constitutive element in its organisation and transformation'. His initial example is the role of published material on marriage, divorce and the family in providing information which can be appropriated and incorporated into decisions about how or whether to enter into specific sorts of relationship with others. He argues that anybody today who contemplates getting married or ending a long-term relationship will already be quite aware of 'what is going on' in this sphere of social action, and as Debra Grodin and Thomas Lindlof (1996: 6) remind us, modernity is 'characterised by questions that were unprecedented in premodern times. ... "How do I raise my child?" or "How do I treat my spouse?"'. The answers to such questions are not fixed and given. They are a matter of debate, open to revision and potentially the cause of anxiety or uncertainty. Television and radio are media through which that debate is frequently channelled. Studio discussion programmes and phone-in shows offer a forum for the expression of opinion or advice, while popular fictions like *Coronation Street* and *EastEnders* confront us with moral dilemmas.

If self-identity is permeated in these ways by electronically mediated communication, then senses of collective identity or 'imagined community' (Anderson, 1983) are dependent to a similar extent on symbolic interactions with the media. For instance, Paddy Scannell and David Cardiff (1991) have charted the role of British public service broadcasting in constructing an accessible and knowable national culture during the inter-war years, providing a common schedule of radio output which was available simultaneously to dispersed millions. From the privacy of their homes, listeners could tune in to the routine fare of news or entertainment and also to the BBC's live coverage of major state or sporting occasions. They were thereby invited to identify with a wider 'general public' and to imagine themselves as members of an abstract community that was reproduced by broadcasting day in day out, week in week out, year in year out. Despite being very much an institution of the modern age, the BBC gradually invented its own traditions, establishing its own national calendar of events. One such 'media event', as Daniel Dayan and Elihu Katz (1992) would have called it, was the monarch's annual Christmas Day message – first instituted back in the 1930s yet accepted soon afterwards as a taken-for-granted part of the festive season. On this special occasion, the head of state spoke directly and intimately to the British people, addressing them both individually and collectively as national subjects.

Today, however, that old feeling of confidence in the existence of the nation as a shared community is not so readily available from broadcasting. Of course, the BBC continues to provide its viewers and listeners with common access to a schedule of national programming – but by the 1990s, several factors have contributed to a shift in the imaginative geography of community and in television's 'electronic landscapes'. Alongside general changes in the spatio-temporal organisation of modern institutions – like the international scale of commerce and politics, and the expanding reach of transportation networks – we are witnessing a trend towards the 'transnationalisation' or globalisation of media industries and audiences. The 'deregulation' of broadcasting and the introduction of new technologies for cable or satellite TV transmission have led to a greater level of competition between television companies. As David Morley and Kevin Robins (1995) note in their recent book on media and collective identities, these policies of deregulation have brought a marked decline in the influence of national public service broadcasting in Western Europe. What they see there is an 'expansionist tendency at work, pushing ceaselessly towards the construction of enlarged audio-visual spaces and markets' (Morley and Robins, 1995: 11).[6]

III

Precisely the same set of issues – to do with arrangements of space and time, experiences of modernity, and constructions of self and community – must also be central to any consideration of our social interactions via the telephone or computer. Before I pursue those themes, though, it would be helpful to pause for a moment and reflect on what marks these media out as different from broadcast TV and radio. Clearly, a basic difference is the capacity which both telephones and computers have for facilitating direct one-to-one interpersonal communication at a distance, either by electronically transmitted speech or written text.[7] A second distinguishing feature is the heightened level of 'reciprocity' which they each allow in comparison with the quasi-interaction of broadcasting. This results in a 'blurring' of the binary opposition between production and consumption. In communications that are mediated via telephone or computer networks, it is less easy to identify performers and audiences – at least as separate groups of people – because users of the technology are continually switching their positions as message producers or consumers.

The fact that the telephone can be used as a sociable medium (Fischer, 1991), as a means of maintaining friendships or for 'kinkeeping' purposes, is evident in the advertising slogans which are employed by the telecommunications industry – 'it's good to talk', 'reach out and touch someone'. Furthermore, the fact that it falls to female callers to do much of this emotional labour has been of considerable interest to researchers such as Ann Moyal (1989) in Australia and Lana Rakow

(1992) in the United States. In their studies of the 'feminine culture of the telephone', they each detail the resourceful ways in which women have appropriated the medium in order to sustain social relationships across space and over time with absent friends and family. Again, technology offers entry to electronic communities of a sort, and the conversational interaction which it enables to take place may serve as a partial substitute for regular face-to-face contact.

However, we must not assume that this electronically mediated communication will always be a satisfactory replacement for physical co-presence with known others. Indeed, while reflecting on her interviews with women in a remote rural area, Rakow (1992: 151) suggests that their use of the telephone might equally be seen as a sign of 'isolation ... boredom or fear'. She is careful to avoid the trap of thinking that mediated experiences can ever simply transcend the problems of 'real life' in a situated locality, an important point to which I return below in my discussion of computer cultures. The reliance of her interviewees on telephone communication was largely down to the restricted control which they exerted over their own physical location. For instance, several found themselves isolated in the country as a result of having moved there with men. So even if phone networks could 'make all points equidistant ... the point from which these women are starting is not necessarily of their own choosing' (Rakow, 1992: 62). Here, then, is a valuable reminder of the material limitations which help to shape symbolic exchanges in modern society. Telephone use in this particular example may well constitute a creative set of gendered cultural practices, but ultimately they are acted out within determinate social constraints.

Thus far, I have focused our attention on mediated interactions and quasi-interactions where the participants are seeking to reproduce a routine experience of familiarity – callers speaking with friends and relatives by phone, or television viewers identifying with screen personalities. Yet on certain occasions, it could be the case that more fleeting and anonymous encounters are being sought. Gary Gumpert (1990) presents a revealing account of such communications in his analysis of 'remote sex' via the telephone and computer. He is concerned with the dynamics and consequences of this erotic discourse between strangers, in which callers or 'keyboarders' engage in a live spoken or written event. Subscribing to services with names like *Fantasy Phone Inc.*, *The Hot Line* and *EROTICOMM*, users are spatially separated but they participate in temporally simultaneous electronic conferences – involving two people or sometimes larger groups.

One of the features of that jointly constructed dialogue is the ability it gives interlocutors to indulge in fantasy narratives and to develop fictional personae for themselves which are quite different from those they inhabit in their ordinary, everyday lives.

Aside from these forms of specifically pornographic communication, there are also numerous other text-based 'virtual realities' now available to us on the Internet, interactive electronic environments in which a participant's own 'presentation of self' is heavily dependent on the description of character and appearance that is offered to others who are known only on the same terms. As a number of recent commentators have argued, such on-line chat sessions and role-playing games – which are enacted collaboratively within the computer network's multi-user domains, or MUDs – allow self-identity to be experimented with in new and interesting ways.[8] Perhaps the most astute social theorist currently writing on this topic is Sherry Turkle (1996). Carrying out her ethnographic fieldwork both in actual places and simulated locations, she looks at the putting together of personal identities in between what MUD inhabitants call RL – real life – and the expanding frontiers of virtual reality or 'cyberspace'.

A fundamental starting point here is the idea that contemporary subjectivities are fragmented and multiple. Of course, as discussed above in the preceding section of my chapter, we will usually try to construct a coherent sense of selfhood through our inner speech or storytelling – but what happens when these narratives appear on a computer screen, and when the stories cast us in roles which are not those played in day-to-day life outside cyberspace? For example, a normally shy graduate student living in modest university accommodation builds an elegant apartment for himself on the MUD, and through an alias becomes romantically involved with a fellow player who logs on from another continent. His fantasy character develops an on-line friendship with hers, which then leads to an 'engagement' and finally to a simulated 'wedding ceremony', a virtual event that is 'witnessed' and celebrated by other computer users. In cyberspace, he is able to interact with a confidence which is lacking in RL, and tells Turkle (1996: 193) how he would like 'to feel that his MUD life is part of his real life'. Yet when it comes to his own co-present interactions in local settings, this young man finds it difficult to draw on any of the confidence he has gained in communication with his absent lover on the global Net. In the end, situated and mediated experience remain deeply divided and his self-identity is split or distributed across different sites.

If MUDs are primarily sites for chat or game playing, albeit serious play for some computer users, then other areas on the Net are devoted to public debate and to a sharing of knowledge on specialist topics – leading a technological optimist like William Mitchell (1995) to enthuse over the formation of 'electronic agoras' for the so-called 'soft cities' of the next millennium. He believes that the Internet will have 'as crucial a role in twenty-first century urbanity as the centrally located, spatially bounded, architecturally celebrated agora did (according to Aristotle's *Politics*) in the life of the Greek polis' (Mitchell, 1995: 8). His utopian vision is one in which on-line communities might enable us, despite our largely privatised existence, to combat an erosion of civil society – as we gather together in virtual locations that substitute for collective meeting places where opinions and ideas are exchanged.

A rather more cautious or pessimistic view is being offered by Kevin Robins (1996), who remains suspicious of those enthusiastic terms in which certain writers are now describing the virtual community. Although their visions may appear to be futuristic, he detects a fundamentally nostalgic imagination at work there, a kind of 'techno-communitarianism' that advocates 'extending the security of small-town "gemeinschaft" to the transnational scale of the global village' (Robins, 1996: 21). Instead of seeking simulated utopian alternatives to our presently existing culture, Robins invites us to look at cyberspace firmly in the context of 'the world we live in', by which he means a material world of social inequalities and power relations. Similarly, when considering the implications of computer-mediated communications for modern public life, Jim McGuigan (1996: 184) reminds his readers of a wide gap between the 'information-haves' and the 'information-have-nots' – pointing out that most of this earth's population still has no easy access to old IT such as the telephone, let alone new computer technologies.

IV

Further sobering thoughts are voiced by Deirdre Boden and Harvey Molotch (1994). It is their bold assertion that – in all the excitement generated by recent developments in media technology – the enduring significance of routine, co-present interaction has actually been under-appreciated. They produce a wealth of empirical evidence which suggests that, even in our technologically advanced modern society where human relationships might be extended across space and time, 'the compulsion of proximity' is alive and well. For instance, while communicating with absent friends or family by telephone or electronic mail, it is not unusual for us to say things like 'I miss you' or 'let's meet up soon' – and when we do meet up, to use phrases such as 'it's great to see you again'. There will obviously be times when mediated interactions are preferred for various reasons over situated encounters. However, the general point here is that electronic communication has not totally removed our desire to be both physically and emotionally close to others. Far from it, because we continue to live in what Giddens (1990: 143) names a 'peopled world' and 'not merely one of anonymous, blank faces'. Modernity, then, is characterised by certain sorts of proximate intimacy – as well as by mediated intimacy at a distance or by the polite, impersonal rituals of 'civil inattention' (Goffman, 1963: 84) between strangers in many urban settings today.

The strength of that case for the continued study of situated interactions need not lead social theorists and researchers away from the media, though. I want to argue that a sociology of the mediated interaction order must also account for the complex ways in which information and communication technologies are knotted into everyday encounters between co-present participants. Those relationships which people form in places like households, neighbourhoods, work and leisure contexts are frequently negotiated around electronic media – in the course of using television, radio, telephones or computers. So in the little dramas of day-to-day living, these technological objects and their symbolic contents may serve as part of what Erving Goffman (1969) once called the 'stage props' and 'scenery' for interpersonal behaviour.

In his analysis of the 'social uses' of broadcasting in domestic situations, James Lull (1990) talks about TV being employed in precisely this fashion – as an affiliation resource with which audience members can engineer shared moments of intimacy, physical contact and family solidarity. One of his examples is a household where, during a period of participant observation, the husband and wife were seen to touch on two specific occasions. On the first of these, he notes that the 'medium' for their playful embrace was the daughter, who returned from school with a humorous story to tell – but on the second occasion, it was the medium of television which provided them with an opportunity for closeness. The husband was tired and 'fell asleep when he watched television at night', while the wife, 'who had been sitting on the floor in the same room … leaned back until her head rested against his bare feet and smiled' (Lull, 1990: 38). Although this particular instance of proximity is profoundly mundane, such ordinary events are the very stuff of social interaction in families.

Of course, households might just as easily be sites of discord and avoidance as havens of harmony or domestic solidarity (Bausinger, 1984). There is a 'politics of the living room', and the broadcast media are often located at the centre of interpersonal struggles in consumption contexts.[9] David Morley (1986: 148) has remarked upon the position of the remote control device in TV viewing arrangements, finding this gadget to be typically 'the symbolic possession of the father (or the son, in the father's absence) which sits "on the arm of Daddy's chair" and is used almost exclusively by him'. Disputes over which programme or channel to watch are frequently resolved in ways that reflect a patriarchal structure of authority in the home. Turning our attention to a different domestic technology, we could point to gendered and generational frictions in family life over access to the telephone, or over the size of the quarterly phone bill. Most people will have experienced these tensions at some time – for example, as teenagers fighting for the right to talk privately with friends and thereby mark out independent identities, or as parents worried about the accumulated expense of those calls. It is therefore necessary for us to see the technology not simply as a means of interacting with absent others, but as a 'fixed prop' for co-present encounters and for situated practices of self-presentation.

Beyond the front door, in the neighbourhood setting, there are also occasions when media technologies can serve as props for the performance of identity – or else for struggles over the meaning of local community. The arrival of satellite dish aerials in the UK during the late 1980s and early 1990s gave rise to what Charlotte Brunsdon (1991) refers to as a 'controversy about siting', a kind of taste war fought out between 'dish erectors' and 'anti-dishers'. For members of the former group, the object was a public sign of their investment in 'the new'. Meanwhile, for the latter group – especially those living in 'respectable' areas of older housing – it posed a threat to the financial or 'heritage' value of their residential properties. Discourses of innovation and conservation confronted each other head on in a curious collision of aesthetic and cultural codes. These circumstances resulted in a range of emotional dispositions being displayed towards the dish on the outside wall of the house, from senses of pride or embarrassment through to feelings of distaste and disgust (Moores, 1996).

Reception analysts in media studies have recently begun to document the circulation of TV narratives in public workplaces and leisure interactions, too. Dorothy Hobson (1989) has investigated routine talk about soap opera amongst female office workers, noting that the consumption of this popular entertainment does not come to an end in the privacy of the home. Instead, continuous serials provide some of the material which is used to generate day-to-day 'gossip' with workmates.[10] Hobson (1989: 150) saw how such talk is 'fitted in around their working time or in lunch breaks', and she heard it taking 'the form of storytelling, commenting on the stories ... moving from the drama to discussing the incidents which are happening in the "real world"'. Charting a similar process in a different context, in this case the peer group interactions of British Asian youths, Marie Gillespie (1993: 27) argues that these 'young people's everyday verbal discourse is informed in significant ways by their soap viewing not simply in its content but also ... in its form'. Discussion of *Neighbours* – a globally distributed Australian fiction – was inextricably linked with utterances about other, more local matters. At first, the two appeared almost indistinguishable to her, as the focus of gossip shifted unselfconsciously between mediated culture and immediate social circumstances.

Just as Hobson challenged the idea that investigations of television viewing can be confined to the domestic situations in which it usually takes place, so Leslie Haddon (1992) contends that 'home computing' must not be seen as a solely home-based cultural activity. Reflecting back on his study of teenage boys and microcomputers, conducted in the 1980s, he encourages us to look at school and leisure settings as important locales for the production of 'computer talk' – a specific type of competitive banter in which the boys would evaluate hardware and software, and compare notes on their game-playing abilities. The consumption of those goods in the household was shaped in part by outside interactions with peers. In turn, their private use of technology became a resource for public leisure in the context of the schoolyard or computer club.

None of this points towards a disappearance of 'thick' co-present communications. Rather, it illustrates the changing 'interaction mix' of daily life in the modern world (Thompson, 1995: 87), in which media use and proximate interpersonal exchanges are either mutually dependent or simultaneously enacted. A further example of this 'blurred genre' of social behaviour is the current emergence of coffee houses in the high street with names like *The CyberCafe* and *Cyberia*. In these places there is an intriguing blend of old and new cultural activities. Customers pay for food and drink, chatting to staff and to other customers as they might do in any café or bar setting – but in addition, they buy access to a computer screen and keyboard, 'surfing' the Net to contact absent interlocutors. Could it be said that sociability is being sustained on two separate fronts at once here – as conversations are held both with those who are nearby and those who are, at least in physical terms, far away?

V

Let us now look at some of the conceptual and practical implications of delimiting our field of study in this way, of defining our objects of inquiry in the manner proposed by my chapter. I will consider four such implications. First of all, we require *an expanded and more inclusive definition of electronic media* than that which has traditionally been employed by media sociologists. There is still a strong tendency, even today, to equate media analysis rather too narrowly with an investigation of 'mass communication' – and even if the recent interest in reception has enabled us to see how television and radio use are intricately bound up with situated interactions in day-to-day life, we do need to pay much greater attention to 'mediated interpersonal' communications conducted via the telephone and computer. Of course, as is clearly acknowledged in my preceding commentary, these different forms of mediated interaction and quasi-interaction have their own distinctive features – yet I am proposing that there is much to be gained by studying them side-by-side in the broader context of debates about communication and modernity. In any event, arguments for a convergence of academic work around the notion of a mediated interaction order are soon likely to be overtaken by technological convergence in the media industries. Manufacturers themselves are seeking to develop a new generation of entertainment and information services which can increasingly bridge the gap between broadcasting, telecommunications and computing.

Secondly, it is also necessary for us to adopt *a modified vocabulary of critical terms* for the purposes of media inquiry. So alongside those key concepts which are found in contemporary media studies – 'ideology', 'power', 'discourse' and so forth – I am suggesting that we recover an alternative series of terms like 'para-social interaction', 'presentation of self' and 'sociability'. These come out of a different strand of modern social theory which has been concerned directly with the performative or experiential dimensions of culture, aspects of symbolic exchange which in my view deserve our careful scrutiny. This is certainly not to deny the ideological or political dimensions of electronically mediated communication, but to propose that they are best approached via basic issues of human interaction and lived experience. Neither is this merely an academic game of words, because concepts which are chosen to describe and interpret various objects in a field of study are absolutely crucial in shaping the perspective taken by social researchers.

Thirdly, I would argue that we must now find adequate research strategies with which *to investigate the complex interaction mixes of daily life in modern society*. This is easier said than done. How might it be practically possible for us to chart a combination of often simultaneous activities involving situated, mediated interpersonal and mediated quasi-interaction – especially when those activities interweave presence and absence, and when some of them are extended or stretched across space and time? Where should our mapping of these kinds of 'hybrid' communication begin? My pragmatic answer is to say that, despite the highly mobile and dispersed character of communications in contemporary culture, it has to start with the everyday practices of particular social subjects in specific places or locales. Recognising the 'permeability' of place, we could then go on to explore the many distant or virtual sites to which people travel imaginatively in their routine existence, utilising electronic media ourselves in the course of the research. The methods of participant or non-participant observation and conversational interviewing, and the analysis of media texts or solicited documentary materials, may provide us with valuable data for constructing detailed ethnographic 'portraits' of interaction patterns.

Fourthly, and finally, it follows that one practical way of examining modernity's mixed or hybrid interactions is *by grounding them in ongoing biographical projects*. At several points in my chapter I have referred to the idea that senses of self-identity or imagined community are put together as part of a reflexive project, as subjects draw selectively on the available symbolic resources. By accessing their narratives of individual and collective identity, it might be possible to discover precisely how they are attempting to combine a range of situated and mediated communications in an orderly and organised fashion. Indeed, there is no reason why – so long as it is only understood as a preparatory step – social theorists cannot take an autobiographical turn and 'look to themselves' for leads here, considering personal stories of self or community as concrete instances of a more general process.

NOTES

In revising the chapter for publication I have drawn on comments made by participants attending the 1997 British Sociological Association Conference at the University of York. Other audiences for this material included seminars in the Department of Film and Television Studies at the University of Warwick, and in the Research Centre for Social Sciences at the University of Edinburgh.

1. The title of my chapter is an intentional reference to that of a paper written by Erving Goffman (1983) shortly before his death. For Goffman, the 'interaction order' was understood primarily as a realm of face-to-face interpersonal contact, 'that which uniquely transpires in social situations ... environments in which two or more individuals are physically in one another's response presence' (Goffman, 1983: 2). Throughout his career as a sociologist, he argued that this face-to-face realm deserved to be taken seriously as a focus of inquiry. It was, he believed, the site of 'a particular kind of activity as in the phrase "the economic order"' – but it was also apparent to him that 'as an order of activity, the interaction one, more than any other perhaps, is in fact orderly' (Goffman, 1983: 5). Late in his academic life he did begin to research some aspects of technologically mediated communication – for example, see the essay on radio talk in Goffman (1981) – yet this was never his central analytical concern. Might it be possible, though, to conceive of a 'mediated' interaction order with its own particular conventions and organising principles?
2. However, there are a few notable attempts to overcome this barrier. For instance, see Joshua Meyrowitz (1985) – who tried to combine the insights of Goffman with those of Marshall McLuhan – and also the essays collected in Gary Gumpert and Robert Cathcart (1986). More recently, Patrice Flichy (1995) has written a social history of modern communications which looks jointly at the development of broadcasting, telephones and computers.
3. In highlighting these themes, it is clear that the agenda for this chapter has been influenced by Anthony Giddens's social theory of modernity (Giddens, 1990; 1991). For a critical discussion of Giddens's key concepts – such as 'time–space distanciation', 'disembedding' and 're-embedding' – and an assessment of their relevance for contemporary media studies, see Moores (1995).
4. There has been a good deal of work in media studies over the past 20 years on matters of consumption, taste and interpretation – for a summary see Moores (1993a).
5. We should note that her performance typology also incorporates styles of acting in television fiction, as well as the frequent screen appearances of lay participants on a 'people-centred game show' like *Blind Date* – where the willed ordinariness and performed sincerity of the celebrity host, Cilla Black, is enhanced by the presence of contestants who are drawn from the general public. For further discussion of the role of the

lay participant in broadcasting, see Sonia Livingstone and Peter Lunt (1994). Their work is concerned with daytime programmes in Britain and the United States which feature studio audiences in discussion and debate. Once again, this is a TV genre that foregrounds the personality of the presenter – reflected by titles such as *Kilroy!*, *Esther*, *The Oprah Winfrey Show* and *Ricki Lake*.

6. In these changed economic circumstances, a crucial question is how viewers in local settings are responding to transformations on the global stage. Any discussion of the impact of new television technologies and 'territories of transmission' has to be grounded in a study of the daily 'domestic rituals' which consumers act out behind closed doors. It is necessary for us to enter the private sphere of the home, in order to ask what difference this altered 'menu' of cultural resources is making to patterns of identification with community. See Moores (1993b, 1996), on the everyday uses and interpretations of satellite TV, for a modest attempt to answer that question.
7. Two minor qualifications to my statement are required. Firstly, as well as the usual person-to-person calls made routinely by phone users, 'teleconferencing' services are now available – while computers can offer access to numerous 'multi-user domains', and topically oriented discussion groups otherwise known as 'newsgroups'. For an analysis of newsgroup discourse, see Nancy Baym (1995). Baym's research focuses on interactions between participants who exchange ideas and information about television soap operas. In addition, computer-mediated communication is no longer conducted solely by means of written text. For example, on the Internet, it is possible to create and visit 'web sites' where images and sounds may be experienced.
8. These commentators include Elizabeth Reid (1995), Heather Bromberg (1996) and Caroline Bassett (1997) – all of whom discuss creative practices of 'identity play' on MUDs where the participants encounter each other as they pass through 'rooms' in virtual architecture. Here, users will usually construct an alias or a series of aliases for themselves, sometimes 'morphing' between different characters and appearances. Inventive as the practices are, they inevitably raise questions about the integrity and sincerity of self-presentation. How can participants be sure precisely who they are in dialogue with? To what extent do screen identities correspond with those performed in life away from the computer?
9. This was clearly so from the beginnings of broadcasting in the inter-war period. See Moores (1988) for an oral history of early radio's entry and incorporation into the private sphere in the 1920s and 1930s, which highlighted the different meanings that new technology had for men and for women. Within masculine discourses, it was constituted as a 'miraculous toy' – a great adventure in technical experimentation – while from a feminine perspective, initially at least, it was experienced as an unwanted intrusion into daily life. Only later did the housewife welcome the wireless, as the listening apparatus was redesigned to resemble a fashionable piece of furniture, and as the broadcasters' schedules started to 'chime in' with the household's rhythms. Radio

gradually came to 'capture time and space' in the home, finding its way into domestic geographies and routines.

10. See Christine Geraghty (1981) for an important account of the role of gossip – both within the continuous serial, where characters offer an ongoing commentary on the narrative action, and outside it as regular viewers speculate on possible outcomes. In doing so, they draw on the knowledge they have gained of the programme's past, using it to predict the future direction of storylines.

REFERENCES

Anderson, Benedict (1983) *Imagined Communities: Reflections on the Origin and Spread of Nationalism* (London: Verso).

Bassett, Caroline (1997) 'Virtually Gendered: Life in an On-Line World', in Ken Gelder and Sarah Thornton (eds), *The Subcultures Reader* (London: Routledge), pp. 537–50.

Bausinger, Hermann (1984) 'Media, Technology and Daily Life', *Media, Culture and Society*, 6(4): 343–51.

Baym, Nancy (1995) 'From Practice to Culture on Usenet', in Susan Star (ed.), *The Cultures of Computing* (Oxford: Blackwell/Sociological Review), pp. 29–52.

Boden, Deirdre and Harvey Molotch (1994) 'The Compulsion of Proximity', in Roger Friedland and Deirdre Boden (eds), *NowHere: Space, Time and Modernity* (Berkeley, CA: University of California Press), pp. 257–86.

Bromberg, Heather (1996) 'Are MUDs Communities? Identity, Belonging and Consciousness in Virtual Worlds', in Rob Shields (ed.), *Cultures of Internet: Virtual Spaces, Real Histories, Living Bodies* (London: Sage), pp. 143–52.

Brunsdon, Charlotte (1991) 'Satellite Dishes and the Landscapes of Taste', *New Formations*, 15: 23–42.

Dayan, Daniel and Elihu Katz (1992) *Media Events: The Live Broadcasting of History* (Cambridge, MA: Harvard University Press).

Fairclough, Norman (1995) *Media Discourse* (London: Arnold).

Fischer, Claude (1991) '"Touch Someone": The Telephone Industry Discovers Sociability', in Marcel Lafollette and Jeffrey Stine (eds), *Technology and Choice: Readings from 'Technology and Culture'* (Chicago, IL: University of Chicago Press), pp. 87–116.

Flichy, Patrice (1995) *Dynamics of Modern Communication: The Shaping and Impact of New Communication Technologies* (London: Sage).

Geraghty, Christine (1981) 'The Continuous Serial: A Definition', in Richard Dyer, Christine Geraghty, Marion Jordan, Terry Lovell, Richard Paterson and John Stewart (eds), *Coronation Street* (London: British Film Institute – BFI TV Monograph 13), pp. 9–26.

Giddens, Anthony (1990) *The Consequences of Modernity* (Cambridge: Polity).

Giddens, Anthony (1991) *Modernity and Self-Identity: Self and Society in the Late Modern Age* (Cambridge: Polity).

Gillespie, Marie (1993) 'Soap Viewing, Gossip and Rumour amongst Punjabi Youth in Southall', in Phillip Drummond, Richard Paterson and Janet Willis (eds), *National Identity and Europe: The Television Revolution* (London: British Film Institute), pp. 25–42.

Goffman, Erving (1963) *Behavior in Public Places: Notes on the Social Organization of Gatherings* (New York: Free Press).

Goffman, Erving (1969) *The Presentation of Self in Everyday Life* (London: Allen Lane).

Goffman, Erving (1981) *Forms of Talk* (Oxford: Blackwell).

Goffman, Erving (1983) 'The Interaction Order', *American Sociological Review*, 48(1): 1–17.

Grodin, Debra and Thomas Lindlof (1996) 'The Self and Mediated Communication', in Debra Grodin and Thomas Lindlof (eds), *Constructing the Self in a Mediated World* (Thousand Oaks, CA: Sage), pp. 3–12.

Gumpert, Gary (1990) 'Remote Sex in the Information Age', in Gary Gumpert and Sandra Fish (eds), *Talking to Strangers: Mediated Therapeutic Communication* (Norwood: Ablex), pp. 143–53.

Gumpert, Gary and Robert Cathcart (eds) (1986) *Inter/Media: Interpersonal Communication in a Media World* (New York: Oxford University Press).

Haddon, Leslie (1992) 'Explaining ICT Consumption: The Case of the Home Computer', in Roger Silverstone and Eric Hirsch (eds), *Consuming Technologies: Media and Information in Domestic Spaces* (London: Routledge), pp. 82–96.

Hobson, Dorothy (1989) 'Soap Operas at Work', in Ellen Seiter, Hans Borchers, Gabriele Kreutzner and Eva-Maria Warth (eds), *Remote Control: Television, Audiences and Cultural Power* (London: Routledge), pp. 150–67.

Horton, Donald and Richard Wohl (1956) 'Mass Communication and Para-Social Interaction: Observations on Intimacy at a Distance', *Psychiatry*, 19(3): 215–29.

Johnson, Richard (1986) 'The Story So Far: and Further Transformations?', in David Punter (ed.), *Introduction to Contemporary Cultural Studies* (London: Longman), pp. 277–313.

Langer, John (1981) 'Television's "Personality System"', *Media, Culture and Society*, 3(4): 351–65.

Livingstone, Sonia and Peter Lunt (1994) *Talk on Television: Audience Participation and Public Debate* (London: Routledge).

Lull, James (1990) *Inside Family Viewing: Ethnographic Research on Television's Audiences* (London: Routledge).

Lury, Karen (1996) 'Television Performance: Being, Acting and "Corpsing"', *New Formations*, 27: 114–27.

McGuigan, Jim (1996) *Culture and the Public Sphere* (London: Routledge).

Meyrowitz, Joshua (1985) *No Sense of Place: The Impact of Electronic Media on Social Behavior* (New York: Oxford University Press).

Mitchell, William (1995) *City of Bits: Space, Place and the Infobahn* (Cambridge, MA: MIT Press).

Moores, Shaun (1988) '"The Box on the Dresser": Memories of Early Radio and Everyday Life', *Media, Culture and Society*, 10(1): 23–40.

Moores, Shaun (1993a) *Interpreting Audiences: The Ethnography of Media Consumption* (London: Sage).

Moores, Shaun (1993b) 'Satellite TV as Cultural Sign: Consumption, Embedding and Articulation', *Media, Culture and Society*, 15(4): 621–39.

Moores, Shaun (1995) 'Media, Modernity and Lived Experience', *Journal of Communication Inquiry*, 19(1): 5–19.

Moores, Shaun (1996) *Satellite Television and Everyday Life: Articulating Technology* (Luton: John Libbey Media – Acamedia Research Monograph 18).

Moores, Shaun (1997) 'Broadcasting and its Audiences', in Hugh Mackay (ed.), *Consumption and Everyday Life* (London: Sage/Open University), pp. 213–46.

Morley, David (1986) *Family Television: Cultural Power and Domestic Leisure* (London: Comedia).

Morley, David and Kevin Robins (1995) *Spaces of Identity: Global Media, Electronic Landscapes and Cultural Boundaries* (London: Routledge).

Moyal, Ann (1989) 'The Feminine Culture of the Telephone: People, Patterns and Policy', *Prometheus*, 7(1): 5–31.

Ochberg, Richard (1994) 'Life Stories and Storied Lives', in Amia Lieblich and Ruthellen Josselson (eds), *The Narrative Study of Lives: Exploring Identity and Gender* (Thousand Oaks, CA: Sage), pp. 113–44.

Rakow, Lana (1992) *Gender on the Line: Women, the Telephone and Community Life* (Urbana, IL: University of Illinois Press).

Reid, Elizabeth (1995) 'Virtual Worlds: Culture and Imagination', in Steven Jones (ed.), *CyberSociety: Computer-Mediated Communication and Community* (Thousand Oaks, CA: Sage), pp. 164–83.

Robins, Kevin (1996) 'Cyberspace and the World We Live In', in Jon Dovey (ed.), *Fractal Dreams: New Media in Social Context* (London: Lawrence and Wishart), pp. 1–30.

Scannell, Paddy (1996) *Radio, Television and Modern Life: A Phenomenological Approach* (Oxford: Blackwell).

Scannell, Paddy and David Cardiff (1991) *A Social History of British Broadcasting*, vol. 1: *1922–1939: Serving the Nation* (Oxford: Blackwell).

Thompson, John (1995) *The Media and Modernity: A Social Theory of the Media* (Cambridge: Polity).

Turkle, Sherry (1996) *Life on the Screen: Identity in the Age of the Internet* (London: Weidenfeld and Nicolson).

12 Junk Mail and Consumer Freedom: Resistance, Transgression and Reward in the Panoptic Gaze

GILLIAN REYNOLDS and
CATRINA ALFEROFF

INTRODUCTION

Unsolicited direct mail – or, as it is more frequently called, 'junk mail' – is an issue about which most people have an opinion. We either love it, or we hate it; it is a pleasure, or a pain. As far as the authors are aware however, the issue has yet to be fully debated by sociologists. This chapter therefore seeks to make a contribution to such a debate. In particular, it addresses some relationships between power, agency and subjectivity, by means of an exploration of attitudes towards junk mail and perceptions of the centralisation of personal data.

The gaze of the 'electronic panopticon' manifests itself in many aspects of our lives. Information processes are central to junk mail, as individuals are re-formulated into binary codes (Baudrillard, 1983). The phenomenon of junk mail is conceptualised here as an extension of the 'electronic panopticon' (Lyon, 1988) by which desired behaviours are rewarded with further junk mail: but in the process, consumers can enact their own punishments and rewards. Through our individual activities and resistance, however, we can – in a limited way – manipulate the clarity of the gaze to our advantage.

The authors' mutual interest in junk mail developed after one of us found herself unexpectedly registered on a database. Several informal discussions with colleagues suggested a fairly widespread ignorance amongst us about how this whole system 'worked'. Accordingly, a small advertisement was placed in a national newspaper, seeking participants in a pilot study, under the heading of 'Junk mail: pleasure or pain?' This generated some interest from both local and national radio stations, and discussions on their programmes led to further expressions of interest from people throughout England, Scotland and Wales, yielding in total approximately 60 responses.

Short postal questionnaires were sent to all these respondents, which included a request to keep junk mail for a number of weeks. At the end of this time, further questionnaires were distributed, which included a section on the frequency of different types of junk mail they had received. People were also asked at this stage whether they would be prepared to take part in an in-depth interview. Limited finances dictated that, where possible, those who lived in geographical 'clusters' were eventually interviewed, usually in their own homes, but occasionally at other venues such as place of employment. Altogether, ten in-depth interviews took place, from the West Country, London and the North of England.[1] The tapes were later transcribed and analysed. Data from both interviews and questionnaires are used here. Those who decided to take part were divided between enthusiastic supporters of junk mail – both as producers and consumers – and those who, for various reasons, had degrees of antipathy towards it. In an under-researched topic, both groups may be conceptualised as 'ideal types', providing much insight for further analysis.

For the purpose of this chapter, 'junk mail' is defined as items of unsolicited mail which are delivered by a postal worker to a named individual at a specific address. The designation on the envelope is usually accompanied by a series of identification numbers which differ from the standard postcode. We do not include unaddressed leaflets which fall out of newspapers and magazines, or which are distributed by hand throughout a local area. Neither do we address the issue of junk mail on the Internet, nor unsolicited telephone marketing.

TECHNIQUE AND THE INFORMATION SOCIETY

Before proceeding further, it is necessary to explain the ways in which the databases for junk mail are collated. The discussion is located within the context of technology, technique and consumerism in an 'information society'.

> Technique has … become a generalised mediation, so that it is no longer possible for us to form relationships of any kind without its intervening between us and our environment.
>
> (Ellul, 1980: 242)

Following Marcuse (1964), Ellul argues that the socially acceptable face of technological advance lies in the principle of technique, the 'cultural mind-set' which enables the integration of technology into society. This occurs as an incremental historical process, in which the solution of one problem by technological means immediately raises a multitude of other problems, resulting directly from those means. Problems, however, may also be perceived as opportunities for technological advance (Ellul, 1965).

During the latter part of the twentieth century these new technological advances have made possible the accumulation, merging and manipulation of vast quantities of data, not only enabling accumulation of huge databases, but also distribution of information in various forms, through either remote terminals or computer peripherals (for example, CD-roms or magnetic tapes). Opportunistic use of these new capabilities has given the marketing sector the opportunity to vastly increase their activities. Mass surveys of potential customers have become a possibility by merging databases concerning the location, financial status, demographic and behavioural characteristics, and lifestyles of millions of individuals (Sleight, 1993). The product of such companies is detailed information on disaggregated 'communities' of potential consumers.

One of the larger listbrokers can supply information on over 50 million adult consumers residing in 22 million households. In their publicity literature this company boasts that '(t)he great strength of this database is in its ability to deliver either mass market coverage or specific markets defined by our families of classification, overlay and index products' (Eurodirect, 1996). Detailed information in these formats is collected from a variety of sources: census returns, geodemographic data including the socio-economic basis of the household, income levels, housing occupation, average age and family pattern, ethnic characteristics, and individual credit ratings collated from County Court judgements. By merging and overlaying lifestyle data derived from market research, information from retailers, and comprehensive national surveys, an idealised profile of individual consumers can be constructed.

Individuals themselves contribute data, whether knowingly or unknowingly, by the use of credit and debit cards, charge accounts and loyalty cards, and responses to special offers, competitions, or prize draws. Taken together, this accumulated and merged information can be manipulated to provide direct mailers with a detailed map of an ideal-type representation of the target consumer. The emerging data can be sold on to target mass or specific markets. Lifestyle data, for example, can be purchased on the basis of addresses by consumer theme: art and music, beauty, current affairs, gadgets, gardening, good food, home-sweet-home, old age, religion and sport (Mar Rel, 1996). Contrary to popular opinion, it is not difficult for producers to avoid financial loss with their unsolicited mail drops: a response rate of 1 per cent is all that is necessary (Sleight, 1993), and publicity gained for products or company may represent added (if less quantifiable) value.

CONSUMER FREEDOM?

Here we address the ways in which consumption replaces work as a central focus of many analyses of contemporary society. Consumer freedom, however, may be circumscribed by the inability to remain unidentified by ever-expanding computer databases.

> [T]he ideology of competition, which under the sign of 'freedom' was previously the golden rule of production, has now been transferred entirely to the domain of consumption. ... The latest such freedom is the random selection of objects that will distinguish any individual from others.
>
> (Baudrillard, 1988: 11)

Although consumer *rationality* has been hotly debated (see, for example, Aldridge, 1994), the concept of consumer *freedom* is now frequently utilised as a crucial link between the individual self and the rational system. Consumer conduct 'moves steadily into the position of, simultaneously, the cognitive and moral focus of life, the integrative bond of society, and the focus of systemic management' (Bauman, 1992: 49). It is clear, then, that 'spatially unconnected' consumer behaviour can be encouraged through the medium of junk mail because enough consumers can be trusted by capital to participate without direct control. As Bauman (1988: 61) comments

> The soliciting of conduct functionally indispensable for the capitalist economic system and harmless to the capitalist political system

> may now be entrusted to the consumer market and its attractions. Reproduction of the capitalist system is therefore achieved through individual freedom and not through its suppression.

These 'enterprising consumers' (Lash and Urry, 1994) live in a society saturated, according to Jameson (1984), with information-laden signs and symbols, which individuals may process as a means of identity-creation. This phenomenon may apply particularly to the new middle class whose backgrounds and biographical narratives encourage a lack of confidence in self-presentation, for which they may attempt to compensate by the acquisition of cultural capital (Bourdieu, 1986). Cultural capital may be observed in the cross-cutting of socio-economic stratification with cultural identification, and the absence of previously understood mass culture, through the practice of 'lifestyle shopping' (Shields, 1992). Shopping for a particular cultural lifestyle involves what Lash and Urry (1994) define as 'reflexive accumulation'. Thus, consumer freedom and reflexive accumulation together force specific choices to be faced:

> Whole areas of lifestyle and consumer choice are freed up and individuals are forced to decide, to take risks, to bear responsibilities, to be actively involved in the construction of their own identities for themselves, to be enterprising consumers.
>
> (Lash and Urry, 1994: 61)

In contemporary consumer society (Shields, 1992) we all not only follow lifestyles, but in an important sense are forced to do so – we have no choice but to choose (Giddens, 1991a). Giddens defines lifestyle as:

> a more or less integrated set of practices which an individual embraces, not only because such practices fulfil utilitarian needs, but because they give material form to a particular narrative of self identity.
>
> (Giddens, 1991a: 81)

For social groups which are defined solely by their lifestyle the only sanction against their non-conforming members is exclusion, if and when their interests change from those of the group (Shields, 1992: 15). Whilst this may be perceived as a form of individual freedom, Ellul (1980: 12) suggests it is freedom by default, in that in these more integrated social groups individuals actualise themselves in consumption, *as individuals* in isolation. This may be because the accelerated pace of change means that the reference points used by individuals in the past to plot their life-courses are disappearing (Melucci, 1996a). Each consumer is progressively confronted with the difficult and anxiety-provoking task of constructing his or her own identity: everyone must ask themselves the questions, 'Who am I?' and 'Who do I want to become?', and – at the end of the day – accept responsibility for the answer (Bauman, 1988: 62). In contemporary times, however, there are clues – often visual – to guide the self towards the construction of identity. Clues come:

> complete with instructions on how to assemble them into total images ... the only job left to be done by the individual himself [*sic*] is to follow the instruction attached to the kit.
>
> (Bauman, 1988: 63)

Junk mail offers the consumer the opportunity to domesticate and selectively control the process of identity-construction in kit form. Because of the individualised targeting of junk mail, the choices which come through the letterbox are – in theory – totally consistent with the perceived self-identity of the recipient, thus removing much of the anxiety involved in shopping in conventional spaces. This means that we can create our own flexible shopping space, using the 'self-assembly' kit, in a drawer, or on a shelf, in our home – an individualised self-service city centre (Alferoff and Reynolds, 1996).

Consumer freedom does, of course, have its limits (Bauman, 1988). The freedom to opt out of receiving junk mail altogether, for example, is severely limited since almost every adult with a home address is potentially a representation on a list. We cannot escape by moving house: Eurodirect point out in their publicity material that they can supply databases on individuals who have moved away from their address. Their 'UK Trace database combines and compares UK Goneaways with UK Movers to provide the complete movement picture' (Eurodirect, 1996). Although the Royal Mail currently operates a 'Mailing Preference Service' which filters out some junk mail, the only way to opt out altogether is to become a wanderer, with no fixable location. Freedom is therefore constrained.

Whereas Bauman (1988: 65) notes that tightly structured 'local' communities have been atomised and transformed into loosely aggregated 'populations' of spatially unconnected individuals, it is clear from the advertising information above that the technology allows individual characteristics and behaviours of the 'populations' to be more tightly aggregated than he implies. In the context of junk mail, the freedom of listbrokers to identify 'individuals' and to categorise them into disaggregated communities sets the territory to our freedom not to be identified. Indeed, in the eye of the electronic panopticon, representations of individuals exist as if in a binary world of yes–no, 0–1 computer coding (Baudrillard, 1983: 116–17). Demographic detail, income, spending and credit card transactions, as well as court judgements, are logged into databases and subsequently merged with other database files from lifestyle questionnaires, retailer returns and market research. Baudrillard claims that the collective function of advertising is to convert us all to this binary code, arguing from a somewhat deterministic epistemology that any infraction of it is more or less charged with guilt. The code is 'totalitarian': our individual flights do not negate the fact that each day we participate in its collective elaboration (Baudrillard, 1988: 19).

AN ELECTRONIC PANOPTICON

At issue here are the development of the 'advanced panopticon', and the problems and complexity of privacy as a social value. The section also illustrates the potential neutrality of the electronic gaze when applied to consumer responses.

> In each respect the advent of the modern state has been distinguished by a vast expansion of surveillance. Now 'surveillance', by its very nature, involves disclosure, making visible. The garnering of information discloses the patterns of activity of those to whom that information refers, and direct supervision openly keeps such activity under observation in order to control it.
>
> (Giddens, 1991b: 127)

The foundations of the 'panopticon' debate are well known and well understood. Based on the Benthamite architectural style of prisons, it became possible for a central controlling agency to monitor the behaviour of the inmates without being seen by them:

> This enclosed, segmented space, observed at every point, in which the individuals are inserted in a fixed place, in which the slightest

> movements are supervised, in which all events are recorded, in which the uninterrupted work of writing links the centre and periphery ... all this constitutes a compact model of the disciplinary mechanism.
>
> (Foucault, 1977: 197)

Foucault goes on to use the *analogy* of the panopticon to illustrate patterns of power relations in wider society. In this way he is able to emphasise the rationalised and co-ordinated methods by which instruments and procedures are used to harness the accumulation of knowledge within an unequal relationship (McHoul and Grace, 1995).

Lyon (1988) suggests that the visibility of the 'watchtower' has been made redundant with the advent of the computer, which vastly increases the capacity for surveillance. This increased capacity for 'invisible' surveillance means that there is an unseen pressure towards 'normalising' behaviour, thus enabling an illusion of greater freedom for, and trust in, the population. Catalogued behaviour is all that is necessary for capital to monitor the process of consumerism. For the keeper of this panopticon, the success of the system relies on patterns of predictable behaviour from *self-monitored* inmates. This is the way in which saleable goods are produced and profits made in the market. 'Making profit will be the sign of being on the right track. Making a loss will serve as a warning signal that the action should be altered' (Bauman, 1988: 25).

Lyon does have some criticisms of the 'electronic panopticon' argument, however. Claiming that the panopticon is often described as though it had some mysterious power of its own, he argues that public concern about computerised surveillance – as with prison disturbances of the nineteenth century – promotes efforts at resistance. People are understandably reluctant, claims Lyon, to lose control over the processes whereby details of their personal lives are disclosed to others. In our study of attitudes towards junk mail, some people were clearly concerned about this issue of privacy. As one male respondent put it:

> It's a matter of concern where companies are keeping information which is not relevant to their ultimate purpose. There's something about computer security, that something isn't necessarily life threatening or lifestyle threatening, but you think, 'Hang on a minute, this is private, why should the world know about it?' That information could get into the wrong hands, such as governments, credit agencies, banks, in the sense that they might start making judgements about the things you want to do, based on misinformation.

Whilst acknowledging that these technological advances represent an invasion of personal privacy, this person also felt a degree of ambivalence about the technique which defines the very mind-set of capitalist culture:

> At one end of the scale this is a huge invasion of privacy: why should AM-EX make money for themselves by enquiring what I've bought? On the other hand, it is brilliant business. I don't know where the dividing line is between those two.

In relation to the issue of privacy, therefore, some respondents did reflect Lyon's concerns; others, however, expressed greater enthusiasm for being known. Some of these people were pragmatic in their attitude to the dispersal of information that is concomitant with advances in communication technologies. As one woman pointed out:

> I just think now that there are so many people who have got my name and address and just keep passing it around – why worry? There's no way that I can stop it now, it's like trying to stop ripples in a pool.

For other respondents, making their identity transparent to a panoptic gaze was an ontological position which could bring its own rewards. As another woman commented:

> I would tell anybody anything about me, if asked ... my interests, my aspirations, my buying patterns.

Those who took part in this study clearly were aware of problems of both privacy and access to information; what seemed important, however, was the right to *control* the degree of private or public knowledge. Autonomy – the freedom to choose whether or not one is 'known' – can seem more important to individuals than privacy *per se*. Michael (1986) acknowledges that privacy and autonomy are interlinked in a complex way in fragmented and individualised societies:

> Laws protecting personal privacy ... depend in part on a simple preference for individuals to have rights to control information about themselves, and this is most sharply presented by the common assertion that only those who have something to hide want to protect information about themselves. Yet many people would

> object to public knowledge of information about themselves which it is difficult to consider as being shameful. ... [The] linking of privacy and autonomy is rather more subtle than the cliché which Bacon's dictum that 'knowledge is power' has become.
>
> (Michael, 1986: 118)

The simple notion of privacy as a social value, suggested by Lyon, is thus rendered more problematic when embedded in philosophies of both autonomy and individualism, as Michael illustrates. The consequences of valuing individual freedom to choose publicity more than privacy in this way can also mean that socially perceived moral parameters of 'good business' are progressively blurred:

> Each time the offer is taken advantage of, the dependence of the individual on the market and on experts and their knowledge is reproduced and reinforced. Individuals depend on the market and the experts for being individual – that is, being able to make free choices and make them without undue risk and psychological costs. Individual freedom becomes an important link in the process of reproduction of the power structure. ... Under the circumstances, the 'panoptic' method of behavioural control (consisting first and foremost in depriving individuals of their freedom of choice) may be suspended.
>
> (Bauman, 1988: 67)

Whilst Bauman implies the 'suspension' of such methods of surveillance, we would rather suggest that, although this 'panoptic gaze' actually remains, it has become more neutral and 'benign' in its attention. It is useful here to reflect upon the issue of junk mail through the analogy of Foucault's archaeology of the plague. In plague-ridden villages a lock-up system operated. Individuals were locked into their homes by the appointed overseers, who catalogued and monitored the progress of their health. At the overseer's command, all members of the household, on pain of death, had to present themselves at the window and report on their current state of health. Basic essentials such as bread and wine were distributed through wooden channels set up between the street and each house (Foucault, 1977: 195). In this instance there is an immanent relationship between making oneself fully visible and receiving sustenance from the overseer. The central point at issue for Foucault, however, is not so much the power accredited to the overseers, but the instruments and procedures that 'normalise' behaviour through disciplinary practices:

> (D)isciplinary power was one of the great 'inventions' of bourgeois society and is the primary means whereby the 'cohesion' of this type of social body is ensured and maintained. But disciplinary power cannot ... be seen simply to 'reflect' the requirements of the economic (capitalist) base.
>
> (McHoul and Grace 1993: 71)

In utilising the instruments and procedures for 'normalising' responses to junk mail, the *electronic* panopticon does not attempt such close scrutiny. Computer profiling is understood best as a technology of surveillance of 'observation before the fact' (Bogard, 1996: 27). Bogard argues that it resembles an 'informated' form of stereotyping and has become increasingly important in the targeting of individuals for specialised messages: unlike traditional stereotypes, profiles exist at the intersection of the actual and virtual worlds, and come to have more 'reality', more 'truth and significance', than the cases to which they are compared. According to Bogard, all that is required, therefore, is that sufficient of a representation is produced for targeted mail to communicate with a hyper-real self:

> The human agent [is] reduced to a machinic–organic interface or, in the case of telematics, the hyper-real 'persons' that inhabit databanks as simulated electronic 'communities.'
>
> (Bogard, 1996: 14)

Bogard describes this situation as a 'virtual panopticon' where a form of play exists between illusion and reality, human and machine, the fluid meanings of power, and the unresolved problem of who is the watcher and who is watched:

> [This] is no longer the source of an absolute gaze, and the ideal of control is no longer that of transparency. ... This is still, if not a system of confinement, at least a system of scrutiny. No longer subtle, but always in a position of exteriority, playing on the opposition between seeing and being seen, even if the focal point of the panopticon may be blind.
>
> (Baudrillard, 1983: 52)

The panoptic argument has clearly moved beyond forms of actual control, the simple idea of regulating social relations, to grapple with the creation of virtual forms of control. The fantasy that drives it is simulation – the point at which the imaginary and the real coincide – specifically where the gap between virtual and actual control disappears. The problem of surveillance from perceptual distance is resolved (Bogard, 1996: 9).

Whereas surveillance apparatus is a machinery for making a surface transparent, and what interests that apparatus is always what lies on the 'other side' of this surface, simulation has a different relation to surfaces. It does not seek to see *through* a surface, but structures perception *across* it:

> Simulation performs its own operation on reality – not to reveal it as an essence or signified behind the surface, but to dispose of it as a visible (perceptible) surface, to dismantle the 'real' surface in order to better 'realise' the appearances.
>
> (Bogard, 1996: 35)

This negating of the 'real' *to some extent* precludes the possibility of acts of resistance by the human actor, either to force the panoptic gaze to focus on the 'real', rather than the hyper-real, self; or indeed, acts of resistance to retake control of the self by rendering opaque, or blurring, the gaze. As with 'electronic eyes', the panoptic gaze is attracted by movement – in this instance, by individual consumer movements which are codifiable by databases. Absence of movement leads to only a vague and less useful construction of a hyper-real individual.

RESISTANCE TO THE FOCUS OF THE GAZE

People react to the focus of the panoptic gaze in different ways. Some people enter into a form of conflict; some subvert the system by 'transgressing' its purpose; others, however, use their freedom as consumers to encourage and reward the perceived acuity of the gaze. Melucci argues that if power were a form of total control, then resistance would be purely reactive. In social practice, however:

> power itself is caught up in the same problem of the ambivalence of its own instruments. ... In the symbolic realm, there is always ambivalence on both sides. Emerging power is increasingly based not solely on material strength, but on the production and circulation of information, it has today decisively exposed itself to its own weakness: where symbols enter the constitution of the field, they

render it open to multiple interpretations and into something that is never under full control.

(Melucci, 1996b: 176)

It is advocated by Ellul (1980) that in this technological society we need to seek evidence of a morality, which would play the traditional role of ethics in preserving the individuals' control over their lives, in order to retain the possibility of development of both society and personal relationships. This, he argues, leaves us with a paradox: we cannot claim to be anti-technique – 'we are deeply implicated in it and cannot be otherwise' (1980: 245). This implicatedness was evident in some comments in this study. As one man put it:

> The more information you have about anything, the more use it is to you, and hopefully, the more use you are to them. ... I can't reasonably think of a situation where information about me could do me any harm.

In advanced technological society, however, technique may also be perceived as problematic, and not all the respondents in this study wished to be so open to view. Some people resist being constituted into these virtual communities which – although imparting meaning to the panoptic gaze – are meaningless to the recipients of junk mail; other people – whilst not resisting the principle – do resist assumptions about their consumer behaviour. 'The forms of enclosure and disclosure which allow agents to deviate from, or flout ... [expected] norms are important features of the dialectic of control' (Giddens, 1991b: 127). A male respondent, who had attempted to resist a particular assumption about his potential consumer behaviour, wistfully commented:

> I've made a serious attempt to try and get them to alter the classification they have put me in. ... If I could convince them that I am 35 instead of 52 I think I'd get more of what I'm interested in. But obviously they've got my age locked away somewhere – at one point I told the truth and forever I shall pay!

Ellul's ethic of freedom means 'adopting an analytical perspective on the technological system': in contemporary times it is necessary to assert that it is 'not technique which frees us, but rather it is from technique that we must free ourselves' (Ellul, 1980: 246). Ellul's stance can be viewed as idealist, and it may be that freedom must be fought for, claimed and affirmed, *within* the technique in order to reclaim an ethical identity. Consumer freedom, for example, may be a specific illustration of resistance: it is a freedom claimed and affirmed in the full knowledge that we 'have no choice but to choose'. Within this idea of freedom, the consumer is no longer a person who merely desires, buys and uses up a commodity. They have come of age; and may choose, buy or refuse to buy; display or not display; feel guilt or have moral qualms; explore or interpret, read or decode, reflect or daydream; pay or steal; need or cherish; love or are indifferent; deface or destroy (Gabriel and Lang, 1995). For Gabriel and Lang and others (for example, Bauman and Giddens), consumer freedom is interpreted as a form of choice, rather than resistance, albeit limited by the negotiated order.

Within the arena of consumer freedom there are different ways, both active and passive, of resisting the perceived determinism of the panoptic gaze. Although technique appears as 'unifying and totalizing', individuals enter into processes of conflict and negotiation by 'punch[ing] holes in the social fabric which technique would wish to remain seamless' (Ellul, 1980: 246). Ellul describes four '*discrete expressions of resistance*' comprising freedom, conflict, transgression, and non-power (1980: 245) by which those processes of conflict and negotiation can be expressed. Unlike others, Ellul perceives freedom as a form of resistance, rather than choice.

Using a conceptual model which, to some extent, bridges these two opposing perceptions of freedom, our analysis suggests that those who resist their junk mail may deploy different tactics of resistance as strategy *within* an overarching negotiated order of consumer freedom. This tactical behaviour may involve either participative or non-participative acts of conflict or transgression. Participative acts may have unanticipated consequences, because the panoptic gaze is attracted, individual details are entered into new databases, and new junk mail begins to arrive. Non-participative acts, on the other hand, may help to blur the panoptic gaze.

THE TACTIC OF CONFLICT

The technological system which enables junk mail to be targeted does not exist in isolation, but in a complex relationship of tension with technique and with the quest for uniqueness in self-identity. In rejecting the whole notion of unsolicited mail, some respondents reacted in a participative relationship of conflict by punishing the sources of such mail:

> I put 'return to sender' on it and when I go out, I put it in the letter-box.
>
> I open it to find out who it is from so that I can send it back. I always return it in their pre-paid envelope, or without postage stamps.
>
> I'll collect it all up and when I've got a pile I'll get a big envelope, and, whoever happens to be the top, I address it to them and send it back ... I don't put a stamp on but ... just put a little note in saying 'How do YOU like getting it?'

This form of resistance can therefore be seen to involve different levels of punishment or revenge. It is, however, ambivalent in its consequences. This is because, although the actions may be negative in intention, they may still have the unforeseen consequence of informing the panoptic gaze of its errors, which may be rectified by a new supply of differently targeted information. This consequence can be avoided by entering into a tactic of conflict as non-participation. Other respondents in this study were using this tactic, sometimes in a 'blanket' fashion:

> I bin it all straightaway;

and sometimes selectively:

> About three days after my fiftieth birthday I got a Saga leaflet dropped through the door. It was binned!

Ellul's ethic of non-power means choosing not to do something; being capable of doing something and deciding against it. A vital principle in setting limits to technique, this ethic involves decisions which must be renewed each time the choice of action is presented (1980: 246); in this case when all, or some, items of junk mail are received. Non-power, therefore, means refusing to engage in any dialogue with the gaze in constructing a hyper-real self. The quotes above thus represent the least ambivalent forms of resistance to the panoptic gaze, because without 'movement' of the hyper-real self, through either negative or positive responses to junk mail, the focus cannot be sharpened. The lens remains masked and unseeing, leaving the real self to enjoy a heightened sense of freedom and empowerment.

THE TACTIC OF TRANSGRESSION

The second form of resistance identified here may be conceptualised as transgression. Ellul's ethics of transgression can only be achieved by challenging the illusions imposed by technique – of progress, achievement, and the seamless blending of the 'material' with the aesthetic, or 'spiritual'. 'It is the transgression of the technological ideology that we have absorbed which allows for the establishment of new limits' of resistance (1980: 247).

In reacting to their junk mail, many people enter into different forms of transgression. Some of these involve bypassing the neutrality of the 'coded' self, by blurring their identity and thus entering into a self-interested, but cynical, relationship with the panoptic gaze; this we have conceptualised as 'participative' transgression. It occurs when recipients of junk mail encourage and consciously use it for purposes which are defined by themselves; a tactic adopted by some people in this study:

> I get the free gifts – pens, vouchers etc. – received for replies to junk mail.

> I sometimes like to fill in questionnaires which come in junk mail, and give false information. This leads to all sorts of fancy offers.

> I tend to look at what people say, and read between the lines. Some junk mail is so banal it tells me quite a lot about the company. If they think I'm that much of an idiot … then I wouldn't deal with them anyway.

These people 'transgressed' the aims of junk mail producers in three ways: (1) by encouraging further junk mail simply in order to receive any free gifts offered for responding; (2) by deliberately giving false information (such as multiplying their income tenfold) in order to encourage a different kind of junk mail; and (3) by using the style of the junk mail presentation to make judgements about the worth of the organisation which sent it out. This tactic of participative transgression does not remove the panoptic gaze from the recipients, for the junk mail will keep coming and – indeed – increase in volume; the transgression does, however, tend to distract the gaze by encouraging junk mail in order to use the benefits (for example, the free gifts) for other purposes, or by manipulating information for their self-interest by providing false information about themselves. 'The minimization or manipulation of conditions of disclosure is ... ordinarily in the interests of those whose behaviour is subject to surveillance' (Giddens, 1991b: 127–8).

Other people in this study 'transgressed' in ways which involved non-participation in a relationship with the senders of junk mail, the consequence of which is to render the gaze opaque, rather than to distract it. This kind of transgression involves using junk mail (which has arrived 'legitimately') for purposes for which it was never intended. These 'subversive' purposes may be aesthetically creative:

> I like colours and patterns so I cut out and keep those, and throw the rest out;

or the simulation of a fantasy self:

> What I really would like is catalogues of stuff I would *almost* wear ... it's a bit like transvestism;

or practical recycling:

> I sort through the junk mail for free offers, competitions etc., recycle all paper, and re-use reply-paid envelopes;

> I shred it all for the horses' bedding.

Again, this form of transgression does not prevent the gaze from noting the individual's existence and holding basic personal information. What it does do is to refuse to give signals which would allow the gaze to construct a clearer picture, regardless of whether that picture 'accurately' reflects the individual. Contrary to Bauman's assertion that 'while enjoying privacy, the individual may be "out of sight", certain of not being watched, and thus able to engage in whatever one may wish to engage in' (Bauman, 1988: 51), we argue that, here, the individual continues to be visible and does not attempt to distract the gaze, but, nevertheless, still chooses to engage in conscious transgressions.

THE TACTIC OF REWARD

Those in this study who had engaged in non-participative transgression clearly gained some reward from their junk mail. Contrary to the more deterministic arguments which suggest that people 'inevitably' perceive their privacy as constrained or threatened by the electronic panopticon, it is also clear that junk mail can be perceived as a technological means of extending and realising consumer freedom. As one female respondent claimed:

> I love it ... I save it up in drawers for when I can afford to buy something.

Some people welcome – indeed would encourage – visual acuity from the gaze because they do not perceive the power relationship as problematic. These individuals – both men – saw it, rather, as a reciprocal relationship involving a process of sharing information:

> The more that is known about us as individuals, the more accurate the mailshots will be. Accordingly, we should be pleased about companies finding out about us because it helps them in contacting people particularly interested in their products.
>
> With modern technology and modern psychology they should be able to direct their marketing much more accurately – which they obviously don't. I'm still 70938 who goes on Saga holidays and has more money than he knows what to do with. It's just that we haven't managed to sell him anything yet!

To summarise, the respondents' comments above are illustrative of three different strands of reaction to the technique which makes possible the distribution of junk mail, and to junk mail itself. Two strands involve tactics of resistance in either conflict or transgression, which do not appear to directly address the enabling technique. The third strand rewards consumerism by encouraging and seeking to perfect both technique and its consequences. It seems apparent from these data, therefore, that debates around consumer freedom are not unproblematic. Consumer freedom involves choice, privacy, resistance, and issues of morality around these principles. It also addresses the nature of the relationships between individuals and technique. In addition, it must also account for self-interested behaviours neither anticipated nor accounted for, by the negotiated order of consumerism.

CONCLUSION

In 1988 (p. 103), David Lyon asked the question, how will the perceived threat by electronic surveillance to privacy be challenged and mitigated? In this chapter we have attempted to respond to Lyon's question in one specific area of research. We have used the theme of junk mail to trace a relationship between technique, technological advances in computing, the construction of hyper-real communities, and real individuals. Thus we have sought to make visible a phenomenon which occurs at the intersection of structure and action, surveillance and freedom, and production and consumption.

Whilst agreeing in principle with the notion of an electronic panoptic gaze, we have explored ways in which the concept may also be problematic for use in discussion of the scrutiny of consumer freedom. The basic purpose of the panopticon in accumulating codifiable actions remains valid, but the normalising principle is much more complex. Our discussion allows for a degree of complexity in acknowledging a more neutral gaze in which the 'normality' for each individual is whatever they are currently signalling as normal in their consumer movements.

This enables the more structuralist arguments of such writers as Giddens (1991a), Michael (1986), and Campbell and Connor (1986) to be problematised. Whilst others have indicated a greater or lesser possibility of patterns of resistance to the panoptic gaze – for example, Lyon (1988), Ellul (1980), Bauman (1988), Baudrillard (1983) – few theorists have taken into account the notion that consumer freedom, because it is used to exercise a degree of choice, may mean that some individuals *choose* to be more visible to the gaze, by embracing the technique with enthusiasm. Bauman claims that the inmates of the panopticon are objects: 'the intention behind their condition is to transform them into something they are not and something they themselves have no intention of becoming' (1988: 11). Clearly, this is not universal, for between the electronic gaze and the self stands the hyper-real self:

> No longer is there any imperative to submit to the model, or to the gaze. 'You are the model!'. ... A turnabout of affairs by which it

> becomes impossible to locate an instance of the model, of power, of the gaze, of the medium itself, since YOU are always already on the other side.
>
> (Baudrillard, 1983: 53)

From Baudrillard's perspective, in the junk mail we receive we are always already a hyper-real self. We have argued here that this 'hyper-real self' is merely a *representation* and therefore is also available for manipulation and remodelling by the real individual in this dialectical and dynamic relationship. The manipulation or remodelling can be conceptualised as resistance, either as conflict or transgression; or it may take the form of an enthusiastic reward for the sharing of accumulated information. All these actions can be viewed as forms of resistance to the determinism of 'technique' as defined by Marcuse and Ellul.

We conclude, therefore, that the panoptic gaze is rendered less than deterministic in its power to constrain the freedom of individuals to reconstitute their 'selves'; indeed, it is rather more the case that an individual decision to reconstitute a 'self' is welcomed and subsequently colonised by agents who make use of the panoptic gaze. Within the arena of consumer freedom, therefore, although the surveillance role of the panopticon is strengthened by technique, its power to normalise consumer behaviour depends largely on the responses of individual recipients of junk mail.

NOTE

1. Travel expenses were supported by the Knowledge, Organizations and Society Research Unit at Staffordshire University.

REFERENCES

Aldridge, A. (1994) 'The Construction of Rational Consumption in *Which?* Magazine: The More Blobs the Better?', *Sociology*, 28(4): 899–912.

Alferoff, C. and Reynolds, G. (1996) 'Junk Mail and the Fragmentations of Shopping Patterns: Games Beyond the City', paper presented to 'City Limits' Conference, School of Arts, Staffordshire University.

Baudrillard, J. (1983) *Simulations* (New York: Semiotext).
Baudrillard, J. (1988) *Selected Writings*, ed. Mark Poster (Cambridge: Polity).
Bauman, Z. (1988) *Freedom* (Milton Keynes: Open University Press).
Bauman, Z. (1992) *Intimations of Postmodernity* (London: Routledge).
Bogard, W. (1996) *The Simulation of Surveillance: Hypercontrol in Telematic Societies* (Cambridge: Cambridge University Press).
Bourdieu, P. (1986) *Distinction: A Social Critique of the Judgement of Taste* (London: Routledge and Kegan Paul).
Campbell, D. and Connor, S. (1986) *On the Record: Surveillance, Computers and Privacy – The Inside Story* (London: Michael Joseph).
Ellul, J. (1965) *The Technological Society* (London: Cape).
Ellul, J. (1980) 'The Power of Technique and the Ethics of Non-Power', in K. Woodward (ed.), *The Myths of Information: Technology and Postindustrial Culture* (London: Routledge and Kegan Paul).
Eurodirect (1996) *Mapping the Future* (publicity leaflet).
Foucault, M. (1977) *Discipline and Punish* (London: Penguin).
Gabriel, Y. and Lang, T. (1995) *The Unmanageable Consumer: Contemporary Consumption and its Fragmentations* (London: Sage).
Giddens, A. (1991a) *Modernity and Self-Identity* (Cambridge: Polity).
Giddens, A. (1991b) *The Constitution of Society* (Cambridge: Polity).
Jameson, F. (1984) 'Postmodernism or the Culture of Late Capitalism', *New Left Review*, 146: 53–92.
Lash, S. and Urry, J. (1994) *Economies of Signs and Space* (London: Sage).
Lyon, D. (1988) *The Information Society* (Cambridge: Polity).
Mar Rel (1996) 1996 catalogue.
Marcuse, H. (1964) *One Dimensional Man: Studies in the Ideology of Advanced Industrial Society* (London: Routledge and Kegan Paul).
McHoul, A. and Grace, W. (1995) *A Foucault Primer: Discourse, Power and the Subject* (London: UCL Press).
Melucci, A. (1996a) *The Playing Self: Person and Meaning in the Planetary Society* (Cambridge: Cambridge University Press).
Melucci, A. (1996b) *Challenging Codes: Collective Action in the Information Age* (Cambridge: Cambridge University Press).
Michael, J. (1986) 'Information Law, Policy and the Public Interest', in M. Ferguson (ed.), *New Communication Technologies and the Public Interest: Comparative Perspectives on Policy and Research* (London: Sage).
Shields, R. (ed.) (1992) *Lifestyle Shopping: The Subject of Consumption* (London: Routledge).
Sleight, P. (1993) *Targeting Customers: How to Use Geodemographic and Lifestyle Data* (Oxfordshire: NTC Publications).

13 Rubbish-Power: Towards a Sociology of the Rubbish Society

MARTIN O'BRIEN

INTRODUCTION

There is a glaring absence at the heart of sociological theory and research. In the most reputable and widely read treatises on consumption, production or everyday life in sociology, nobody talks about waste. It is as if, for the discipline of sociology in general, and for sociological theory in particular, nobody ever throws anything away or ever carries out the bin-bags for a 'waste management authority' to deal with. It is as if, when you go to a shop, restaurant, club or place of work, you work, consume or take your leisure without ever producing rubbish or detritus of any kind. Sociology treats 'waste' as if it were literally immaterial, as if it existed in a world apart from the one we inhabit in our daily, routine lives. Sociology has failed signally to acknowledge that every day of our lives someone, somewhere – either ourselves or others – has to deal with waste. This chapter outlines some of the sociological insights that researching rubbish can provide, and suggests that a sociology of the rubbish society can take forward sociological contributions to understanding the relationships between social and environmental change.

NOT FOR THE HISTORICAL RECORD

In 1979 Michael Thompson opened his eloquent survey of the creation and destruction of value (*Rubbish Theory*) by reminding his readers of an old riddle, *viz*: what does a rich man keep that a poor man throws away? Answer: snot. The riddle recalls a time when the docker's handkerchief spread far and wide beneath the poor man's feet whilst the rich man's silken cloth secreted his private phlegm from public scrutiny. Thompson used this riddle to alert his readers at the outset to the cultural frameworks that give meaning and substance to rubbish. Muck, garbage, trash, snot, filth or waste are not incidental ephemera of society's productive activities. Rather, they are themselves at the centre of any of meaningful or co-ordinated social activity at all.

How right he was! Entire sectors of social and economic activity are driven by the management and exploitation of rubbish. Whether to burn it, bury it, sell it, swap it, recycle or re-use it; reduce it, minimise it, detoxify it or disown it; mine it, sort it, co-dispose of it or dump it: these issues are central to the conduct of individuals and organisations alike. On examination, they reveal that rubbish is not an unwanted by-product of some other economic, cultural or social system. They reveal that rubbish expresses a political dynamic that drives social change and that the endemic conflicts that surround rubbish – local opposition to incinerators or nuclear storage facilities, legal challenges to the awarding of operator contracts, European-level disputes over national definitions of and arrangements for managing wastes, and so on, – are only the most visible tensions in a society awash with conflict and compromise over detritus: a rubbish society.

Why, then, has sociology ignored rubbish? There is, after all, a sociology of the media, the family, work, sport and leisure, amongst many others, but there is not a sociology of waste and wasting. There is no canon in which to situate a social theory of wastage comparable to those for production or consumption. It seems strange that sociology has apparently ignored rubbish, for two reasons. First, in its widest sense, waste and wasting comprise experiences and activities that, at least on the face of it, sociologists appear to share among themselves and with non-sociologists. Second, 357 million tonnes of agricultural and mining waste is produced in the UK annually. Sixty-nine million tonnes of industrial waste, 47 million tonnes of commercial and construction waste and 20 million tonnes of domestic waste is also produced annually. Every decade approximately 5 billion tonnes of waste emanates from what is produced, consumed and used by people and institutions in the UK alone. Under the weight of all this debris, why do systems of production and consumption fail to collapse? How is it possible to walk or drive anywhere? How come your house, your workplace, where you take your leisure are not inaccessibly submerged in junk? The answer is of course obvious: you, and someone else, are collecting, transporting and routing, storing, treating, burying or burning it. But if it is the case that the processes of dealing with waste are so essential that production and consumption could not persist without them, why is this manifest fact absent in sociological theory? One of the political characteristics of rubbish is precisely this silencing process: the removal or dispersion of shared meanings and experiences of waste and detritus and their reconfiguration in codified or hierarchical meanings and experiences. In this chapter I am going to suggest, in a broader sense, that an analysis of the dispersion and reconfiguration of the social relations of wasting comprises at least a starting point for a sociology of waste.

How much do you recycle? Household waste can be recycled via several routes, including local bottle or paper banks and kerbside recycling schemes. Kerbside schemes are often vaunted for the convenience factor: they enable lazy recycling for the fit and active and a needed service for the less active or mobile. However, they also display other qualities. They make visible your private habits and routines: they tell your neighbours that you are a bit of a soak or that you have a fetish for Nutella chocolate spread or that you are a *Guardian* or a *Sunday Sport* reader. Kerbside recycling is the public revelation of your household's industrial allegiances. What goes into the recycling box reveals things about your body and ideals, your commodity fetishes and dependencies, your emotions and income. What you put into it, therefore, is a public act, at least in part a statement about yourself and your relationships to the social world. Do you want to tell your neighbours that you drank 20 cans of lager and/or 10 bottles of wine last week (again)? Or do you have a light week this time and recycle only seven of them? Do you recycle your hard-core bestiality magazines or do you consign them to the social and historical dustbin? Kerbside recycling exposes a visibility/invisibility tension in people's relationships to different wastes. Some qualities and quantities of objects are publicly validated resources – glass, paper and so on – yet the containers or materials (the glass, the paper) of those objects themselves may make visible publicly taboo practices. The problem is not confined to the kerbside but also characterises the bottle and paper bank system. Do you take several trips with small numbers of whisky bottles or do you unload a large number in front of strangers (or familiars)? Recycling schemes are an ongoing public record of industrial–domestic life that people generate as they dispose of industrial–domestic commodities. Wasting is a kind of translation: each person's public/private location of waste objects translates industrial commodities through a domestic waste stream into new kinds of industrial commodities. If you put some bottles and cans into the bin and some into recycling baskets you supply industrial production in both cases. In one case your waste may be traded on competitive markets for incineration or landfill. In the other case your waste may be traded in competitive markets for secondary use. The percentages of glass, paper, plastic, aluminium, and so on that are regularly collated by academic, charitable and governmental organisations may represent quantities collected, but they do not represent the labours of wasting that got the materials into the percentages or the different disposal routes that industrial objects take.

Where does your life go when you die? If you are poor and alone it is likely that your possessions – your letters, photographs, books, clothes, ornaments and implements – will be collected by a waste-contractor and buried or burned in the local landfill or incinerator. What tokens and records of yourself that you leave behind will be classified as waste in the common-sense meaning of the term: as a superfluous, pointless nuisance. The contents or personal significance of those tokens and records are unlikely to have any social consequence or enter into social memory. If you are rich and connected some of your tokens and records will probably comprise historical archives: monuments to the passage of time. Their historical location and significance – their contents and their meaning – will pass into institutional memory. The social remnants that comprise the historical records of contemporary society did not 'survive' a psychological process of mass forgetting: they simply avoided burial in the earth or burning in the flames. Today, the power to burn and bury other people's histories is formulated in environmental departments and pursued in the name of environmental health and waste management. Landfills are graveyards for the poor's personal histories and incinerators their crematoria.

THE RUBBISH SOCIETY

In the two cases above, some aspects of people's lives maintain a visibility: the remnants persist as public expressions of who you are (or were); some aspects of people's lives sustain an invisibility: the remnants are destroyed or hidden from public view. The question of public visibility does not apply only to the post-consumption phase of objects in the industrial–domestic complex. What is and is not visible about waste on a wider scale is an equally illuminating indicator of the power of rubbish to influence or drive social change. Two further examples illustrate the shifting visibility and impact of waste on social relations and social labours. The first concerns clinical waste, the other concerns one aspect of the discourse of waste.

Ivan Illich (1976) famously observed that the treatment of health causes illness: that any curative system supports iatrogenic consequences. Cross-infections, inappropriate treatments, accidents, the creation of conditions for disease cultures are embedded in the means of health intervention. The shifting and many-stranded management of clinical wastes adds a new dimension to Illich's assessment.

Until the late 1980s the major disposal route for clinical waste was hospital incineration. However, problems like the poor quality of these incinerators, the cost of running and upgrading them and the break-up of statutory Health Authority responsibilities were compounded by the removal of Crown Immunity from hospitals. At this point, medical waste disposal facilities became subject to the same pollution and environmental health regulations as private and public waste disposal facilities. The maintenance of high-grade, efficient incinerators was beyond the capacity of many hospitals and clinical waste entered private and public waste management systems. More recently, the NHS and Community Care Act, combined with efficiency drives in the NHS, has resulted in large increases in community nursing and consequent large increases in the quantities of clinical waste circulating within communities. Since the Environmental Protection Act (1990, section 34), nurses are subject to the Duty of Care compliance regulation and are accountable for clinical wastes they handle. These kinds of statutory duties and professional responsibilities are themselves means (albeit ambiguous ones) of locating wastes in public/private spaces. For example, the work of community nurses involves a lot of personal and hygiene care as well as medical care and administration. Not only are they responsible for ensuring secure disposal of soiled dressings, they are also responsible for the wrappings and any unused open dressings. If they cut toenails in someone's home the clippings regularly go into the domestic refuse but if toenails are cut in schools or retirement homes they are classified as clinical waste and pass into specialised refuse management routes. Toenails in your own home are not clinical wastes (usually). Toenails in an institution are clinical wastes. What determines the status of toenails as clinical waste is not the substance of which they are composed but their location in public/private, domestic/institutional settings.

Clinical wastes, particularly low-grade clinical wastes, are acquired and routed into the municipal waste stream by a very wide range and a very large number of individuals and groups, some of whom I have noted above, with the consequence that the distributive framework for these materials is fractured into many different networks. Whilst there are specific arrangements relating to clinical waste and the pharmacy, nursing homes and hospitals, health centres and other health service-controlled establishments, the applicability of these arrangements to private (or public) residential homes, supermarket pharmacy franchises, home-carers, and so on has not been studied. The circulation of clinical wastes through these latter networks means that different people are defining 'clinical' wastes in different ways, are claiming and disclaiming responsibilities for these wastes and are – knowingly or otherwise – passing on both the hazard itself and its management to different sectors of the community. Clinical waste exhibits, in a compressed form, the ambiguous social and political existence of rubbish. It illustrates how the public visibility of wastes and the targets and indicators through which it is managed are dependent on political reorientations in wider social policy (community care policy, for example) and the labours of networks of people in divided organisational and community settings. The estimates on clinical waste arisings list the different sources of clinical wastes but they do not indicate the nature or quantity of special wastes in the municipal waste stream. They also do not indicate the nature or quantity of controlled wastes (wrapping paper, unused dressings, for example,) in the clinical waste stream. In short, the indicators and targets themselves conceal important social processes of wasting – the routing of objects into different managerial solutions (Collins, 1991; Phillipp, 1993; O'Brien *et al.*, 1996a, 1996b).

Behind the reported increases in the ebb and flow of clinical wastes around cities and countryside alike are identifiable changes in the social relations of wasting: in the networks and organisations through which wastes are defined, channelled and controlled. The policy discourse on the waste 'problem' views rubbish as a loss of utility: as a depletion in use-value but at the same time as an (increasingly lucrative) source of exchange value. Consequently, the discourse partially reveals and partially conceals the political economy of waste. It reveals some of the work of managing the contradictory push and pull of wastes – the simultaneous decrease in use value and increase in exchange value – and it obscures other elements of this work. The EPA itself expresses the contradiction in its own definition of waste as:

(a) Any substance which constitutes a scrap material or other unwanted surplus substance arising from the application of any

> process; and (b) any substance or article which requires to be disposed of as being broken, worn out, contaminated or otherwise spoiled. Any thing which is discarded or otherwise dealt with as if it were waste shall be presumed to be waste unless the contrary is proved.
>
> (EPA, 1990, section 75)

The first sentence defines waste as unwanted surplus but the second allows that the surplus might itself be valuable (i.e. it might represent a scarcity). It allows for the contrariness of waste: its capacity to be its own opposite, to have no apparent value and yet potentially to be valuable. The second sentence of the definition is actually the policy in its entirety: to prove that waste has value by opening up channels – ways of dealing with waste – for its exploitation. Simplified examples of these channels include incineration, recycling and re-use. Each of these channels represents a political economy of waste that draws on different forms of labour, encourages different technological developments and transacts different values for the same objects. I will use recycling as an example.

The simplest definition of recycling is to pass objects through a productive process again: recycled paper, glass and metal, for example, comprise materials that have been formed into a second or third, or further product. But there are different ways of getting the paper, glass, metal, or other material, back into a productive process for a second or third, or further, time. For example, in the UK, in 1996, a County Council (Berkshire) examined bids from 100 companies from all over the world to begin 'mining' a full landfill site in search of valuable plastics, glass and metals. These valuable items are the accumulated wealth of 15 years of the dumping of household and commercial waste into a hole previously left by sand and gravel quarrying. The valuables could be sorted on site and the remaining semi-rotted materials reburied (Schoon, 1996) – presumably for someone else to come along in 15 years and discover that other components are also 'valuable' enough for further 'mining'. Mining landfill, which has been under way in the USA for some time, is considered to be a serious option for extracting value out of garbage.

Currently, the most common means for returning objects through productive processes, however, is recycling. The labours of recycling differ from mining in several important ways (Schultz, 1993). Schultz's analysis refers to the German system for collecting, sorting and recycling waste, but has wider implications for gendered labour and labour relations in the rubbish society. She observes that in Germany, as in other industrial economies, materials and resources have tended to flow along a linear track: from the extraction of raw materials through product manufacture, distribution and consumption to disposal. Currently, there is more emphasis on the recycling or re-use of materials throughout an economy: there is a trend towards a circular economy where secondary (waste or residue) materials – rather than primary, raw materials – become the first stage in the process of manufacture. Over the last two decades, but especially since the mid-1980s, rates of household recycling, sorting, and re-supplying have increased markedly. Schultz points out, however, that the recycling of industrial–domestic commodities is a form of labour. It involves sorting, sometimes washing, storing and delivering objects to appropriate collection points as well as collecting the wastes that become raw materials from several different sources. Even if it were not inflected by gender it remains a form of labour that supplies raw materials but generates no income, but Schultz argues that a disproportionate share of this labour is undertaken by women. Also, the elimination of household wastes – by planning a minimum-waste cooking regime, for example, repairing and re-using items – as well as their recycling, is labour for which householders are not paid. Schultz argues that the focus of 'environmental education' and local recycling schemes has been on convincing women in the home to take responsibility for wastes whilst the major industrial manufacturers profit from their unpaid sorting and recycling labours.

A number of implications follow from this analysis. For example, the (economic and environmental) consequences of a circular system will be affected significantly by the costs of gaining access to the commodity materials in the waste stream – just as the benefits and burdens of mining, drilling, quarrying or chemically synthesising 'primary' materials affect the costs of a linear system. Access can be gained to by 'mining' wastes after disposal (as in the Berkshire example, above) or by sorting and routing the materials prior to disposal. The first system connects with the socially organised labour of men in traditional male industries. The second system connects with the domestically organised labour of women in traditional female unpaid roles. The change in gendered relationships around extractive labour occurs not by incorporating women into men's occupations and associated benefits (or vice versa), but by resiting or relocating the focus of materials extraction into the domestic arena. Thus, the circular economy signals a reiteration of the gendered division of labour in the extractive industries:

men exploit depleting resources, women exchange fixed resources. In this way the new organisation breaks down entrenched distinctions between production and consumption, 'official' work (paid work in the public sphere) and 'unofficial' work (unpaid work in the private or domestic sphere), whilst reaffirming the gendered division of labour in resource exploitation.

Note, however, that this reconfigured political economy undermines the classical view of production – the translation of raw materials via desired objects into unwanted debris. Instead, the productive process itself is a breach in the debris. The existence of objects-as-goods is a temporary social form as they pass from the status of waste to the status of waste. The political economy of recycling is thus the passage of an object not through a productive process again, but through a process of wastage again: the return of the object to its concealed status. The rubbish society is an 'apogenic'[1] society, a society whose means of *permanently disposing of* or removing waste creates its own opposite: the appearance of a *temporary value* in industrial commodities. The sociology of the environment has been criticised for ignoring the dimension of time in its analysis. The criticism has force only so long as 'time' is understood as distinct from struggles over value. The rubbish society brings to centre stage a (now open, now hidden) struggle over the social time of objective value, over what values are invested in materials as they phase in and out of different circuits of use and exchange. These struggles are endemic to the rubbish society's political economy: they give social substance to material value and provide a more or less ordered temporality for the social circulation of 'depleted values' (i.e. the values of things that have been always–already exchanged, always–already used). The range and scope of these struggles is too large to address here but they include disputes around the quantity of value that remains in unwanted or superfluous materials (such as conflicts over targets for recovery and recycling from municipal wastes or setting the price of incinerator ash in competitive waste markets – see Chepesiuk, 1991), as well as disputes over who gains and who loses from the distribution of the valuable and non-valuable elements of wastes. The most common examples of these latter disputes are community conflicts over the siting and operational characteristics of landfills or waste to energy plants, for example. It should be noted, however, that such conflicts pale into numerical insignificance beside the wranglings between competing waste operators and waste disposal authorities for lucrative contracts. The award of a contract to bury, burn, ship, transport or manage wastes in any way is far more likely to be the subject of a legal dispute between companies about the tendering process than a community conflict about the environment. Wasting is not the exit of value *from* systems of production and consumption. It is a contested entry–exit–re-entry of economic and cultural values *as* systems of production, consumption and exchange. Wasting, in fact, underpins such 'systems': without the social process of wasting they could neither exist nor continue to operate: rubbish is temporally, socially, politically and economically *dynamic*.

REALISING AND IDEALISING RUBBISH

The dynamic of rubbish – its entry–exit–re-entry – is a process of dispersion and reconfiguration: both material objects and the meanings invested in them translate from status to status, location to location. The translation is not, however, an autopoietic reproduction of economic and cultural values. It is a site, as I have noted, of political–economic conflict, and also a site of cultural resistance.

The dynamism of rubbish is apparent in the different layers of the translation of objects and meanings between the status of nuisance, utility, beauty and commodity. These statuses or forms are configured differently in everyday and institutional life: objects in a 'commodity phase' (Appadurai, 1986) in some locations are in a phase of 'nuisance', 'utility' or 'beauty', elsewhere. The same object is commodified and beautified in different places. For example, empty or used plastic containers are a common constituent of domestic, commercial and industrial waste. They are objects whose bulk contributes to the 500 million tonnes annually of UK waste. The contexts of their entry–exit in this flow of rubbish combine networks of social relationships and political discourses. For example, note that the environmental assessment for a waste-to-energy (wte) plant observes that:

> Landfill is the only alternative for some types of waste, e.g., inert building waste and incinerator ash and the plant will help to preserve the increasingly scare commodity of landfill.

and that:

> The plant will create energy from waste. Energy as a commodity may rise substantially in price in the medium to long term.

Here, the plastic container in my example is a discursive vehicle of commodification: it supports the 'commodity' of landfill and is supported by the 'commodity' of energy: it exists in a 'commodity context' (Appadurai, *op. cit.*). In this regard, the discursive context of the plastic container is a network of dependent commodities through which to co-ordinate its social movement. The context also comprises a network of institutional relationships. Among other divisions of responsibility and benefit, the company controlling the wte plant to which the statement refers consists of three contractual sections: construction and operations contracts (private members of the company); sale of electricity (Electrical Supply Industry); and supply of refuse (sponsoring Boroughs). Each of these groups holds different responsibilities and has different interests in the system's commodities, a difference that is apparent in the temporal routing or organisation of wastes-as-commodities. The Borough Authority involved in the plant stipulates a condition on its acceptability to the effect that the business will:

> (ii) not expose the authorities to unacceptable risk and offer flexibility/protection from market forces
>
> (*ibid.*, p. 3)

The Borough agrees to provide the commodity 'waste-fuel' in exchange for protection from 'the market' during the operational phase of waste-throughput – which comprises a financial life of 20 years in the first instance (with an initial five-year renewal option). The commodity context of the plastic bottle as a waste-fuel is thereby made conditional on market protection and established temporally (the phase lasts for 20 years). At the same time, its commodity phase is divided into three discrete, albeit connected, units: operation, (energy-) service supply and fuel (or 'raw materials') supply. The 'commodity' of the plastic bottle as a waste-fuel is not a single object traversing a unified institutional matrix. It comprises, at least, three commodified objects in a disfigured or disorganised (after Lash and Urry, 1987) institutional complex.

This is not, however, the sole being of the empty or used plastic container. This object circulates simultaneously in other social relationships and political discourses:

> Look at this bottle, here. It's a beautiful thing, really, all these things [household 'waste' items on a table], colours. It is designed

> to look beautiful, attractive to buy it, sell it, what's in it. It's such a shame to throw it away because of my son [i.e. who will grow up in a world of discarded objects] and it is a nice package and well presented and when I am throwing it in the bin, I feel so guilty about it.
>
> Sometimes I cook I feel like crying because I keep on throwing this, throwing this. One time I kept them and my house was full of bits and I had to throw them all away. People do not take me serious but it gives me a serious headache.[2]

The same plastic bottle that is a waste-commodity is also a nice, beautiful, attractive cultural form; an object that inspires guilt and headaches and induces tears. Like the commodity-bottle, the beauty-bottle is located in a network of dependent objects that substantiate its value but establish a counter-discourse of rubbish. The plastic bottle in my example here comprises a discursive vehicle, not of commodification, but of beautification: a vehicle for beautifying rubbish. The bottle's role, however, is ambiguous. It is one of the beautiful 'bits' that fill houses but it is displaced by 'junk':

> I think everybody's got a junk drawer or a junk cupboard, I know we have. You think it might come in handy and put it in the drawer and it gets so full you can't open the drawer.
>
> If you had a big house with four bedrooms you would have a junk house.[3]

Again, like the bottle, 'junk' is neither waste nor not waste: it is doubt-inspiring yet avarice-inducing:

> Well, you usually think of them ['little bits of junk'] as waste because we don't use them again, it's there and what are you going to do with them. It's not waste, I don't know.[4]
>
> And, in fact, that's almost a virtue [keeping 'junk'] if you are interested in the environment, isn't it? I mean in the past we used to feel a bit guilty if we hoarded things and felt that you should throw these things out but now once you realise that you should be trying to reuse a lot of things, um, avarice becomes a virtue.[5]

From plastic bottles to little bits of junk, 20 million tonnes of ostensible waste are the subject of discourses of beauty and virtue which contrast sharply with a discourse of commodity. Junk is a familial and spiritual object of desire:

> you still, if you've enjoyed a book or something on tv or whatever you still do want to keep it. It is a strange thing and even though you probably know you might not do it again, read it or see it again, you still have this desire, you try to resist it sometimes but ...[6]

In this discourse, junk is a foundation of life, giving meaning and memory to personal, familial and social change. It is a kind of historical substance to everyday life whose changing constituents provide social and industrial markers of personal history:

> My son's bedroom ... always looked reasonable on the surface but underneath there was masses of stuff in drawers and in cubby-holes and masses and masses of stuff and since he has left home it is largely still there because when he left he just left it behind him on the whole and occasionally we think we ought to clear it out, we've thought of it.[7]

> I've got a sort of cupboard which is sort of, which has got my old files and information cupboard and I mean I do move bits of paper around the house from downstairs to upstairs to this cupboard and try and file it [*laughter*] and try to keep it organised but I'm aware I'm always doing that and the older I've got, thinking about old things that you don't use, ... brought to mind things like videos and I mean this is sort of new technology. I mean we tape things from the telly and say 'Oh, must keep those', that set of Victoria Woods, or whatever, ... I mean we have got loads and loads of videos that some of them we would want to keep and others we don't know what's on them because you haven't looked recently or you haven't got the time to keep finding what's on them so this is new technology isn't it? And then the next thing is computer disks ...[8]

Junk, thus, is things that belong in a 'spiritual category ... I wouldn't want to throw them, I wouldn't regard them as waste, they may not be useful on a day to day basis but I want them around me in my life.'[9] Whereas the institutional relationships that relayed the plastic bottle through a commodity network divided the object into (at least three) discrete entities, the social networks that relay junk through a beauty network reveal a different configuration in people's relationship to used/waste objects of many descriptions. Junk is beautiful, spiritual because its networks include, amongst others, 'my son' and 'getting older', rather than the commodity values of energy and land. The management and organisation of junk locates objects in different discursive and social relationships and invests them with different social and economic significances. Insofar as junk is dispersed and reconfigured in commodity networks it will express the commodification of all resources and objects – including land, energy, water, air, flora, fauna. Insofar as junk is dispersed in familial, communal and historic networks it will express the socialisation of all resources and objects. The social relations of rubbish exert power over action and meaning: they translate objects between forms and statuses, investing them with values and counter-values, they provoke both institutional and personal change and provide social and industrial markers of that change.

CONCLUSION

Rubbish is everywhere. It is in the home, the street, the factory, the office, the soil, the seas and the atmosphere. The rubbish society is awash with debris. But the dispersion of rubbish across all of these contexts is not a chaotic or unforeseen by-product of something else – a system of production or consumption, for example. Rubbish is reconfigured through identifiable social relationships and political discourses into many different forms. Without some forms of rubbish, life would be immeasurably poorer, without others it would be immeasurably richer. Does sociology know which is which? In particular, are there sociological theories of social change which address the crucial contribution of wasting to the activities of production and consumption? In turn, does a social theory of wasting contribute to sociological theories of production and consumption? These questions are for the next instalment of the rubbish society. What I have tried to show, in this chapter, is that wasting is, in its own right, a social process, embroiled in social meanings and social practices, achieved through networks and institutions, a process involving desire, spirituality and beauty as well as commodities, profits and resources.

ACKNOWLEDGEMENTS

This chapter was first presented as a paper at the 1997 British Sociological Association Annual Conference: *Power/Resistance*, University of York, 7–10 April. It is a first draft of my ideas for a project on the rubbish society. Most of it is new material, some parts of it, and/or the research materials on which the paper is based, can be found in published form in: O'Brien, 1995; O'Brien *et al.*, 1996a, b; O'Brien and Penna, 1997, 1998. Thanks to Jeff Hearn for advice on previous drafts of the essay.

NOTES

1. I am not a Greek or Latin scholar. I have combined the root of '*aporipto*' – to throw out/away – with '*genesis*' (from Greek/Latin). Thanks to Anna Tsatsaroni for help with this – any mistake is mine!
2. Section (LFG1: 9, 17) of a transcript of a focus group conducted for the Economic and Social Research Council/Engineering and Physical Sciences Research Council research project funded under the Global Environmental Change programme, award number L320253136: 'An Environmental and Social Life Cycle Comparison of Coal and Waste as Fuels'. 'LFG' and 'GFG' refer to anonymised focus group discussion transcripts.
3. *Ibid.*, 11.
4. *Ibid.*
5. GFG1, 11.
6. *Ibid.*, 17.
7. *Ibid.*, 15.
8. *Ibid.*, 16.
9. *Ibid.*, 17.

REFERENCES

Appadurai, A. (1986) 'Commodities and the Politics of Value', in A. Appadurai, (ed.), *The Social Life of Things: Commodities in Cultural Perspective* (Cambridge: Cambridge University Press).

Chepesiuk, R. (1991) 'From Ash to Cash', *E: The Environmental Magazine*, July/August, p. 3.

Collins, H. (1991) 'Treatment and Disposal of Clinical and Laboratory Waste', *Medical Laboratory Science*, 48(4): 324–31.
Illich, I. (1976) *Medical Nemesis: The Expropriation of Health* (New York: Pantheon).
Lash, S. and Urry, J. (1987) *The End of Organised Capitalism* (Cambridge: Polity).
O'Brien, M. (1995) 'Representing the Commodifications of Waste', presentation to the meeting of the Environmental Research Group of the Institute of British Geographers and the British Sociological Association Risk and Environment Study Group, *Commodifying the Environment: Consumption, Production and Representation*, Middlesex University, 3 July.
O'Brien, M. and Penna, S. (1997) 'European Policy and the Politics of Environmental Governance', *Policy and Politics*, 25(2): 185–200.
O'Brien, M. and Penna, S. (1998) 'Environmentalism', in M. O'Brien and S. Penna (eds), *Theorising Welfare: Enlightenment and Modern Society* (London: Sage).
O'Brien, M., Clift, R. and Doig, A. (1996a) *An Environmental and Social Life Cycle Comparison of Coal and Waste as Fuels: A Report to the Economic and Social Research Council*, University of Surrey, private print.
O'Brien, M., Clift, R. and Doig, A. (1996b) *Social and Environmental Life Cycle Assessment: Report of a Research Project*, University of Surrey, private print.
Phillipp, R. (1993) 'Community Needlestick Accident Data and Trends in Environmental Quality', *Public Health*, 107(5): 363–9.
Schoon, N. (1996) 'Significant Shorts', *The Independent*, 15 July, p. 2.
Schultz, I. (1993) 'Women and Waste', *Capitalism, Nature, Socialism*, 4(2): 51–63.
Thompson, M. (1979) *Rubbish Theory: The Creation and Destruction of Value* (Oxford: Oxford University Press).

Index